Us versus Them

Us versus Them

Race, Crime, and Gentrification in Chicago Neighborhoods

JAN DOERING

OXFORD

UNIVERSITY PRESS

Oxford University Press is a department of the University of Oxford. It furthers
the University's objective of excellence in research, scholarship, and education
by publishing worldwide. Oxford is a registered trade mark of Oxford University
Press in the UK and certain other countries.

Published in the United States of America by Oxford University Press
198 Madison Avenue, New York, NY 10016, United States of America.

CIP data is on file at the Library of Congress
ISBN 978-0-19-006658-1 (pbk.)
ISBN 978-0-19-006657-4 (hbk.)

1 3 5 7 9 8 6 4 2

Paperback printed by Marquis, Canada
Hardback printed by Bridgeport National Bindery, Inc., United States of America

Contents

Contents

Acknowledgments

From its early planning stage to the point of publication, this project has taken me ten years to complete. Over those years, I received help from countless people, and I apologize to anyone I may have forgotten to mention here. I conducted the fieldwork for this book as a graduate student at the University of Chicago. There, I enjoyed the singular intellectual experience that this strange institution affords. I am particularly indebted to my doctoral advisor, the inimitable John Levi Martin, whose sincere commitment to scholarly craftsmanship completely changed the way I think. John read and greatly improved practically everything I wrote over the last decade. He was a tireless advocate. And he reminded me of the pleasures of actual intellectual engagement. Thank you! I am also grateful to the additional members of my dissertation committee—Nicole Marwell, Kristen Schilt, and Richard Taub—whose profound expertise benefited my work in myriad ways. Furthermore, I gladly acknowledge the support of Andrew Abbott, James Evans, Andreas Glaeser, and Omar McRoberts. And I thank those scholars whose mentorship initially enabled me to pursue a PhD, especially Günter Albrecht and Kurt Salentin at Bielefeld University.

Among my fellow graduate students in Chicago, I thank first and foremost Jessica Borja, Chad Borkenhagen, Rick Moore, Thomas Swerts, and Christopher Takacs—truly encouraging and inspiring friends. During my final years at the University of Chicago, I participated in the Urban Doctoral Fellows Program, led by Joshua Garoon, which permitted me to clarify and develop my ideas. After completing my doctorate, I joined an excellent writing group of University of Chicago graduates: Gordon Douglas and Danielle Raudenbush, as well as Michaela Soyer, who had graciously hosted me during my first academic visit to Chicago and later passed on to me her beautiful Hyde Park apartment when she left town.

My fieldwork and dissertation were supported by a Doctoral Dissertation Research Improvement Grant (SES-1303625) from the National Science Foundation, research grants from the University of Chicago's Center for the Study of Race, Politics, and Culture and the Midwestern Sociological Society, and a Mellon Dissertation Completion Fellowship. While conducting fieldwork, I received precious guidance from Larry Bennett, an expert on all things Uptown, and Wesley Skogan, an expert on everything related to crime and policing. I also got advice from Ellen Berrey and Japonica Brown-Saracino, who had themselves conducted fieldwork on the Far North Side. Furthermore, I had the great fortune of studying Rogers Park at the same time as Florian Sichling, then a student at the University of Chicago's School of Social Service Administration. Florian greatly expanded my understanding of youth and Latino life in Chicago and helped me make sense of my fieldwork experiences as we worked in Andersonville bars and coffee shops.

I thank the study participants from Rogers Park and Uptown for speaking with me and letting me spend time with them. I think that many of them will not like this book very much, because it contains neither the vindications nor the indictments they may have desired. In my defense, I can say that I have done my best to incorporate their viewpoints and experiences without unduly distorting them. If the book elicits a grudging "fair enough," I will be happy.

I wrote much of the manuscript as a postdoctoral fellow at the University of Toronto. For making my unusual position there possible in the first place, I thank Richard Florida, whose generous support endowed me with much-needed time for research and writing, as well as access to a Swiss coffee machine. I am also grateful to my ninth-floor colleagues, especially Vass Bednar, Melanie Fasche, Ian Gormely, Michelle Hopgood, and Lauren Jones. Daniel Silver and Zack Taylor taught me much about Toronto and urban politics in general. Clayton Childress and Neda Maghbouleh kindly shared with me the prospectuses of their rightfully celebrated books and were also just very nice to me.

Many scholars have provided me with comments on earlier drafts of chapters in this book. Aside from my dissertation committee, they are Delia Baldassarri, Larry Bennett, Japonica Brown-Saracino, Jeffrey Denis, Laura Doering, David Engel, Robert Eschmann, Corey Fields, Gary Fine, Philip Goodman, Lauren Jones, Rory McVeigh, Andrew Papachristos, Jeffrey Parker, Poulami Roychowdhury, Nitasha Sharma, Eran Shor, Florian Sichling, Daniel Silver, Wesley Skogan, Forrest Stuart, and Thomas Soehl. I humbly thank them all. In addition, I acknowledge the feedback I received from departmental and workshop audiences at the University of Michigan's Department of Sociology, the International Center for Comparative Criminology at Université de Montréal, the Social Theory and Evidence Workshop at the University of Chicago, and Northwestern

University's Ethnography Workshop. Different versions of chapters 4 and 6 were published, respectively, in *Social Problems* and *Sociology of Race and Ethnicity*. I thank the reviewers and editors for helping me improve them.

At McGill University, I cherish my fellow faculty members' marvelous collegiality and intellectual stimulation. Truly exciting work is happening within these concrete halls. I thank all of my colleagues in the Department of Sociology and especially Sarah Brauner-Otto, Barry Eidlin, Jennifer Elrick, Matthew Lange, Céline LeBourdais, Poulami Roychowdhury, Eran Shor, and Thomas Soehl, as well as John Hall, who helped me complete the manuscript by memorably telling me that "the key to publishing a book is just to finish it and then write another one." I suppose his record proves him right. Four excellent (former) McGill students—Toma Itar Beit-Arie, Evan Mancini, Nora Shaalan, and Elise Soulier—read the complete manuscript and provided helpful feedback.

I thank all my friends in Jülich, Berlin, Bielefeld, San Diego, Chicago, Toronto, and Montreal—I cannot list them all, but they know who they are. Especially my friend Patrick challenged and taught me more than he could possibly know. I am also grateful to my fellow jazz friends, who gave me the opportunity to apply my mind to a very different set of problems and puzzles. I also thank my family. After initially trying to talk me out of majoring in sociology, my parents, Udo and Ulrike, my brother, Ingo, and my cousin, Britta, have consistently expressed unshakable trust in my academic future ("Du machst das schon."). I actually found this trust exasperating at first, since it seemed to offhandedly discount the many anxieties and obstacles the academic track entails, but eventually I found great comfort in it. I believe it must have empowered me somehow, because I cannot explain how I made it through in any other way.

Except by talking about Laura. Now, Laura and I will sometimes read out or make up acknowledgment lines when talking to each other, because we enjoy the delightful cringing they produce. So here I go. Laura has shared with me her graceful lightness and iron discipline, her unbending stubbornness and boundless empathy, her saltless calzones and bizarre songs, her high expectations and seemingly unconditional love. Without Laura, it really wouldn't be very much fun at all.

1

Introduction: The Battle over Race, Crime, and Gentrification

On a balmy Sunday evening in the early summer of 2012, a group of white residents assembled at around 9 p.m. on a street corner in Rogers Park, a racially diverse neighborhood on Chicago's North Side. The residents were members of a "positive loitering" group, which meant that they regularly walked the neighborhood together in order to deter crime and to report suspicious behavior to the police. By holding these events, the positive loiterers—I will call them the Lakesiders—wanted to signal that the community in this neighborhood was vigilant and not going to tolerate street crime. For about a year, this largely residential area of four-story apartment buildings had seen an increase in gang activity on the part of the Gangster Disciples. Several gang members had moved there and started dealing drugs from a unit on a rundown rental block and, occasionally, on nearby street corners. Because of a conflict with a different group ("crew") of Gangster Disciples from another part of the neighborhood, an uptick in shootings had occurred, and two people had been killed. After the shooting of one young black man, whom the police later identified as an innocent bystander, some residents had come together to form the Lakesiders.

As usual, the first to arrive that night was Bob, a retired, working-class man in his midfifties, bringing as always his dog, an ageing Labrador. Bob had founded the group. He scheduled the events and maintained the group's email listserv. Bob had receding gray hair, which he wore short and gelled back, a mustache, and thin-rimmed glasses. The second to join was Howard, a chubby and slightly disheveled-looking man. Bob and Howard were currently not on speaking terms. At the loitering event the night before, Bob had harshly criticized Howard for splitting off from the group and following a man whom the positive loiterers suspected of being a Gangster Disciple in order to find out where he lived. Bob had complained that Howard's action had been too dangerous.

Us versus Them. Jan Doering, Oxford University Press (2020) © Oxford University Press.
DOI: 10.1093/oso/9780190066574.001.0001

Having locked up my rusty mountain bike at a pole, I greeted the men, and we waited for additional members in silence, punctuated by my occasional unsuccessful efforts to start a conversation. Bob smoked a few cigarettes to pass the time. By around 9:30, the group was complete for the night, having reached a size of twelve. It now consisted evenly of men and women, including younger and older residents. One woman was East Asian; the rest were white. In addition, for a part of the night, the Lakesiders received an escort of two police officers in a patrol car, because yesterday one young black man—another gang member, according to the Lakesiders—had approached the positive loiterers to speak with them, which the group had interpreted as a threat. Those who had missed the event asked Bob to recount what had happened. Bob laconically repeated the conversation with a wry smile. The young man had asked what the positive loiterers were doing (Bob's reply: "Nothing."), why the residents were watching him and his friends from across the street (Bob: "Because we can."), and what Bob was writing on his notepad ("Just things."). The young man had then returned to his friends. After Bob had finished the story, the positive loiterers started to move through the neighborhood. The police officers remained in their car. At sporadic intervals, they started the engine and caught up with the group.

This specific night was unusually eventful, but it unfolded the same way the Lakesiders' positive loitering events generally did. Every so often, the Lakesiders came across a group of black adolescents who were hanging out, talking, laughing, or listening to music on their cell phone speakers. When the positive loiterers found such a group, they stopped across the street and watched them. After a short while, the young people then usually dispersed or walked away—tonight they certainly did so as soon as the police cruiser drove up. As the teenagers walked off, some of them complained, saying things like "I am not doing anything" or "I am just walking" without clearly addressing anyone in particular. That night, the positive loiterers had proceeded this way for about an hour and a half when the police officers left for the evening. But at around 11, the positive loiterers encountered yet another group of young black residents who were standing in front of a church building.

To me, the three men and two women in their late teens or early twenties looked like they were dressed to go out, perhaps to a club. They were engrossed in conversation and did not notice us at first. The Lakesiders lined up under a row of shady trees while their targets stood across the street in the open, under a streetlight. For two or three minutes, the young people ignored the positive loiterers and kept talking, but as the Lakesiders continued to scrutinize them, they began to look over. After another couple of minutes, one of the men walked up to the curb on his side of the street and started to shout at the positive loiterers: "Trayvon Martin! Trayvon Martin! Trayvon Martin!" His voice increased in volume and assertiveness as he repeated the exclamation. He then turned on his heels and walked back to his friends, who cheered him and exchanged high fives. They demonstratively resumed their conversation, making it a point to ignore the Lakesiders from then on.

By this evening in the summer of 2012, the death of Trayvon Martin at the hands of a neighborhood watch volunteer in Sanford, Florida, had already become a national flashpoint, a tragic icon for the harassment and violence black Americans are experiencing under the guise of crime fighting. In shouting "Trayvon Martin," the speaker was able to situate the encounter with the Lakesiders in this political context and, by extension, accuse the positive loiterers of racism. The Lakesiders, however, did not respond to this racial challenge and continued to watch for another minute. Finally, they quietly walked off and relocated to a different street corner, two blocks away. I asked Bob why we had left the prior corner. I saw that the other positive loiterers listened with interest. Bob replied: "They weren't going to move. They were digging in their heels." Despite the event's obvious emotional intensity, no one else commented on the incident. Soon, the Lakesiders decided to quit for the evening, and everyone went home.

In an email to the members of the listserv, which Bob sent the next day, he reported that the Lakesiders had successfully dispersed several groups of "bangers" until a final group had tried to provoke the positive loiterers. He commented: "I am very proud of the group's lack of response so that it did not 'feed' the situation!" But the racial challenge that the young man had leveled at the Lakesiders in shouting "Trayvon Martin" was never discussed.

Between 2011 and 2014, I studied the politics of crime and race in Rogers Park and Uptown, two racially integrated neighborhoods on Chicago's Far North Side. The confrontation between the Lakesiders and the group of black teenagers I just described represents one specific instance of a more general community conflict I observed in settings ranging from street corners to electoral campaign debates. Many residents regarded the fight against gang activity, shootings, and drug dealing as the most important local issue that had to be addressed in Rogers Park and Uptown. Like the Lakesiders, some became actively involved in public safety initiatives: they attended community policing meetings that enabled them to discuss local

problems with police officers and shape the police's priorities and strategies; they joined or formed block clubs that monitored crime and disorder
and also sought to influence local development decisions; and they participated in positive loitering events to reclaim public space. They also lobbied
for more police officers, and they called on the city to go after "problem
buildings" and "problem businesses" they suspected of abetting criminal
activity.

Others were less concerned about crime than the displacement and marginalization of low-income and minority renters. These residents argued that
the real question Rogers Park and Uptown were facing was not how to reduce
crime but how neighborhoods could remain racially and socioeconomically
diverse in the face of gentrification, which was slowly increasing the ranks of
middle-class whites at the expense of low-income black, Latino, and immigrant residents.[1] In highly segregated Chicago, these residents felt, these rare
integrated spaces had to be protected, especially on the prosperous North
Side, where nearby neighborhoods, such as Lincoln Park and Lakeview,
were already prohibitively expensive. As far as crime was concerned, any
interventions needed to target "root causes"—poverty, unemployment,
underfunded schools, and bad housing conditions—without making life
harder for low-income residents.

These competing views divided locally involved residents into two camps.
Following the activists' self-descriptions, I call them the "public safety" and
"social justice" camps. Each camp's members exhibited quite a bit of hostility
and distrust toward the other, and there was very little overlap in membership. As Eric, a middle-aged public safety activist from Uptown, said: "there
is an 'us versus them.' People in subsidized housing look at safety initiatives
as, you know, the evil condo owners teaming up, trying to get rid of everybody and gentrify the neighborhood." This perception of "us versus them"
reached deeply through the two neighborhoods and occasionally erupted
as full-blown conflict between neighbors, community organizations, and
candidates for public office.

Many of those opposing gentrification were convinced that public safety
activism—at least in the form in which it was conducted in Rogers Park and
Uptown—did not make anyone safer and was not even intended to do so.
Instead, they portrayed safety initiatives as barely covert racist practices.
The actual goal, they charged, was to intimidate, incarcerate, or simply
displace black, Latino, and low-income residents so as to fulfill hopes of
increasing home values and rents that would match those already found in

the surrounding highly gentrified areas. Social justice activists thus regarded public safety initiatives with scorn and sometimes directly attacked them. Due to their particularly belligerent practices, the Lakesiders, whom I will describe in more detail in chapter 6, drew more attributions of racism than other groups, but justice activists regarded most public safety initiatives as racially suspect.

By contrast, public safety activists and their organizational and political allies argued that all law-abiding citizens—including African Americans, Latinos, and immigrants—deserved to be safe. Block clubs, positive loitering groups, and community policing meetings were not about racially targeting residents or fostering gentrification but about reducing crime and ridding the neighborhoods of incorrigible, dangerous offenders. Unlike the Lakesiders, some safety activists engaged their critics and took proactive steps to demonstrate that their efforts were not rooted in racial animus or fears. But others complained that social justice activists were simply harping on race because it allowed them to discredit their opponents. The hosts of *Uptown Update*, for example, a blog that reported and commented on crime in that neighborhood, became so infuriated by charges of racism in the blog's comment sections that they explicitly forbade such charges and pledged to delete any entries that contained them.[2]

This book provides a detailed analysis of community conflicts about crime, race, and gentrification. In doing so, it makes two broad contributions to the state of sociological knowledge and theorizing. First, it contributes to research on the link between crime and gentrification, showing how anticrime initiatives can amplify gentrification and contribute to the marginalization of low-income, black, and Latino residents. Second, the book closely traces how individuals and organizations invoke race as they negotiate the politics of crime and gentrification. Analyzing Rogers Park and Uptown as arenas for the making of racial claims, I will examine the ways residents, activists, and politicians tried to influence the direction of neighborhood change by strategically deploying racial meanings—discrediting an intervention as racially divisive, charging an opponent with racism, defending a particular initiative as racially benign, and so on. As I will show, these struggles over racial meanings shaped important local outcomes. But before elaborating on these points, I must first establish some historical and structural context about the links between race, crime, and residential integration. These links are by no means unique to Rogers Park and Uptown but are essential aspects of the racial order of the United States.

Race, Crime, and Racial Integration

Crime and punishment have left a durable spatial mark on American cities and suburbs. At least since W. E. B. Du Bois's (1899) classic study of Philadelphia's black community, scholars have noted how whites' exaggerated fears of black crime have served to justify racial segregation, forcing African Americans into undesirable and underserved neighborhoods. After World War II, the issue of crime became even more pivotal for America's urban structure as whites moved to the suburbs in part to flee from the perceived lawlessness of the growing black population. African Americans were left behind in segregated neighborhoods deprived of services and resources. With the decline of urban manufacturing, many of these neighborhoods slipped by the late 1970s into severely concentrated poverty, from which many have not recovered to this day.[3]

Segregated and high-poverty neighborhoods lack both realistic opportunities for upward social mobility and the resources and collective efficacy needed to prevent crime. In these environments, hopelessness and alienation allow risky behavior and crime to thrive.[4] All of these problems are directly linked to racial segregation. On the basis of an ambitious study of crime and inequality in American neighborhoods, Lauren Krivo and Ruth Peterson (2010:114) concluded that the combination of racial segregation and poverty "is largely responsible for the dramatic inequalities in crime, particularly violent crime, that exist across urban neighborhoods."

The criminal justice system's focus on punishment rather than prevention and rehabilitation further destabilizes black neighborhoods. Over the last two decades, social scientists have assembled a vast scholarly literature that overwhelmingly demonstrates the negative effects of incessant police stops, institutional surveillance, and harsh punishment especially on African Americans.[5] These harmful impacts continue to gain visibility and prominence in black politics. Michelle Alexander's (2010) book *The New Jim Crow*, which identifies the criminal justice system as the heart of racial oppression in the post–civil rights era, has become a national bestseller. The nationwide social movement Black Lives Matter has emerged in response to high-profile cases of vigilantism and police brutality. Time and time again, cases like Trayvon Martin, Michael Brown, and Laquan McDonald rattle the nation. It is not surprising that many African Americans distrust the police, perceiving them not as a provider of security but as a hostile force that harasses, discriminates, and marginalizes.

Since racial segregation reproduces poverty and crime in black neighborhoods, residential integration could conceivably alleviate both of these problems.[6] There are some reasons for optimism in this regard. As scholars like Patrick Sharkey (2018) and Franklin Zimring (2007) have shown, crime has fallen dramatically in America's cities since its peak in the 1990s, although the neighborhood distribution of crime remains highly uneven. In principle, the general decline in crime means that white resistance against integration could soften. However, perceptions of black criminality remain deeply ingrained in American culture, complicating residential integration.

Many whites continue to shun neighborhoods with sizable black populations and oppose measures that might contribute to desegregation, such as the construction of affordable housing in largely white neighborhoods.[7] Aggregate measures of racial segregation are declining—which has led the economists Edward Glaeser and Jacob Vigdor (2012) to declare "the end of the segregated century"—but this trend reflects a steady influx of immigrants into urban neighborhoods more than increasing acceptance of black-white integration among whites. Thus, while racial segregation has decreased since the 1960s, black-white segregation in particular remains high.[8]

Against this background, it makes sense that crime would be a volatile topic in racially heterogeneous neighborhoods like Rogers Park and Uptown. From the perspective of most whites, low crime is the sine qua non of residential integration. Whites tend to feel unsafe and systematically overestimate crime rates in black and integrated neighborhoods. Both empirical studies and general theories of race and racism—such as the works of Lawrence Bobo (1999) and Eduardo Bonilla-Silva (1997)—suggest that whites' limited tolerance for racial integration hinges on keeping a tight lid on crime.[9] African Americans on the other hand often appreciate the superior conditions that integrated neighborhoods typically offer over segregated ones, but they can feel aggravated by the selective focus on black street crime that the police and their white neighbors tend to exhibit—as well as whites' inability or unwillingness to distinguish between the majority of law-abiding black residents and the minority of criminal ones.[10] Indeed, the confrontation between the Lakesiders and the group of young black residents I've described illustrates just this type of conflict. It is therefore easy to imagine that the issue of crime could divide entire neighborhoods along racial lines.

This potential for conflict is by no means limited to Rogers Park and Uptown. Without focusing on this particular issue, studies of diverse or gentrifying neighborhoods, including books by Lance Freeman (2006) and Evelyn Perry (2017), pinpoint crime as one major area of contention. Related stories can also be found in the news media. A 2017 piece in the *Atlantic* describes tensions over policing and surveillance in Brooklyn, concluding that "gentrification and aggressive policing are two sides of the same coin" (Fayyad 2017). Furthermore, many of the recently publicized cases of whites calling the police to request interventions in response to black people engaging in lawful and mundane behaviors like sitting in a coffee shop, barbequing, or using a swimming pool reveal a potent sense of threat whites experience in racially heterogeneous environments.[11] Whites' fear of black crime aggravates racial division.

At the same time, a smaller set of studies suggests that the fight against crime could produce the opposite outcome and actually coalesce urbanites of all backgrounds into strong communities. On the neighborhood level, blacks and whites have incentives to work together to ensure low crime, even if they disagree about larger questions of racial justice. Safety is a public good that all law-abiding residents need and want. According to George Kelling and Catherine Coles (1996:8–9), the main exponents of broken windows theory, public safety work "does not divide rich from poor, black from white, or one ethnic group from another. Instead, it unites diverse neighborhoods against those who behave in outrageous ways." Neighbors collaborating in grassroots initiatives, such as positive loitering groups or block clubs, could build trust and relationships across racial boundaries. In support of this claim, some studies have shown that anticrime initiatives can indeed strengthen the fabric of racially heterogeneous neighborhoods.[12]

These conflicting perspectives served as the initial puzzle that led me to study crime and race in Rogers Park and Uptown. I wanted to understand whether crime would unite or divide residents across racial lines. But very soon it became clear that this question was the wrong one, because it assumed that there was one correct answer—that black and white people formed cohesive political blocks that were either at peace or at war. Instead, I found both conflict *and* cooperation. In the public safety camp, whites strongly preponderated, but I also encountered African American safety activists.[13] The latter did not at all agree that fighting crime had anything to do with race or racism. Among the social justice activists, there were certainly more African Americans but also many whites. And of all the confrontations about the racial implications of fighting crime that I observed, most actually involved whites struggling with other whites. The political lines of alliance and opposition were thus too complex to fit my initial question.

As a result, I shifted my attention from the politics of racial groups to the politics of racial claims-making. How and when did specific actors invoke race? What could they hope to accomplish in doing so? What strategic value did specific racial narratives have? Asking these questions, I used Rogers Park and Uptown as sites for a fine-grained study of racial politics and its impact on the urban environment. As political microcosms, which exhibit partly independent political dynamics and feature a manageable set of relevant actors, these integrated neighborhoods afforded an excellent opportunity to do so. Following this approach provided much more interesting insights into racial politics and urban change than my initial question could have allowed.

Studying the Politics of Crime and Race in Rogers Park and Uptown

To examine the politics of crime and race, I conducted three and a half years of ethnographic fieldwork in Rogers Park and Uptown between the summer of 2011 and the spring of 2014. Rogers Park and Uptown are located along the lakefront of Lake Michigan on Chicago's Far North Side (see figure 1.1). Given that Chicago remains one of the most segregated cities in the United States,[14] the two neighborhoods represent anomalies. In 2010, 27 and 20 percent of Rogers Parkers and Uptowners, respectively, identified as black or African American; 25 and 13 percent as Latino; and 38 and 52 percent as non-Hispanic white. These neighborhood demographics reflect more closely than most neighborhoods the overall composition of Chicago, in which each of three groups—African Americans, Latinos, and whites—constitutes about 30 percent of the population. In this sense, it is accurate to call Rogers Park and Uptown "integrated."[15] This is not to say that at the time of my fieldwork all aspects of community life in these neighborhoods reflected their racial diversity. Echoing findings from other studies of integrated neighborhoods, I found that specific establishments and spaces frequently revealed micro segregation.[16] For example, only a handful of non-Hispanic whites attended the local high schools, despite the fact that they were the largest population group in both neighborhoods.[17] Neither does "integrated" mean that residents' networks were necessarily racially diverse. In speaking

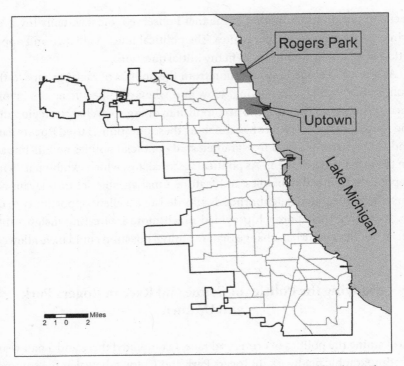

Figure 1.1. Rogers Park and Uptown in Chicago. Map created by the author.

of "integration," I mean to communicate only that residents lived close to members of other ethnoracial groups and thus had to engage or actively avoid one another in public life.

There were strategic and methodological advantages to studying Rogers Park and Uptown. Their proximity made it possible for me to conduct fieldwork in both neighborhoods at the same time, regularly going back and forth between them on the same day of fieldwork. Studying two neighborhoods increased the sheer number of opportunities for observing community events and identifying interviewees from rare populations, such as black safety activists. Having access to two neighborhood contexts also provided useful analytic and interpretive leverage for understanding each case better. Rogers Park and Uptown resemble each other in terms of their sociodemographic composition, crime rates, and vibrant traditions of community activism. Their match along these dimensions, all of which are central to the study, allowed me to compare how the politics of crime and race diverged or converged in similar environments.[18] In this process of contextualizing the findings, I could build not only on my own data but also on several accounts of community life and politics other scholars have published over the years.[19]

In order to study how residents negotiated the racial implications of fighting street crime, I observed positive loitering events, block club and community policing meetings, antigentrification protests, aldermanic town halls, and much more. I listened as social justice activists rehearsed protest songs on the way to picketing the home of a wealthy developer; I heard exasperated residents tell stories about notorious offenders who had accumulated hundreds of arrests; I witnessed black teenagers describe volatile police encounters at a racial justice book club; I helped block club members pick up trash while discussing the causes of crime. In this way, I created an extensive set of field notes. I also conducted interviews with seventy-eight African Americans, whites, Asians, Latinos, and Africans of all ages and backgrounds. Furthermore, I gathered a sizeable corpus of newspaper articles, blog posts, electoral campaign flyers, organizational documents, and secondary data, such as crime and census statistics. Together, these data create a richly detailed portrait of local politics and urban change. For more information on my methods and data, I refer interested readers to the methodological appendix.

I began this study with an interest in racial politics, but the book's substantial focus on crime emerged inductively from the fieldwork. During exploratory observations in 2010, I realized that crime was the right issue through which to examine local racial politics. Like most neighborhoods across the United States, Rogers Park and Uptown have seen steep declines in crime and violence since the 1990s. Their crime rates were also consistently lower than those in the highly segregated neighborhoods on the city's South and West Side. Nonetheless, it quickly became clear that crime was a major concern for many residents as well as a salient political issue.

The main problem residents invoked in this regard was the presence of criminal street gangs. In the territories they considered their turf, the gangs claimed parks, street corners, and parking lots where they would hang out and deal drugs. Residents felt intimidated by the gang members and the aggressive demeanor of the "code of the street" that Elijah Anderson (1999) has described, but beyond anything they feared the attendant shootings. Gang shootings distinguished Rogers Park and Uptown from surrounding neighborhoods. Anywhere else on Chicago's North Side gang shootings were very rare, but in Rogers Park and Uptown they claimed several lives each year. In 2012, for example, six people were killed in Rogers Park and five in

Uptown.[20] Furthermore, shootings were more frequent than these figures suggest. In 2013, shootings killed only one person in Uptown, but at least twenty more were injured.[21] In the aftermath of shootings, the police usually reported that the victims had themselves been involved in gang activity, but it was clear that uninvolved residents were sometimes hit as well. In 2014, a pedestrian was mistaken for a rival gang member in Rogers Park and shot dead in a drive-by shooting. According to the *Chicago Tribune*, the victim, a professional photographer, and his wife had moved into the neighborhood only two weeks earlier.[22]

Shootings caused a great deal of anxiety and anger, particularly when incidents clustered as a result of prolonged cycles of retaliation. During such outbursts of violence, residents frequently expressed outrage that "known gang members" could live freely in Rogers Park and Uptown, perhaps even in publicly subsidized housing. Why were they not arrested, or at least evicted and chased out of the neighborhood? Why should residents have to endure shootings while adjacent neighborhoods were evidently safe and thriving? Some residents decided to pack up and leave, claiming that one could not live or even raise a family where one had to worry about "thugs" and stray bullets.

Almost all Rogers Park and Uptown residents agreed that street crime and especially the shootings posed a serious problem, but the topic brought out heated disagreements over competing visions of neighborhood change. A sizeable segment of residents believed that the main challenge for the two neighborhoods was not crime but gentrification. Since the 1990s, the proportion of whites had grown in Rogers Park and Uptown, while the number of minority and immigrant residents had declined. The median income was rising fast, and homeownership rates were increasing while they were stagnating in the city as a whole.[23] Accordingly, critics of gentrification regarded public safety initiatives simply as a tool of racial displacement. For example, when I asked Phil, a white resident of Rogers Park, about organizations from the public safety camp, he said:

"A lot of the neighborhood organizations strike me as a nice middle-class version of gang turf wars. We don't like the gangs fighting for turf, but we're willing to fight for our turf as property owners and I'm not sure I see much difference between the two. The African American folks see gentrification happening and see it largely as white folks coming in and taking property that they'll never be able to have and making it less hospitable for them."

Given these conflicting priorities—to stop gentrification or to fight crime— residents, community organizations, and other local actors approached many local issues from two very different standpoints. What should be done about deteriorating rental towers? Who should be the next alderman? How should the police deal with loiterers on street corners? Members of the public safety camp answered these questions by assessing whether the available options would help to reduce crime. Social justice activists instead assessed the impact on gentrification and racial marginalization. Bitter conflicts—often framed in racial terms—broke out when residents engaged each other across this political divide. As I will show, these conflicts between the public safety and social justice camps deeply shaped the neighborhoods and their political fields.

The Field of Neighborhood Politics and Racial Claims-Making

Rather than portraying Rogers Park and Uptown in their entirety, as community studies traditionally aspire to do,[24] I zoom in to the neighborhoods' political fields and their influence on urban change. In doing so, I follow Neil Fligstein and Doug McAdam's (2012:9) helpful definition of a field as a "mesolevel social order in which actors (who can be individual or collective) are attuned to and interact with one another on the basis of shared (which is not to say consensual) understandings about the purposes of the field [and] relationships to others in the field." For analyzing neighborhood conflict, this definition turned out to be quite useful. Politics in Rogers Park and Uptown unfolded through the continuous interplay of community organizations and activist residents, who recognized one another as allies or foes and who tried to influence the direction of neighborhood change.[25]

The political fields' fundamental characteristics were similar in both neighborhoods. The fields' most consistent participants were the local aldermen, community organizations, and heavily involved activists who often worked with several organizations at the same time. Relationships between these core actors were often rooted in memories of conflicts and alliances that could span decades—the struggles of the past were very much alive in Rogers Park and Uptown.[26] Aside from the core actors, the fields' participants fluctuated. Otherwise-uninvolved residents were sometimes swept into the public safety camp through crime spikes in their immediate residential areas. The members of the Lakesiders, for example, had not been very active in Rogers Park before they started their positive loitering group in response to a sudden uptick in gang activity. On the other side, some tenants temporarily joined the social justice camp when their buildings were threatened by gentrification. In addition, nonresidents occasionally entered the fields by way of their professional roles: journalists, developers, the police district commander, and so forth.

I tried to observe and speak with the broadest possible range of local actors, including those who were active only on the margins—for example, posting messages on community blogs in order to influence their neighbors. In doing so, I aim to show how various levels of community dynamics—relationships between neighbors but also between local organizations, activists, and civic leaders—intersected and shaped one another. This approach ties into the tradition of work Matthew Desmond (2014) has described as relational ethnography. It is also informed by scholarly admonitions to move urban ethnography beyond the observation of street corners so as to incorporate a wider set of forces that structure urban life, including organizations, politics, and historical pathways.[27]

Remarkably, I found that almost all participants in the local political fields were either non-Hispanic white or African American. A few were Latino. But only very rarely did I encounter Asians, Africans, or members of additional ethnoracial groups at community policing meetings, antigentrification protests, or other events I observed. This is surprising, because Rogers Park and Uptown are home to sizeable Caribbean, African, and Southeast Asian communities. In the neighborhoods' political fields, however, these communities remained almost invisible, despite the fact that they had community organizations, such as churches, cultural associations, and social service agencies. In chapter 8, I describe several immigrant communities' perspectives on gentrification and crime, which are important and interesting in their own right. But in the ongoing conflicts I observed during my fieldwork, neither individuals nor organizations from these communities emerged as influential participants, and with the exception of chapter 8, they therefore play only a marginal role in this book.

Mirroring the racial composition of the neighborhoods' political fields, racial discourse about the politics of crime and gentrification revolved around "white" and "black" as reference points. Thus, social justice activists frequently charged that whites (sometimes class qualifiers were added: "white condo/home owners," "rich white folks," etc.) were using the police and other crime-fighting tools to target African Americans. This discourse framed public safety initiatives as a form of white-on-black aggression, and debates about this conflict eclipsed discussions of other ethnoracial groups and their experiences. This was true even in those parts of the neighborhoods where Latinos were the largest minority group. For example, Gary, the citizen facilitator for community policing in a police beat with a large Latino presence, remarked on this issue: "I find it particularly fascinating here that race is often a black and white conflict. There are actually more Hispanics [in this police beat]. Sometimes I think it's just an easy card to use." Safety activists and their allies—including police officers and other institutional agents—vigorously rejected the use of what Gary called the race "card," but usually the categories of "white" and "black" nevertheless remained the reference points in their defenses.

The dominance of the black-white relationship in local politics in Rogers Park and Uptown must be interpreted in a larger context. First, this axis has a special resonance in the American imagination—as Michèle Lamont and her colleagues (2016:56) write in a recent book, "tensions between whites and blacks remain particularly deep." In addition, the local issues that were at stake—gang activity and street crime on the one hand, racial profiling, harassment, and displacement on the other—fit squarely into existing fault lines of America's racial politics. Since the most important gangs in Rogers Park and Uptown (the Gangster Disciples, Black P. Stones, and Conservative Vice Lords) were considered "black gangs," their presence symbolically affirmed the broader "conflation of blackness and crime" (Wacquant 2002a:56) in American culture, although neither all offenders nor even all gang members were black or African American. For racial claims-making, all of this meant that blackness and whiteness were the most potent and thus also the most frequent points of reference in Rogers Park and Uptown. In the following section, I discuss racial claims-making in more detail.

Negotiating Racial Identities: Racial Challenges and Neutralizations

To conceptualize the dynamics of racial claims-making, I deploy two concepts: *racial challenges* and *racial neutralizations*. Like the "Trayvon Martin" shouts, racial challenges are utterances that hold individuals accountable for their behavior or views against the moral backdrop of their racial category. Racial challenges first and foremost consist of charges of white racism but also include any other statements that frame behaviors or views as racially problematic. Restrained statements of racial disapproval thus fall into this category as well. For instance, a person might express dissatisfaction with the fact that a company board is all white or that the syllabus for a social theory class includes only white writers. Furthermore, while racial challenges are often addressed to whites—the dominant group in American society—this is not necessarily always the case. For instance, a family member might challenge an African American woman over her involvement in the Republican Party.[28] None of these utterances qualify, in any immediate sense, as charges of racism, but they do establish situations of racial accountability, situations in which the addressees of racial challenges are expected to account for their actions and views against the background of their racial category.[29] Conversely, the concept of racial neutralization refers to any defensive or reparative "face work" that denies, downplays, or excuses alleged racial failings.[30] Racial neutralizations may be made in response to racial challenges but also occur in preemptive form, to prevent challenges from being made or from appearing plausible in the first place.

Racial challenges and neutralizations frequently draw on what C. Wright Mills (1940) called "vocabularies of motive." Some motives, such as racial animus, are socially unacceptable springs of action in the eyes of most Americans.[31] When challengers ascribe such motives to people, the latter generally defend themselves by explaining their actions in racially benign ways. If neutralization is impossible or unlikely to convince the relevant audience, the accused can still try to excuse their behavior as temporary lapses of judgment and promise to do better in the future.[32] But if they fail to neutralize or apologize—or to do so convincingly—they may have to accept, as Erving Goffman (1963) put it, a "spoiled identity" that can entail public scorn, disrupted relationships, and other adverse outcomes.

Racial challenges and neutralizations are consequential discursive practices. In John Austin's (1975) terms, they are illocutionary speech acts, which produce social changes in the world simply by being uttered by the right person under the right circumstances. And since they may bring about specific practical outcomes, racial challenges and neutralizations can be used for strategic purposes. The philosopher Mikhail Bakhtin (1986:94–95) suggested that all utterances are strategic in nature, but his arguments apply all the more to racial challenges and neutralizations: "from the very beginning, the utterance is constructed while taking into account possible responsive reactions, for whose sake, in essence, it is actually created. . . . When constructing my utterance, I try actively to determine this response.

Moreover, I try to act in accordance with the response I anticipate, so this anticipated response, in turn, exerts an active influence on my utterance (I parry objections that I foresee, I make all kinds of provisos, and so forth)." Racial challenges and neutralizations can bring about a whole range of practical outcomes. They produce emotional responses, such as anger or shame. They affirm favorable, but also confer unfavorable, social identities—bigot, racist, race-baiter, Uncle Tom, and so on.[33] Furthermore, they may reshape social relationships. After all, the ways individuals are positioned in relation to race influences the ways they can and cannot position themselves toward one another. Perhaps most important, racial challenges and neutralizations influence future conduct, because many lines of action require a certain degree of legitimacy to proceed. As C. Wright Mills (1940:907) wrote: "in many social actions, others must agree, tacitly or explicitly. Thus, acts often will be abandoned if no reason can be found that others will accept." While racial challenges and neutralizations are discursive practices, they therefore have consequences that transcend discourse itself.

Without using these particular concepts and definitions, scholars have previously studied racial challenges and neutralizations.[34] Most famously, Eduardo Bonilla-Silva (2003:70) has analyzed the neutralizations whites deploy as they attempt "to restore a color-blind image" after engaging in speech or actions that betray their negative views about racial minorities.[35] As for racial challenges, Leslie Picca and Joe Feagin's (2007) interviews show how some whites challenge other whites over racist stereotyping and jokes. Rarely are racial challenges and neutralizations examined together and in process, however. This is unfortunate, because the interplay of challenges and neutralizations shapes everything from interpersonal relationships to policy-making in the United States. Whenever it is unclear or contested whether an object of interest—whatever it might be: an action, a statement, or even a physical object, such as a Confederate memorial—is racially problematic or not, racial challenges and neutralizations rhetorically remove this uncertainty, often with vital practical consequences.

Racial challenges and neutralizations are always made in a concrete historical, political, and structural context that shapes the form these practices take, when they occur, and what their outcomes are. Until very recently, scholars argued that white Americans have become more responsive to challenges of bigotry and racism, embracing what the political scientist Tali Mendelberg (2001) has termed the "norm of racial equality." According to Mendelberg, whites have increasingly condemned overt racism, albeit without necessarily supporting comprehensive measures to address racial inequality.[36] The election and presidency of Donald Trump put the norm of racial equality in doubt, however. There are signs that at least some whites now discount charges of racism whole cloth.[37] This could mean that the political dynamics of challenges and neutralizations are undergoing fundamental historical changes. Nevertheless, it currently remains true that credible racial challenges engender robust public interest and that those who are targeted by them generally have to (and often do) neutralize their behavior, apologize, or resign. As Mustafa Emirbayer and Matthew Desmond (2015:162) write, "charges of racism brought by a well-organized movement can cost a political candidate an election or force a police chief to submit his resignation." Whether the Trump presidency indicates a lasting shift in racial norms remains to be seen.[38]

With this book, I provide a thick empirical case study of the dynamic interplay of racial challenges and neutralizations, which unfolded on interlocking levels of community life between neighbors, activists, community organizations, and political leaders in Rogers Park and Uptown. I ask: When and how do racial challenges and neutralizations occur? When do these strategies succeed? And what practical effects do they have?

Integrated neighborhoods represent ideal sites for examining racial challenges and neutralizations. And specifically the subject of crime can serve as a "key hole issue," to use Arlie Hochschild's (2016) term, that reveals larger features of America's racial politics. Americans are embroiled in an emotional debate over crime and criminal justice. Arguably, Chicago epitomizes this debate more than any other large American city. Chicago continues to witness rates of crime and violence that most other large cities have long left behind. Although Chicago's crime and homicide rates are still well beneath their 1990s peak levels, more homicides occurred there in 2016 than in New York and Los Angeles combined.[39] During his electoral campaign and presidential tenure, Trump has repeatedly invoked Chicago, President Barack Obama's hometown, as a prime example of the alleged disarray of America's cities, arguing that African Americans and Latinos "are living in hell, because it's so dangerous." He has promised to return Chicago to a state of "law and order" by allowing the police to be "very much tougher" and reinstating the unconstitutional practice of stop-and-frisk. Murder rates, he has suggested, remain high in Chicago primarily because police officers are forced to be "overly politically correct."[40]

Even without the Trump presidency, Chicago would still constitute a charged case. Nicole Gonzales Van Cleve (2016) has documented the way Chicago's criminal justice system aggravates racial inequality. As one stark sign of this bias, Black Lives Matter and other racial justice groups launched a successful campaign in 2016 to oust state's attorney Anita Alvarez from office for stalling in the case of Chicago Police Department officer Jason Van Dyke, who in 2014 killed Laquan McDonald, an unarmed black teenager, by shooting him sixteen times without any apparent justification or need.[41] During the final months of the Obama administration, the US Department of Justice released a scathing report about the Chicago Police Department's civil rights violations, which disproportionally hurt African American and Latino Chicagoans. As a result, the Chicago Police Department has now been put under federal oversight in order to implement reforms.[42]

These two long-standing problems—street crime and gang violence on the one hand, racial discrimination and harassment on the other—were very salient in Rogers Park and Uptown. I will discuss the way residents, activists, and politicians clashed over crime and gentrification. In this context, racial challenges and neutralizations emerged as key political strategies. The book will show that the struggle—a tug of war, really—over the racial meanings of fighting crime left a deep imprint on Rogers Park and Uptown. It shaped relationships between neighbors, uniting some of them while dividing them from others; it shaped the dynamics of the local political field and the alliances, battles, and even survival of community organizations; it shaped the neighborhoods' material form, such as the housing stock, and thereby also processes of sociodemographic change; it shaped electoral politics and the neighborhoods' representation in Chicago's city council. In short, racial challenges and neutralizations profoundly affected the cultural and material landscapes of Rogers Park and Uptown. In examining this impact, the book contributes to scholarship on racial politics as well as urban change and neighborhood processes.

Contributions to Urban Sociology

In addition to the study of racial politics, findings from this book advance work on gentrification, integration, and crime in urban neighborhoods. Given the fateful link between crime and neighborhood change, eminent urban scholars—including Harvey Molotch (1972), Elijah Anderson (1990), and Richard Taub and his colleagues (1984)—have long been interested in how integrated neighborhoods deal with crime. These classics are now quite old, however. Urban ethnographers since then have certainly acknowledged the importance of crime in community life but have rarely put the politics of crime front and center.[43] Two important urban transformations suggest that new work on this issue is needed.

First, many police departments have adopted community policing programs since the early 1990s.[44] These programs differ from place to place but often provide residents with additional channels of communication, resources, and tools to address crime. Civic public safety initiatives are nothing new in American neighborhoods, but one would expect that immediate support from, and access to, the police would change the way those initiatives proceed. How does this affect the politics of crime in integrated neighborhoods? Second, gentrification has accelerated and also become more contested in American cities since the 1990s.[45] One may therefore expect that interventions and initiatives to fight crime in gentrifying neighborhoods may incite more racial challenges and resistance today than they did in the 1970s and 1980s. To reveal the contested efforts of fighting crime in the age of Trayvon Martin, I will closely examine how safety activists justified and how justice activists resisted and countered anticrime initiatives in Rogers Park and Uptown.

Resistance against gentrification and associated forms of social control is an important subject in urban sociology, but results are often limited by researchers' study designs. A large segment of gentrification research draws primarily on interviews, which can trace both personal experience and involvement in local activism but not the actual processes of local struggle as it unfolds.[46] Other researchers approach neighborhood conflict largely through a mesosociological lens, mapping the organizational landscape and examining organizational coalitions and clashes within and beyond the neighborhood.[47] These studies provide valuable insights into political dynamics, but they often miss the microsociological footing that interview-based studies or street-level ethnographies can provide. I combine these approaches, studying formal politics and organizational contexts while also tracing community conflict in less structured environments, such as interpersonal encounters at positive loitering events and town hall forums.

A necessary step for analyzing resistance, of course, is to actually examine *what* was being resisted—in this case specifically public safety activism under the institutional umbrella of community policing. Patrick

Carr (2005), Archon Fung (2004), and Wesley Skogan and Susan Hartnett (1997) have previously analyzed civic participation in community policing. This book contributes to that literature by discussing public safety initiatives in detail and uncovering how they galvanized community conflict. Perhaps the closest precedent for this approach is Mary Pattillo's (2007) study of gentrification in a black neighborhood on Chicago's South Side. Indeed, some of the dynamics I observed reminded me of Pattillo's findings. As in Pattillo's North Kenwood-Oakland, efforts to crack down on crime imposed costs primarily on low-income residents. But what made conflict over the politics of crime particularly charged in Rogers Park and Uptown was the added layer of racial difference. The racial implications of local struggle engendered a strong degree of emotional, visceral commitment on both sides of the political divide. It made the politics of crime not only contested but bitter.

Analyzing public safety initiatives and how they may affect racial marginalization, this book complements work on racial inequality and its reproduction, especially in gentrifying areas. Victor Rios (2011) has revealed the everyday marginalization that black and Latino youth in Oakland, California, experience at the hands of the police and other agents of social control while the city around them gentrifies. As Rios argues, this marginalization produces resilience and valuable survival strategies but it can also render young people unable to succeed in school or the labor market, keeping them disempowered.[48] Illuminating another angle of marginalization, Matthew Desmond and Nicol Valdez (2013) have shown how Milwaukee landlords evict tenants in order to reduce their buildings' volume of 911 calls, because high numbers can lead the city administration to fine landlords for violating "nuisance" or "problem building" ordinances. Desmond and Valdez report that such ordinances are applied more stringently in the racially mixed parts of the city. Adding to this important body of work, I show that there is a demand side to these phenomena. Police harassment, "problem building" interventions, and evictions do not just occur naturally or as a result of the city administration's initiative. They are connected to the deliberate efforts of residents and community organizations to *use* the criminal justice system for the purpose of constraining and displacing unwanted neighbors. Analyzing how this occurs uncovers important mechanisms of gentrification and its various manifestations—from "condofication" to the quotidian battles over public spaces that recent cases like those of "Sidewalk Sally" and "BBQ Becky" have highlighted.[49]

Finally, this book contributes to scholarship on the politics of race and gentrification by revealing the complex lines of conflict and collaboration among diverse residents. In his influential work on the "revanchist city," urban geographer Neil Smith (1996) portrayed gentrification as a rather straightforward battle between different classes and races. Since then, gentrification scholars have painted a more complex picture. Japonica Brown-Saracino (2009) and Derek Hyra (2017) have shown that gentrifiers are heterogeneous in terms of race, politics, sexuality, and other factors. Lance Freeman's (2006) work on Harlem demonstrates that low-income, black residents often feel ambivalent about gentrification, expressing support for at least some aspects of the process. Building on and extending this work, I will show that the lines of conflict in Rogers Park and Uptown did not always match the boundaries of race and class. Some black, low-income residents reliably sided with the police and white public safety activists, their civic allies. Conversely, many of the most vocal gentrification critics were white and middle-class. Conflict sometimes pitted white against black residents, but also whites against other whites and blacks against blacks.

In their political claims-making, activists often simplified these complex divisions, using racial challenges and neutralizations to do so. When safety activists exclaimed "we're all in this together," they neutralized the politics of crime and rhetorically conjured a united community, thereby trying to render this unity a real thing. And when their adversaries stated that safety activism was all about white homeowners pushing out black residents, they conjured a racially divided community through racial challenges. Clear political alignments were projected in situations that were almost always racially ambiguous. Eventually, I realized that such statements were not only statements about perceived discord and cohesion but were actually meant to strategically *summon* these patterns. To no small measure, racial unity and strife were rhetorical accomplishments.

Outline and Scope of the Book

The book is organized as follows. Chapter 2 sets the urban stage on which the scenes I describe in subsequent chapters play out. It begins by describing the problems of street crime and gang violence and then recounts Rogers Park and Uptown's urban development, from their early histories through racial integration and the arrival of gentrification. Returning to the present, the chapter then introduces the fields of neighborhood politics and their main actors.

Chapter 3 homes in on grassroots strategies for fighting crime. What did the safety activists actually do and what grounds were there for claims that their efforts were racist? This chapter examines the ways the activists tried to harness state services by systematically calling 911, imposing stricter sentencing through court advocacy, "reclaiming" public space for law-abiding citizens, and attacking "problem buildings" and "problem businesses." All of these practices were ostensibly race-neutral but often had racially disparate impacts. The chapter also begins to show how critical residents challenged these practices and how safety activists justified them.

Chapter 4 examines one context that crucially shaped local dynamics in both neighborhoods: electoral campaigning. Aspiring aldermanic candidates frequently highlighted the prevalence and dangers of street crime and framed opponents (especially incumbents) as soft on crime. But those opponents could, in turn, make racial challenges and claim that tough-on-crime campaigning amplified and marshaled whites' racial fears. The chapter analyzes how aldermanic candidates framed the fight against street crime as racist or race-neutral and uncovers preconditions of making successful racial challenges in that context.

Electoral politics had significant implications for the relations between social justice and public safety organizations. Justice activists in Rogers Park and Uptown equally despised the safety initiatives, but during my fieldwork overt and systematic interorganizational conflict materialized only in Uptown, where justice organizations fought bitterly to prevent accelerated racial displacement after an ostensibly progentrification alderman was elected in 2011. Chapter 5 analyzes their resistance. Uptown's justice activists were able to score a symbolic victory against the alderman and his allies, but their campaign also further divided the neighborhood, which undercut the efficacy of public safety initiatives as well as CeaseFire, a violence prevention program, during a spike in gang violence.

Chapter 6 offers an in-depth examination of two positive loitering groups, one from each neighborhood. The chapter analyzes how safety volunteers responded to the neighborhoods' different climates of racial contestation. In doing so, it reveals an irony of racial politics. Because crime was a hotly contested topic in Uptown, a local positive loitering group self-consciously engaged African Americans and avoided practices that could have exposed the positive loiterers to racial challenges. These efforts fashioned the group into a site of interracial cooperation in a polarized neighborhood. By contrast, the positive loiterers in Rogers Park did not expect to face racial challenges and developed an aggressive style that alienated black and Latino residents. In addition, this chapter reveals that black and Latino residents did not oppose public safety activism monolithically—some of them joined positive loitering initiatives to promote peace and safety, although the Rogers Park group failed to accommodate them.

Chapter 7 focuses on the imperfect alignment between racial categories and the politics of crime and gentrification. It introduces several black and white residents whose cases complicate a simple reading of community conflict as a battle between whites and African Americans. Rather, the chapter shows that neighborhood politics elicited discord not only between but also within racial groups. Uncovering the entire range of conflict and collaboration, the chapter produces a more complete description of the dynamics of racial politics and, in doing so, calls for a less deterministic approach to interpreting the link between race and political decision-making.

Residents with immigration backgrounds rarely participated in neighborhood politics and activism. What was their perspective on crime and gentrification, and how did they position themselves when they had to take sides? Chapter 8 provides a snapshot of three immigrant communities: Uptown's Southeast Asian enclave, Rogers Park's Latino-dominated Clark Street, and a community of African immigrants residing in both neighborhoods. The chapter uncovers some reasons for their low levels of political involvement and shows how ongoing neighborhood conflicts affected them.

The conclusion elaborates the book's contributions to the field of race and racial politics as well as to several areas of urban sociology: residential segregation and integration, crime and neighborhoods, gentrification and resistance. The appendix expounds the methods and data that provide the empirical foundation for this book.

Not all chapters systematically distinguish between findings from Rogers Park and Uptown. The different political contexts in the two neighborhoods had substantial effects on the shape of local racial politics, and this sometimes has necessitated separate analyses. Those neighborhood-level differences become visible especially in chapters 4, 5, and 6. At the same time, I also found extensive similarities and thus combine the findings in other chapters to provide a more general account. The strategies of public safety work I describe in chapter 3 were the same in both neighborhoods, and so were the challenges activists faced in reconciling their racial identities and political positions, as outlined in chapter 7.

Before proceeding, I should note that this book is primarily a sociological and not a criminological study. Throughout, I remain agnostic about the impact particular anticrime or prevention initiatives may have had on crime. I also do not report detailed information about criminal gangs because the gangs stayed on the sidelines of neighborhood politics—they tended to be the objects, not the subjects, of local debates.[50] Instead, I examine the meanings people *projected onto* the gangs and the closely related but broader phenomenon of street crime. Why was street crime and gang activity happening in Rogers Park and Uptown? How big a problem were these things? How ought they be addressed? And were existing interventions effective or useless, just or unjust, racist or benign, divisive or unifying? These are the questions residents, activists, and politicians battled over and the book describes.

2

A Brief History of Living Together

Mimi and Mahandra married in 2010 and joined households in Mahandra's Uptown condo the following year. The condo, located in the Clarendon Park area, was a large and fully refurbished two-bedroom apartment that featured exposed brick walls, a large patio with access to a shared backyard, and a small balcony that Mimi lovingly spruced up with plants and flowers. Mahandra had bought the condo in 2007 after living a few blocks to the south for several years.

Mahandra knew that Clarendon Park was a racially mixed area that exhibited stark socioeconomic contrasts. Aside from the recently renovated six-flat buildings that drew new middle-class residents to Uptown, the area's housing stock also included Chicago Housing Authority townhouses and apartment buildings that had clearly seen better days. Most of the storefronts along the main streets were occupied by African stores that catered to recent immigrants, laundromats, convenience stores, and social service agencies that supported low-income residents of all racial backgrounds.

Mahandra also knew that Uptown experienced occasional bouts of gun violence, but he did not know that the condo was located right in the center of the Conservative Vice Lords' turf. When he bought the condo, the gang presence was at a longtime low—he later heard that some of the gang members were in jail at the time. He did not even become aware of the Vice Lords until 2009, when he began to notice a group of black teenagers and young men who were hanging out on the corner the condo's balcony overlooked. In 2010, he heard gunshots for the first time and also realized that drugs were being sold on the corner.

One Sunday afternoon in the summer of 2011, Mimi was out on the balcony watering her plants when she heard loud gunshots. She defensively dropped to the ground. There were shouts, and as she got up, Mimi saw a young black man lying on the street; a pool of blood was forming around his leg. She called the police. In the street below, another man used his T-shirt to apply pressure to the victim's leg while others loudly called for revenge. As

Us versus Them. Jan Doering, Oxford University Press (2020) © Oxford University Press.
DOI: 10.1093/oso/9780190066574.001.0001

the police and paramedics arrived, the crowd dispersed. That same night, a retaliatory drive-by shooting occurred several blocks to the west in the territory of the Black P. Stones. One twenty-three-year-old man was shot in the head and died; another person was severely injured. This violent day started a gruesome cycle of violence that, over the following months, brought many more shootings, more injuries, and several more deaths.

The gang presence became a focal point in Mimi and Mahandra's lives. Mahandra grew quite anxious about the situation and started to, in Mimi's words, "obsessively" monitor the corner where the Vice Lords loitered. Mahandra, who worked as a physical therapist, had been raised in Thailand by Indian parents; he said, "I'm an immigrant in this country. I wanted to come to America, get a job, make money. Last thing I wanted to do is live in a place where there are shootings going on. I just want to live my life, be happy. And all of a sudden I'm thrust into this situation and I'm like 'Damn these kids!'" Mimi, a music teacher, had grown up working-class and felt a responsibility to empathize with the young men, who seemed scared and vulnerable to her. She made a point of greeting the Vice Lords when she walked by. Once, she handed them a tray of homemade cupcakes that she had brought back from her students' music recital. She enjoys recalling their stunned surprise at being treated with kindness and how they would subsequently call her "Ma'am."

As the gang activity continued, Mimi and Mahandra began to attend community policing meetings, joined a positive loitering group, and became members of the local block club. When Mimi and Mahandra realized that several Vice Lords lived in a nearby Chicago Housing Authority townhouse, they took pictures of those leaving and entering the building and shared the pictures with the police and Alderman James Cappleman, their city council representative. An investigation began. The Chicago Housing Authority found that the lease-holding woman no longer inhabited the unit in question. Violating the terms of her lease, she had allowed her son to move in with her after he was released from jail. She had soon moved out thereafter—now, only her son and his friends lived there. Given that the legal context was straightforward, the Chicago Housing Authority evicted the tenants. Mimi told me that she felt torn about this outcome, as well as her work with the anticrime initiatives in general. After all, she said, the men had to live *somewhere*. It felt wrong to her to push them into another neighborhood that would presumably be poor and racially segregated. Still, she didn't know what else could have been done.

The eviction reduced but did not end the drug dealing and the shootings close to Mimi and Mahandra's condo. They continued to worry and frequently pondered their options for leaving Uptown. They could sell the condo but told me that they would have to accept a stiff loss due to the recent crash of the housing market. According to them, renting the unit out would bring in less than they had to pay toward their mortgage in monthly installments. When I spoke with Mimi and Mahandra, I never knew what their plans currently were—sometimes, they were sure that they were going to move; at other times, they had made a final decision to stay. When I asked her about this, Mimi said: "it's kind of like every day we change our minds. If there is no body outside or no shootings, we're like, 'We can stay here forever,' and then if there's a shooting, we're like, 'Oh my god, we have to move.' It's a daily thing. We just can't make a decision." But in 2015 they finally sold, leaving Uptown and moving northwest to Edgewater. Their new apartment was just over a mile away from their Uptown home, but to them it felt like a different world, located at a safe distance from any gang-related shootings.

Mimi and Mahandra's experience was not unusual. When interviewing Rogers Parkers and Uptowners, I would first ask about the best and the worst experiences they had had living in their neighborhoods. Many talked about the gangs when answering the second question. Several had been caught in crossfire. Gretchen, a white Rogers Parker bound to a wheelchair, reported being outside with her dog when gunfire erupted between the far ends of the alley she was traversing. Some mentioned limiting their time outside, hoping that they would not be personally affected. This was especially true for immigrants. In Uptown's Southeast Asian enclave around Argyle Street, Mr. Wong, a social worker, constantly tried to persuade Chinese and Vietnamese residents not to ignore street crime but to call the police when they saw drug dealing. However, some who refused to look away had been exposed to dangerous situations. Kay, a middle-class African American, recounted what happened when she went to investigate a car that had parked behind her house in Rogers Park's dense and majority-black North of Howard area:

The car was bouncing up and down so some guy was out there with some female and I went out there and I said "Excuse me, you are in a private parking space. You have to move," and they didn't pay any attention to me. The guy just sort of turned around and looked at me and kept doing what he was doing. And so this time I said it a little louder. "Excuse me, you have to

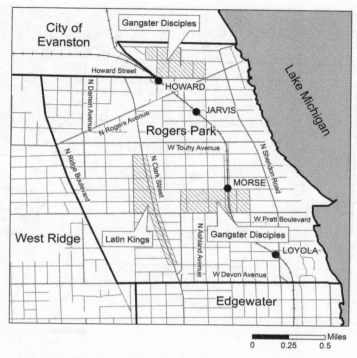

Figure 2.1. Gang territories in Rogers Park. Map created by the author.

get out of my parking space." And he just sort of reached down and I guess he just had the gun under his seat and he just sort of pulled it out and stuck it out the window.

Not all residents came into regular contact with street crime. Much of the gang activity remained limited to specific areas in both neighborhoods (see figures 2.1 and 2.2). In Uptown, there were three areas: Clarendon Park, the area in southeastern Uptown where Mimi and Mahandra lived; a section of Sheridan Park (to the west of Clarendon Park) between Wilson and Montrose Avenues; and the area between the Lawrence and Argyle "L" train stops. In Rogers Park, there were mainly two areas, the blocks south of Morse Avenue (Gretchen lived there) and the North of Howard area, where Kay lived. Other parts of the neighborhoods saw occasional flare-ups of drug dealing and other forms of street crime—sometimes related to gangs, sometimes not—but for the most part people could live there without thinking about crime.

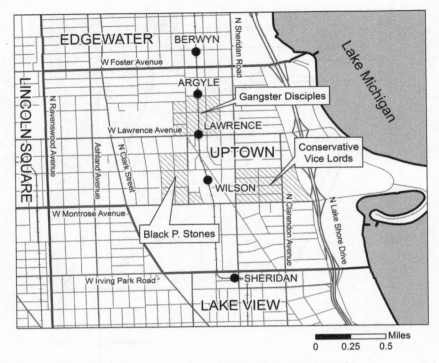

Figure 2.2. Gang territories in Uptown. Map created by the author.

The gangs sold drugs, including crack cocaine, heroin, and marijuana. They had to adapt to the local context, however. As increasingly middle-class neighborhoods with strong community organizations, Rogers Park and Uptown received a significant amount of police attention. Although each gang crew had a street corner that served as their default hangout, some of the crews regularly walked the block, which made it less likely for people to call the police and harder for the police to engage them. The Conservative Vice Lords in Clarendon Park did so, for example. After observing them for a while, Mimi commented, "It's a shitty life. I see these kids walk the circle 500 times a day because if they loiter on this corner, somebody calls the police. If they loiter on that corner, somebody calls the police." When the police appeared, the young people usually dispersed or relocated. Some entered nearby buildings. Others used holes in park fences to escape through backyards or alleyways. To the frustration of those calling 911, they would frequently return to their corners a few minutes later.

The gangs who sparked the most debate and fear in Rogers Park and Uptown—the Black P. Stones, Gangster Disciples, and Vice Lords—were considered "black gangs," although several had Latino and African members.[1] In Rogers Park, Clark Street was associated with the Latin Kings, but residents almost never talked about this gang. The Latin Kings did not maintain a steady public presence. During the time of my fieldwork, they were also at peace with the other gangs in the neighborhood and did not become embroiled in drive-by shootings. In the politics of crime, they therefore played only a very small role. I discuss the Clark Street community and the Latin Kings in more detail in chapter 8.

On average, about five people were killed annually in each neighborhood over the ten-year period 2009–2018. For both community areas, this corresponds to a rate of approximately nine homicides per 100,000 residents; the average rate for Chicago's seventy-seven community areas was seven homicides per 100,000 residents.[2] When assessing these figures, one must recall Robert Sampson's (2011) finding that many Chicago neighborhoods have very low homicide rates, while segregated and low-income black and Latino neighborhoods have very high ones. When residents compared their violent crime rates to the highly gentrified and mostly white areas on the city's North Side, Rogers Park and Uptown certainly stood out.

Nearly all of the victims were African American; a few were Latino. The police classified the vast majority of homicides as "gang-related" and the victims as "gang-involved," although family members and friends typically disputed these classifications. The police acknowledged that uninvolved people were occasionally injured or killed. According to the police and CeaseFire, a violence prevention program, the violence had less to do with turf wars than with interpersonal slights and rivalries. Some residents believed that the gun violence resulted from gentrification forcing the gangs to compete over the shrinking territory where they could still operate. Nevertheless, almost all violence was related to long-standing and very local histories of conflict. Shared gang affiliations meant little in this context.[3] In Uptown, all three gangs fought each other, although the Conservative Vice Lords and the Black P. Stones are generally considered allies because they are members of the People Nation alliance. In Rogers Park, most of the violence unfolded between two Gangster Disciples crews, the ICGs (Insane Cutthroat Gangsters) from the Morse area and the LOCs (Loyalty Over Cash) from North of Howard. As Pete, a senior community organizer and director of Rogers Park's CeaseFire program, explained:

No one's trying to . . . they're not fighting to take over a territory. They're fighting because of interpersonal conflicts. Because you've killed my buddy, I'm going to kill your buddy. It's not about drugs. That sort of stuff is intended to kill people to make a point or to get back at other people. I've had years of experience being on the ground and talking to everyone that's been involved with the conflict—that's what I'm hearing.

Naturally, the shootings greatly increased the attention community leaders and the police paid to the gangs, which undermined the economic potential of drug dealing. Television shows like *The Wire* and Sudhir Venkatesh's (2008) book *Gang Leader for a Day* depict gangs as relatively commercially minded organizations, but this was not the case in Rogers Park and Uptown. Here, business interests often took a backseat to the interpersonal altercations that Pete described.[4]

Rogers Park and Uptown's police-reported crime rates were relatively low when compared with Chicago's more distressed neighborhoods on the South Side and West Side. Figure 2.3 shows the index crime rates for Rogers Park, Uptown, and Chicago from 1998 to 2018. These rates are simple sums of several types of offenses, including homicide, sexual assault, and motor vehicle theft.[5] Of course, one may question how these rates reflect the local experience of crime—oddly, the index treats one homicide as the equivalent of a stolen car. However, residents frequently relied on this figure to assess trends in crime, which means that it had political significance.

Rogers Park and Uptown have consistently had index crime rates below the Chicago average. Of course, the Chicago average is elevated by the extraordinarily high rates of crime in low-income and racially segregated neighborhoods,[6] and accordingly, many residents argued that crime in Rogers Park and Uptown *was* high in comparison to crime in nearby North Side neighborhoods such as North Center or Lincoln Square. More important, however, there was a widespread *perception* that gun violence in particular was getting worse. I could not discern any such pattern in homicide trends—the number of homicides had remained fairly constant over the previous decade—but residents holding very different political attitudes about the topic of crime agreed that violence was escalating.

This agreement matters. As the following chapters will show, social justice activists claimed that white homeowners exaggerated crime so as to advance

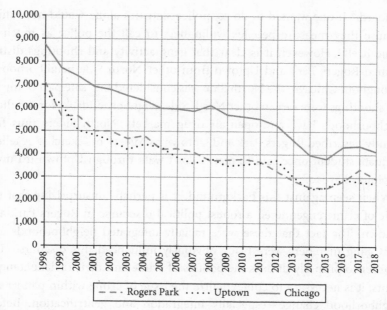

Figure 2.3. Index crimes per 100,000 residents in Rogers Park, Uptown, and Chicago (1998–2018).

Sources[7]: Chicago Police Department annual reports (for 1998-2010 data), Chicago Police Department Research and Development Division (FOIA request for 2011-2013 data), Chicago Data Portal "crimes–2001 to present" dataset (for 2014-2018 data).

gentrification. But this charge of strategic exaggeration did not apply to violence—gentrification critics found the shootings just as horrifying as the public safety activists. For example, I once observed an Uptown group of social justice activists as they held a "speak-out" with teenagers during an afterschool event that aimed to promote peace. One of the activists, an African American man named Wes, became increasingly agitated as he talked about the violence he was witnessing in Uptown, where he had been born and had lived all his life. His voice shaking, he said, "I'm thirty-three years old, and I've *never* seen this place like this. It's like the Wild, Wild West. I'm scared for my son! I'm scared for you all!"

For the politics of crime, perceptions carry more weight than the actual prevalence of crime, and I therefore did not try to establish whether Rogers Park and Uptown *really were* high-crime areas according to some objective standard.[8] If one wanted to do so, police statistics alone would not suffice because they measure people's willingness to call the police as much as crime itself.[9] However, it is clear that gang activity and shootings distinguished Rogers Park and Uptown from other North Side neighborhoods. Throughout Chicago, the North Side was considered the "safe part of town," and shootings were rare in other North Side neighborhoods.[10] Nor did these neighborhoods have any open-air drug markets. North Siders thus frequently described Rogers Park and Uptown as "dicey" or "sketchy." A fellow graduate student once said to me: "I don't walk through Uptown if I don't absolutely have to."

When seen against this background, it is perhaps unsurprising that the topic of crime engendered a robust political discourse in Rogers Park and Uptown. The fact that these were racially integrated neighborhoods and most gang members were black obviously influenced this discourse. But in order to properly discuss the politics of crime and their racial entanglements, it is necessary to contextualize the issue of crime within patterns of neighborhood change—especially integration and gentrification. Before returning to present-day politics later, I will present here a brief history of how the neighborhoods integrated and how, more recently, gentrification has changed them.[11] These processes made Rogers Park and Uptown into the arenas of political and racial conflict that I examine in later chapters. In addition, the processes themselves reflect larger societal changes, and their local manifestations reveal the ways the cases I examine in this book were constituted through the interaction of larger structures and forces.[12]

Before Integration

Chicago turned into a booming town around the middle of the nineteenth century, especially after the Illinois and Michigan Canal connected the Chicago River to the Mississippi.[13] The area where Rogers Park and Uptown are located today, however, remained rural until the early twentieth century, when the elevated rail service (called the "L" by Chicagoans) reached the area, bringing rapid access to downtown. Rogers Park and Uptown quickly developed into attractive residential areas that offered a respite from the industrial city. Chicago was within reach, but urban dwellers could live and play here away from the city's chaos, pollution, and poverty, which novelist Upton Sinclair (1906) so intensely captured in *The Jungle*. Of course, their distance from the city also isolated Rogers Park and Uptown from the Great Migration of African Americans who were streaming into Chicago and other industrial cities from the South during the early 20th century. Uptown had a small settlement of about 500 African Americans, but it derived from an earlier era of paternalistic race relations, when the presence of black people was perceived less as a threat and more as a status marker.[14] As the *Local Community Fact Book* suggests, the settlement "probably started when the Uptown area was one of single-family homes of wealthy people who had Negro servants."[15]

For several decades, Uptown was Chicago's *en vogue* neighborhood and attracted large numbers of young and well-to-do whites. Between 1907 and 1917, Uptown was home to the Essanay Studios, which briefly made it the center of the American movie industry and brought film stars like Charlie Chaplin and Gloria Swanson to the neighborhood. Ballrooms and nightclubs sprouted, including the Aragon, the Riviera, the Uptown Theatre, and the Green Mill, all of which still exist today. The blocks around the Wilson "L" station turned into an upscale shopping district. While Rogers Park never developed quite the same ritzy reputation, its development nonetheless mirrored Uptown's. As in Uptown, entertainment venues emerged, especially along Howard Street, where visitors from nearby Evanston frequented taverns to circumvent Evanston's liquor ban. In the southeastern corner of Rogers Park, Jesuits founded Loyola University in 1909.

Throughout the metropolitan area, construction ground to a halt with the onset of the Great Depression in 1929 and did not really resume until after 1945. In the 1940s, a housing shortage emerged as workers from around the country moved to Chicago in search of employment in the defense industry. Responding to the unmet demand, landlords subdivided their units, often in violation of city building codes. Uptown's spacious apartments in particular proved well suited for subdivision. By the end of the war, both neighborhoods' appeal had declined considerably.

More important, a period of major urban change began that fundamentally reshaped Chicago and indeed many American cities. State-subsidized housing loans and a massive highway construction program initiated a push in suburbanization that steered white Chicagoans to the suburbs. At the same time, aggressive real estate practices, including blockbusting and fearmongering about the city's black population, further encouraged whites to leave. Previously, Chicago's African Americans had been forced to reside in the South Side's overcrowded Black Belt, whose geographical expansion had been slow and met with violent resistance. Suburbanization policies, however, facilitated white outmigration and opened up new inner-city neighborhoods to black Chicagoans. Through white flight, these neighborhoods soon became as segregated as the Black Belt had been.[16]

The North Side initially remained insulated from this sweeping racial change. On the North Side too, however, vacancy rates soared, rents plummeted, and the housing stock deteriorated as more and more of those who could do so moved to the suburbs. Uptown had to confront this problem sooner than Rogers Park. After the war, Uptown, with its cheap subdivided apartments, received a large influx of poor white southerners from Appalachia, who migrated to the cities as a result of the mechanization of the coal industry.[17]

Racial Integration

By the late 1960s, Southeast Asian refugees, Native Americans, and immigrants from Mexico and Latin American had joined Uptown's southern whites.[18] Uptown's commercial vitality and housing stock had reached a low point. The homeownership rate reached a historic low of less than 5 percent in 1970, while the overall rate for Chicago stood at 35 percent. Homeless shelters, mental health services, halfway houses, and soup kitchens appeared.[19] In 1974, an article from the *Chicago Tribune* declared Uptown Chicago's largest "skid row."[20]

It was during this period of decline that the neighborhood opened up for African Americans.[21] In 1970, blacks still constituted only 4 percent of Uptown's population, but their share of the population continued to grow, reaching 15 percent in 1980 and then 25 percent in 1990 (see table 2.1). In Rogers Park, disinvestment occurred later and more slowly than in Uptown. Black inmigration began in the North of Howard area, which had turned into a sketchy row of taverns that continued to serve visitors from Evanston.[22] The 1970 Census identified approximately 6 percent of North of Howard's residents as black, but Rogers Park overall was still virtually entirely white. However, its black population increased steadily, from just 1 percent in 1970 to 5 percent in 1980 and 27 percent in 1990 (see table 2.1). During this period,

Table 2.1. Ethnoracial and sociodemographic composition of Rogers Park and Uptown, 1970–2010.

		1970[a]	1980[a]	1990[a]	2000[b]	2010[b]
Rogers Park	Population	60,787	55,525	60,378	63,484	57,559
	White (%)	96	77	55	32	38
	Afr. Am./Black (%)	1	9	27	30	27
	Asian (%)	N/A	8	9	6	7
	Hispanic/Latino (%)	5	12	20	28	25
	Poor families (%)	5	12	16	18	20
	Median family income	$11,306	$18,784	$27,330	$34,999	$51,211
	(% in relation to Chicago)	(110)	(100)	(89)	(82)	(96)
Uptown	Population	74,838	64,414	63,839	63,551	54,995
	White (%)	88	57	47	42	52
	Afr. Am./Black (%)	4	15	25	21	20
	Asian (%)	N/A	23	15	13	12
	Hispanic/Latino (%)	13	23	22	20	13
	Poor families (%)	16	23	28	22	21
	Median family income	$8,524	$14,455	$22,378	$38,755	$58,195
	(% in relation to Chicago)	(83)	(77)	(73)	(91)	(109)

[a] Hispanic/Latino is counted as a cross-cutting ethnic identity.
[b] Racial categories for 2000 and 2010 exclude Hispanics/Latinos.

Sources: Data are drawn from American Community Survey 2008–2012; US Census 2000; Chicago Fact Book Consortium (1984, 1995).

the initially dreadful housing conditions for African Americans gradually improved.[23]

Racial integration produced a great deal of alarm among whites and community organizations who were anxiously trying to defend the neighborhoods' middle-class character. In 1980, the director of the Uptown Chicago Commission, an umbrella association of block clubs, warned that the ongoing development of subsidized housing might trigger white flight and racial turnover: "if we start drawing in middle-class property owners, Uptown's diversity will continue. . . . As I see it, if we can't make the community more middle class, it is possible that we will go in the direction of a single racial area. Subsidized low income buildings in Chicago are 90% black."[24] The response in Rogers Park was similar. In 1980, the Rogers Park Community Council—the neighborhood's main community organization at the time—demanded a moratorium on the construction of subsidized housing. As Gail Welter, a graduate student from Loyola University, reported in her dissertation, the moratorium "was based on the argument that the community already was more diverse than the 1970 Census indicated. . . . It was also contended that government agencies were not sensitive to the impact of further subsidized housing on Rogers Park." She noted that Community Council members also discussed the danger of looming "ghettoization" (Welter 1982:53). Around the same time, the director of the local community development corporation told a reporter for the *Chicago Tribune*: "we want to have room for everyone, but they [developers] shouldn't target specific neighborhoods for the vast majority of subsidized housing. They're just re-creating economic and racial segregation."[25]

This resistance shows how middle-class activists and community organizations attempted to limit the construction of subsidized housing in Rogers Park and Uptown in order to cap the neighborhoods' black populations. Rather than serving current residents in need, the activists posited, subsidized housing would bring in more low-income African Americans. Allegedly, a situation had emerged in which any additional subsidized housing would lead to "ghettoization," white flight, and racial turnover.

Gentrification

According to Neil Smith (1996:32), gentrification is "the process . . . by which poor and working-class neighborhoods in the inner city are refurbished via an influx of private capital and middle-class homebuyers and renters." In Rogers Park and Uptown, the arrival of gentrification in the 1980s contradicted prior claims of impending racial turnover. For several decades, gentrification had been approaching the Far North Side as neighborhoods closer to downtown were redeveloped into the heartland of Chicago's professional elite.[26] In Uptown, this process initially progressed much more slowly than developers had expected, in part because of Uptown's skid row reputation, which proved sticky.[27] With the support of several development incentives,[28] however, gentrification made sputtering progress and eventually picked up steam in the

1990s. In Rogers Park, direct access to the lake, unencumbered by Lake Shore Drive, and comparably low prices made condominiums attractive to young families—first along the lakefront and later throughout the entire neighborhood.[29] Longtime Rogers Parkers spoke to me of a veritable "condo craze" that swept through the area in the late 1990s.

Gentrification has significantly altered the neighborhoods' racial composition (see table 2.1).[30] In both neighborhoods, the share of non-Hispanic whites has been increasing since 2000. Uptown's black population has been declining since 1990, when blacks constituted a quarter of the neighborhood's population. In 2010, 20 percent of Uptowners still identified as black or African American.[31] Black population decline was slowed by Uptown's substantial stock of project-based housing, which is relatively safe from gentrification and houses many low-income African Americans. The Latino and Asian populations shrank much more quickly; each group made up a quarter of Uptown's population in 1980 but only an eighth in 2010. Since gentrification reached Rogers Park slightly later, the black and Latino populations there peaked only in 2000—at about 30 percent—and had shrunk slightly by 2010.

By contrast, the white population in both neighborhoods is growing in tandem with the rate of homeownership, which reflects the ongoing conversion of rental housing into condominiums. Between 2000 and 2010, Rogers Park and Uptown each lost over 3,000 rental units, while gaining about 2,000 owner-occupied units.[32] The vast majority of the increase in homeownership reflects the growing ranks of non-Hispanic white homeowners—88 percent in Uptown and 79 percent in Rogers Park, respectively. The number of Hispanic and African American owners remains small—in Uptown, it actually declined over this period. Gentrification, therefore, is a composite process that simultaneously reshapes the neighborhoods' class structure, racial composition, and housing pool.

Given its considerable racial impact on Rogers Park and Uptown, gentrification has sparked racial contestation. Just as integration mobilized middle-class residents and their community organizations, gentrification and racial dislocation have rallied social justice activists. Examples of local conflict abound. For instance, in the early 2000s, Loyola University asked the City of Chicago to establish a tax increment financing (TIF) district in Rogers Park's southeastern corner to support commercial development and the construction of new housing.[33] An antigentrification organization launched a campaign against the TIF district. As one protester charged, "[the TIF district] would result in displacement of nonwhite people unless there is some kind of commitment on the [part of the] TIF to save low cost housing and diversity. The result would be the whitening of the neighborhood."[34] As supporting evidence of the plan's racial biases, the antigentrification group invoked the fact that the task force that had been assembled to evaluate the TIF district was all white. A critic commented: "they should be ashamed of themselves and apologize to the community. There has been no effort to include minorities in the planning group. It's all white. It's awful. Apparently they don't know any good members of the minority community for membership on the planning group."[35]

As only one example of the broader politics of gentrification, one can see from this case how social justice activists used racial challenges in campaigns against gentrification. Describing the TIF project as "the whitening of the neighborhood" and attributing the project's purported biases to the absence of nonwhites from the TIF's task force, the activists portrayed the project as fundamentally illegitimate on racial grounds. Consequently, they demanded that the project be either abandoned or that an affordable housing component be added. Similar racial conflicts over gentrification regularly occurred—and still occur—in both Rogers Park and Uptown.[36]

Discussions of gentrification frequently spilled over into the politics of crime. Social scientists have found no straightforward relationship between crime and gentrification, but a lot of residents—whether supportive of gentrification or not—believed that such a relationship existed.[37] Some argued that "development," a word they preferred over "gentrification," was justified in part because it would benefit all by reducing crime. New businesses and owner-occupied housing would add committed stakeholders, who would prevent gang members from loitering on their sidewalks. Some justice activists agreed with the claim but drew the opposite conclusion. Jessica, a white Rogers Parker in her twenties, once said to me:

> There are a lot of community members that will call this "ghetto" when there is gang violence going on and I think I've had this kind of feeling . . . that those people will then decide to leave. Which I guess I have this unchecked feeling for gratefulness for because there are a lot of gentrification issues here.

At the same time that gentrification started to gather force in Rogers Park and Uptown in the early 1990s, the city implemented a new policing strategy that enabled civilians to help the police combat crime—community policing. Given the presumed connection between crime and gentrification, community policing specifically empowered those residents and community organizations who were seeking lower crime, more development, or both. Community policing afforded them a state-supported platform with privileged access to the police and other services and resources. As I will discuss later, it also deepened the split of engaged residents into two competing political camps—public safety and social justice.

Community Policing and Public Safety Initiatives in Rogers Park and Uptown

"Community policing" refers to an overall program of police reform that seeks partnerships between the police and the citizenry.[38] Through mutual coordination, citizens and police officers are supposed to identify persistent problems and devise effective interventions.[39] Community policing departs from the police doctrine of "rapid response," under which departments simply dispatch officers in response to service requests (calls to 911) as quickly as possible. Instead, by deprioritizing certain service requests, community policing frees up manpower for targeted interventions. At least some police officers are supposed to patrol only their assigned beats, hence enabling officers and the locals to communicate, build relationships, and develop trust. Toward the same end, community policing programs provide institutional support for civic public safety initiatives, such as neighborhood watch programs and anticrime marches.

Chicago's community policing program, CAPS (Chicago Alternative Policing Strategy), was launched in the early 1990s.[40] The program aimed not only to reduce crime but also to improve trust in the police and to fight disorder, which could lead to inflated perceptions of crime. In addition to serious crime, therefore, CAPS also addressed more mundane problems, such as public drinking, unlit parks, and other so-called quality of life issues. According to Wesley Skogan's (2006) evaluation, CAPS has been quite successful in achieving these goals. The program increased Chicagoans' trust in the police and reduced their fear of crime.[41]

Civic anticrime initiatives, in Chicago and elsewhere, predate CAPS.[42] In Rogers Park and Uptown, block clubs, the Uptown Chicago Commission, and the Rogers Park Community Council had long worked to control crime and disorder. When CAPS was implemented, they seamlessly transitioned to become the program's main organizational partners.[43] As a result, these organizations now received valuable institutional support from CAPS. Each police district maintained a CAPS office that employed a designated CAPS sergeant, several staff members, and a community organizer. Residents could draw on help from the CAPS office in organizing block clubs, positive loitering groups, and other safety initiatives. In addition, CAPS dispatched officers to coordinate with residents or to offer protection for specific events. Furthermore, working with CAPS, residents and organizations were able to access other institutions of the state, such as the state's attorney and the sheriff's office, which enforced evictions. And CAPS provided other useful resources: crime data, "gang awareness" and burglary prevention seminars, do-it-yourself graffiti removal kits, and more.

In addition to supporting safety initiatives, CAPS held regular beat meetings—usually called "CAPS meetings"—in schools, churches, and other public spaces, where residents and police officers discussed trends in crime and engaged in so-called problem solving. Problem solving could take many different forms—it could mean something as simple as establishing a regularly timed police patrol if neighbors complained that teenagers congregated in a particular alley to smoke marijuana after school let out.[44] It could also mean tracing criminal activity to a particular building or apartment, as Mimi and Mahandra did, and then evicting the tenants. (Whether these and other interventions really *solved* problems is debatable, of course, but CAPS generally considered problems solved when their local symptoms subsided.) Furthermore, CAPS meetings served as a forum to recruit new members for grassroots safety initiatives.

At least in theory, CAPS and other public safety initiatives held the promise of uniting residents—whether white or African American, working-class or middle-class—against the threats of street crime and gun violence. Everyone was free to join these initiatives. And residents could find there a ready-made platform for mutually striving toward a shared goal: safety. Consequently, these groups fulfilled the conditions of positive intergroup contact that the social psychologist Gordon Allport outlined in his work on prejudice.[45] As chapters 6 and 7 will show, safety initiatives sometimes did unite blacks and whites in this way. But I also found a considerable amount of distrust and plain hostility. These negative perceptions resulted in part from the way CAPS and safety initiatives were positioned in the local political field. In essence, CAPS had altered the balance of power among Rogers Park and

Uptown's community organizations in favor of those who might desire not only security but also gentrification. The success or failure of safety activism at uniting people across racial boundaries cannot be understood without considering these field dynamics.

The Field of Local Politics in Rogers Park and Uptown

A field is an arena of strategic action, a mesolevel social order that consists of individuals and organizations whose actions are mutually attuned to one another because they cannot accomplish their own goals without directly affecting other actors in the field.[46] In Rogers Park and Uptown, the goals actors pursued in the local political fields revolved around neighborhood change: defending the stock of affordable housing, upgrading an unattractive strip of businesses, reducing shootings, and so forth. In working toward the goals they considered most important, local actors sought strategic resources (funds, members, etc.) and allies, and occasionally sabotaged their opponents.

I have already noted that the political fields in both neighborhoods were divided into two camps. Here, it makes sense to describe these camps in some more detail. Using the activists' description of their civic efforts' purposes and aims, I call the first the "public safety" or simply "safety" camp. These residents mainly worked with initiatives that were administered in collaboration with CAPS. They consistently argued that the biggest problems in Rogers Park and Uptown were street crime and the gangs and that any local decision had to be evaluated first and foremost in terms of how it would affect crime. Some but not all of these activists also demanded more "development," by which they meant increasing the stock of nonsubsidized housing, attracting more or "better" businesses, and neighborhood beautification.[47] Unsurprisingly, this subset of activists also criticized low-income housing and certain social services, such as homeless shelters or methadone clinics, for their purported contributions to street crime. In terms of their overarching political beliefs, safety activists were diverse. While one could accurately describe their opponents, the social justice camp, as "progressive" or "leftist," it would be misleading to call the members of the safety camp "conservative." Most of them identified as Democrats, held liberal views about such things as gay rights, abortion, and the minimum wage, and supported strict gun control laws.

The safety camp included block clubs as well as positive loitering groups and the regular attendees at the monthly CAPS beat meetings. In Uptown, block clubs covered the entire neighborhood territory, though several of them were dormant. Their umbrella organization was the Uptown Chicago Commission, which led the charge when it came to political lobbying. These groups and organizations were active players in neighborhood politics. They hosted events, such as neighborhood cleanups or electoral debate forums, and took public positions on development projects and other local issues. In Rogers Park, the safety camp was less centralized. There were fewer active block clubs than in Uptown, and—notably—neither of the two areas that regularly experienced gun violence, North of Howard and the Morse area, had a block club when I began fieldwork in 2011. The Rogers Park Community Council, which had served as a neighborhood association of block clubs similar to the Uptown Chicago Commission, had transitioned into a social service agency and no longer constituted a visible political actor.[48]

The second camp I call the "social justice" or "antigentrification" camp, following again the activists' self-description. The members of this camp employed both terms to describe their work; I will use them interchangeably. This camp prioritized the struggle against gentrification and attendant dislocation. Social justice advocates fought to maintain social services and affordable housing options for low-income and minority residents. In relation to crime, social justice activists demanded prevention and rehabilitation instead of what they frequently called "criminalization." Any measures to reduce crime and violence had to do so without further marginalizing black and low-income renters by increasing police harassment, incarceration, and displacement. Accordingly, a lot of justice activists simply talked about the safety camp as "the gentrifiers." Beyond the level of the neighborhood, the justice activists reliably sided with the political left—they were prounion, opposed charter schools, and demanded tax increases for corporations and the wealthy.

Two key social justice organizations, the Organization of the Northeast (ONE) and Northside Action for Justice (NA4J), were active in both Rogers Park and Uptown. There were other such organizations in both neighborhoods, but these two were the most consistent and generally most important ones. The Organization of the Northeast served as a political platform for a set of social service organizations, religious congregations, and ethnic associations.[49] Locally, ONE and some of its member organizations employed professional community organizers, who mobilized residents around such projects as tenants' rights and voter registration. The mission of NA4J resembled ONE's, but NA4J was a true grassroots organization without paid staff members. Both organizations engaged in political organizing, held rallies and protests, and lobbied the city, the county, and the state for social service spending and progressive policy changes.

In addition to their core focus on affordability, social justice organizations sometimes fielded violence prevention initiatives. Most notably, ONE implemented the CeaseFire program in Rogers Park and Uptown.[50] CeaseFire hired former gang members to serve as "violence interrupters," using their connections and street credibility to break cycles of retaliation. The violence interrupters brokered peace agreements and also provided other services, such as supporting gang exit through job training. Since violence prevention programs like CeaseFire sought to reduce violence, they could thus have served as bridges between the social justice and the public safety camps. But in practice, this was not the case—ideological differences and distrust between the camps ran too deep. In chapter 5, I discuss why this was the case.

A crucial actor in the neighborhoods' political fields was the alderman, the area's city council representative. Aldermen are elected every four years through ward-based elections. Ward boundaries do not match neighborhood boundaries perfectly, but for reasons of convenience I will refer to the aldermen of the 46th and 49th Wards, respectively, as the aldermen of Uptown and Rogers Park.[51] Occasionally called "mayors" of their wards, they had considerable control over zoning, development, and the implementation of city services, including even policing.[52] Both the safety and the justice camps thus coveted access to this position, hoping to install (or defend) an ally in office. They also targeted or tried to sway aldermen through political action—lobbying, protests, writing op-eds, and so forth. During my fieldwork, Rogers Park's alderman was Joe Moore, a longtime incumbent, who was neither a clear ally of the public safety nor of the social justice camp. In Uptown, Helen Shiller, a very firm supporter of that neighborhood's social justice camp, left office as I began my research. She was replaced by James Cappleman, who is widely regarded as a progentrification and tough-on-crime alderman.

The political fields' most striking feature was the great degree of distrust that separated the justice from the safety camp. Social justice activists frequently framed this distrust in racial terms, making racial challenges to discredit anticrime initiatives as tools of racial displacement. For example,

Elliot, a white, middle-aged member of NA4J from Rogers Park, said during an interview: "let's be clear: the entire mobilization reaction to crime is about race." He described how safety activists would neutralize their speech to "pretend they're not really racist." In a mocking tone, he imitated them: "Well, we're not blaming people. We just understand that people in bad situations are more likely to engage in criminal behavior." He commented, "Oh, is that what you are saying? Give me a break! I know this white drug dealer who worked out of a building over by the lake for years and he was a white guy, and he was friendly, and he did yoga. Everybody knew he was a drug dealer and no one complained. The same people who are cool with the veggie yoga dealer dude were up in arms about black kids selling something down the block." Safety work, Elliot charged, was all about race, not about crime. Racial neutralizations in the form of sanitized speech were simply an attempt to distract from that fact.

Given this polarization over the issue of crime, the question arises: what were Rogers Parkers and Uptowners actually doing under the umbrella of public safety work? How, precisely, did they try to reduce crime? What basis could be found for the claim that their efforts aimed to bring about racial displacement? And how did the safety activists respond to racial challenges that aimed to undermine their work? These are the questions I discuss in the next chapter.

3

Racial Displacement in Action?

Safety Activism and Its Racial Entanglements

Lawrence House was a rundown, thirteen-story rooming house, located just off the Lawrence "L" station in Uptown. It offered cheap studios that tenants rented on a weekly or monthly basis. Lawrence House had once been an illustrious, glamorous place. During Uptown's time as a hub of silent film production in the 1910s, Charlie Chaplin resided there while working at the Essanay Studios. The basement still contained the original ornately tiled swimming pool, which had been sitting empty for decades. The top floor, also unused, housed a theater and a majestic ballroom. With Uptown's gradual decline after World War II, Lawrence House first became a retirement community. But over the previous decade or so, it had simply turned into a rooming house. The building had fallen into disrepair (see figure 3.1); bedbugs, rodents, and mold were omnipresent. The landlords had ceased to make any major renovations, instead trying to squeeze the building for its final dregs of profit. They also neglected to screen prospective tenants or monitor the premises for criminal activity in any meaningful way.

Among many Uptowners—not just the inner circle of the safety camp—Lawrence House evoked overwhelmingly negative associations. The building and the densely populated area that surrounded it were perceived as a cauldron of trouble. A group of Gangster Disciples hung out down the block from the building in the parking lot of a small shopping plaza. Some of the gang's customers allegedly used Lawrence House to consume the drugs they had purchased, whether they were tenants or not. In 2011, an elderly woman was robbed in one of the building's elevators. There was talk that sex offenders and violent ex-felons inhabited the building. Area residents also complained about loitering outside it. In the summer months, black seniors

Us versus Them. Jan Doering, Oxford University Press (2020) © Oxford University Press.
DOI: 10.1093/oso/9780190066574.001.0001

Figure 3.1. Lawrence House in 2012. The scaffolding provides makeshift protection against bricks falling from the building's crumbling façade. Photo by the author.

would congregate here, sitting on empty milk crates to escape the heat and socialize. They drank out of paper-bagged bottles and played music on old cassette players. Some engaged female pedestrians with uninvited sexual overtures.[1]

In 2011, local block clubs and community policing groups launched a campaign to fundamentally change Lawrence House and its surroundings. When talking about the building, these safety activists claimed that tenants were living in squalor and at constant risk of being victimized by violent criminals. The activists denied that their goal was to eliminate affordable housing or to displace black tenants. I spoke about this with Frank, one leader of Uptown's safety camp, over coffee at a local bakery. Frank was a mild-mannered, tall man in his fifties. Empathetically, he invoked the position of fearful tenants: "the residents [of Lawrence House] don't feel safe. All I want is for these buildings to be safe!"

Gentrification critics and the tenants I met agreed that things had to change. Lawrence House was in desperate need of repairs and better management. But they rejected the claim that the ongoing "safety" campaign really had anything to do with crime. Janelle, a black social worker, acknowledged that there were good reasons to be concerned about crime in the neighborhood. "A shooting on Broadway and Wilson [Uptown's busiest intersection] at two in the afternoon—that's a problem," she said. But if the safety activists wanted to curb serious crime, why did they complain so much about such things as the black men loitering outside Lawrence House, who did not pose a threat to anyone? Janelle argued that many whites living in Uptown had grown up in all-white neighborhoods or suburbs and were thus afraid of "a group of black people standing on the corner." From Janelle's perspective, these whites were simply using the shootings and other serious incidents as a justification for displacing low-income African Americans. She concluded: "so, in the end, money and race is what it comes down to."

As the safety activists' campaign progressed, it became clear that Lawrence House would eventually change hands. Prodded by the safety activists and Alderman Cappleman, the city had sent inspectors to examine the building, finding serious code violations, including mildew and mold, a unit that posed an active health risk because it was "loaded with garbage," and a dangerously dilapidated building façade.[2] Rather than addressing these violations, the owners let Lawrence House slide into foreclosure. In the spring of 2012, the tenants had to endure a week without heat or hot water, because unpaid bills led the utility company to disconnect the gas line (Bowean 2012).

The case went into housing court. For some time, no one knew what would happen to the building and its occupants. Justice advocates called on Alderman Cappleman to use his zoning powers to force any new owner to keep the building affordable. When Cappleman refused do so, claiming that this would constitute extortion, they organized protests in front of the alderman's office and the home of the CEO of FLATS Chicago, a developer who had by then expressed an interest in buying Lawrence House.

The protests drew heavily on the fact that many Lawrence House tenants were black. Protesters carried signs such as "FLATS: Fashionable Segregation!," "Diversity RIP," and "Alderman Cappleman, stop exporting our diversity!" An Organization of the Northeast (ONE) flyer for one protest stated: "Uptown is one of the most racially and economically diverse communities in Chicago, but our neighbors are being PUSHED OUT [sic]. This is re-segregation." Instead of fighting crime by displacing residents, Cappleman was admonished to support "community-based violence prevention efforts," by which ONE meant CeaseFire (discussed in chapter 5). Framing the redevelopment of Lawrence House in terms of racial turnover, the protesters challenged Cappleman and the developer to either step back from the deal or agree to keep the building affordable. In addition, ONE brought in the *Chicago Tribune*, which published an article that sympathetically portrayed tenants' fears of displacement.[3]

Ultimately, FLATS Chicago bought the building in 2013 and terminated all tenants' leases in order to upgrade it.[4] In 2014, it reopened as rental housing, for which FLATS now targets recent college graduates. In collaboration with Alderman Cappleman, FLATS earmarked several units as subsidized housing, noting that this would help "preserve diversity on the North Side lakefront,"[5] but critics like Janelle dismissed this commitment as vastly insufficient, a mere token devised to silence critics.

The case of Lawrence House can serve as an example of how other buildings on the Far North Side gentrified as a result of anticrime initiatives. Accordingly, these initiatives palpably aggravated racial inequality in Rogers Park and Uptown. Safety activism engendered evictions and the conversion of entire buildings into middle-class housing, which hastened the neighborhoods' ongoing shift toward larger white and smaller black (and overall minority and working-class) populations. As I will furthermore show, the initiatives also fostered more extensive and intensive policing.

Such measures of social control not only transform urban spaces but also have severe and lasting effects for the people who are directly affected. Matthew Desmond (2016) has revealed how evictions and precarious housing entrench individuals in poverty. Victor Rios (2011) has shown how the aggressive practices of what Patrick Sharkey (2018) calls "warrior policing" engender racial marginalization. This chapter uncovers the demand side to these social control interventions. Many members of the public safety camp were fully aware that their initiatives sometimes produced racial displacement, although they contested any charges that this outcome motivated their activism.

In order to prepare and begin the analysis of racial conflict over crime and affordability, this chapter examines the main practices of public safety work in Rogers Park and Uptown. What were neighborhood activists actually doing to combat crime? What kinds of racial implications could be attributed to their efforts? And how did the safety activists deal with the potential of facing charges of racism as a result of their efforts? The chapter addresses how safety activists fought "problem buildings" and "problem businesses," secured additional policing, imposed heftier sentences on offenders, and "reclaimed" public space. A final section investigates the steps the safety activists took to neutralize racial challenges.

Fighting "Problem Buildings" and "Problem Businesses"

Lawrence House is a good example of what safety activists called a "problem building," a property suspected of facilitating criminal activity. Safety activists regarded these buildings as the gangs' backbones—this was where some gang members resided (almost always "off the lease") and also where they stashed drugs, money, and weapons and took shelter from the police or hostile gangs during an assault. Police officers suggested that cracking down on problem buildings (and "problem businesses") was crucial for reducing crime—even more crucial than making arrests. If the gangs and drug dealers lost their spatial anchoring points in Rogers Park and Uptown, they said, the gangs would no longer be able to operate here.

How did the safety activists deal with problem buildings? In the case of Lawrence House, they convened a task force that included Alderman Cappleman, business representatives, and block club members. They pressured nearby businesses to more vigilantly report loitering and gang activity to the police. They held positive loitering events across from Lawrence House. But most important, they established a paper trail of emergency service requests—they encouraged residents to systematically call 911 and link their calls to this specific building. For Lawrence House as well as other buildings in Rogers Park and Uptown, this triggered a spiral of events: the city sent building inspectors; the building inspectors identified code violations; the owners failed or refused to fix their buildings; the owners sold or lost their buildings in housing court; and the tenants had to move out as the buildings were upgraded.

Once the police had logged a substantial number of calls to 911, the alderman and the city could pressure the owner to take remedial actions by threatening to bring in the city's inspectors to search for code violations the owner would then have to resolve. Interestingly, these code violations did not need to have anything to do with the 911 service requests—violations I learned about included defective sprinkler systems, rodents, and broken alley gates. Since practically any building or business violates at least some city codes[6], this threat was potent and often sufficed to ensure the landlord's cooperation. For example, I observed one meeting at an alderman's office in which the alderman, a police officer, and several safety activists collectively pressed an increasingly intimidated landlord to file eviction papers for two leaseholders who were suspected of sheltering gang members. The landlord was reluctant to cooperate because he said that he had seen one of the tenants carry a gun, but he eventually yielded when it was explained to him that the city would otherwise impose expensive code violation fines and possibly even initiate a lawsuit.

As in the case of Lawrence House, problem building interventions could accomplish more than just one or two evictions. Some landlords lost their properties in housing court after failing to bring them up to code. Others decided that keeping the buildings was not worth the trouble and sold them to a developer. Whether the transfer was voluntary or not, developers usually converted the buildings into condos or upscale rental housing.[7] Problem building interventions could thus clear the path for gentrification. And social justice activists charged that this was precisely why these buildings were being targeted in the first place—to displace the low-income black and Latino tenants and to create more housing for the white middle class.

Frank and his peers rejected the notion that they were seeking to shut down affordable housing and instead claimed that they were acting on behalf of the common good. Lawrence House again illustrates the point. After the task force had been founded, Frank told me: "there are rumors that we want to shut down Lawrence House entirely, but when people say that I always say, 'No, where do you get that from?'" Frank explained that the safety activists had previously improved another large building in Uptown without shuttering it. Through their intervention, the building had received better management and evicted tenants with felony records. "You'd never know it was affordable housing," Frank said. During a positive loitering event across from Lawrence House, Alderman Cappleman struck a similar chord when he told the participants: "we want affordable housing, but it has to be done in a way that it doesn't frighten people."

The process for dealing with problem buildings depended on whether the building in question was privately owned or not. It was typically difficult to evict tenants from public housing. Since public housing landlords—either the city's housing authority or nonprofit housing providers—generally followed legal procedure to the letter, all evictions had to be court-ordered. Private landlords on the other hand were more pliable because they risked losing a lot of money if the building inspectors were called in.

Given the considerable impact that problem building interventions could have, it is not surprising that anticrime activists conferred to identify and target buildings and businesses that they considered particularly problematic. One CAPS beat facilitator kept in her apartment a handcrafted map of the buildings on her street. It listed each building's street address so that she could make all of her 911 calls count toward a specific building, and she encouraged others to do the same.

To deal with "problem businesses," the city could also simply withdraw licenses. For instance, one week after a man—whom the police later categorized as a gang member—was shot and killed inside a small Rogers Park convenience store on Howard Street, the city closed the business. A city notice posted on the storefront cited the "dangerous condition" of the store's electrical system, but at the next CAPS meeting for the area the police commander freely divulged that the city had closed the store for abetting gang activity. The code violation was simply the official justification.

Securing Police Service: Reporting Crime the "Right Way"

Most of the time, of course, safety activists called 911 not about strategic issues like problem buildings but to address immediate concerns like drug dealing. How to mobilize police support in such cases was a major topic of conversation at CAPS meetings and other public safety events. The question arose because residents found it increasingly difficult to secure the kind of attention they wanted from the police, the CAPS program notwithstanding. In the 1990s the police department had supplied CAPS with significant resources, but continued cuts meant that these resources had disappeared or become harder to access. While systematic police interventions could sporadically still be secured through CAPS, calling 911 had again become the main conduit for obtaining police service, as it had been under the doctrine of rapid response that had preceded the era of community policing. Peter Moskos (2008:92), who wrote a book about his time as a police officer in Baltimore, describes how calls for service shape policing under the doctrine of rapid response: "more than any tactical strategy or mandate from the police administration, citizens' telephone calls control the majority of police services. The emphasis on radio calls means that in busy districts, officers can do little other than answer dispatched calls for service. A system allowing all citizens unlimited and equal access to police services is, at its core, very democratic. The reality, however, is anything but. Police service is not unlimited." Residents who frequently called 911 were well aware of this. Attendees at CAPS meetings complained all the time that nothing appeared to happen in response to their calls or that patrol cars would arrive so long after the fact that the problem—suspected gang loitering, more often than not—had by then resolved itself. When a patrol car did respond in time, officers sometimes drove by without engaging the alleged gang members, to the frustration of the callers. A related outcome was that 911 operators or the responding officers could conclude that nothing illegal was going on and thus ignore the service request. This was particularly challenging for residents reporting gang activity. Usually, all that they had observed was a group of loitering black men whom they believed to be gang members. But loitering is not illegal.[8] Even when callers felt certain that the loiterers were dealing drugs, they still had to convince the 911 operators that criminal behavior was actually going on. In fact, several activists recounted experiences with 911 operators who had lectured them about racial stereotyping when they called about supposed gang loitering.

Consequently, safety activists had to take steps to substantiate their requests in order to direct police services and resources to their neighborhoods. This required organized efforts; as Gretchen—a regular participant at CAPS meetings in Rogers Park—put it, "the squeaky wheel gets the grease." One way to improve police response was to increase the sheer volume of service requests. Safety activists could use the "democratization" of police service via

911 to their advantage—communities that systematically requested more policing would ultimately also receive more. This applied not only to the day-to-day process of steering police officers to Rogers Park and Uptown but also to the long-term distribution of resources throughout the city. Occasionally, the police department reallocated police officers between police districts—and the number of 911 calls per district was a major criterion that determined how many officers each district was entitled to have.[9]

Some block clubs formed "911 phone trees" that allowed their members to report the same issue to the police multiple times, giving it more weight than a single call would have had.[10] In addition, they discussed ways of describing suspicious activity in such a way that the 911 operator would take the service request more seriously. At beat meetings, the CAPS sergeants regularly offered advice in this regard. For example, if they did not see any hand-to-hand drug deals, callers could point out that the supposed gang members were blocking the public way, were drinking alcohol, or were congregating in a spot where a shooting had recently occurred. All of these things made it more likely that a patrol car would be dispatched.

In sum, anticrime activists were trying to funnel more police services to their neighborhoods. But for black residents, increased policing could also mean increased scrutiny and harassment. Justice activists were therefore not shy about making racial challenges. Elliot, a Rogers Parker and member of NA4J, said: "there are lots of cops that get it, who say, 'Look, I can come out here and arrest people constantly. That's not going to do anything!'" But white homeowners were immune to pragmatism, Elliot said: "I've seen this at CAPS meetings. It's always the white homeowners telling the cops 'No, we want you to come out and arrest them.' [Imitating a police officer] 'But they're just standing there.' [Imitating a white homeowner] 'Exactly! They're standing there! I don't want them standing there!' They want someone with a gun to go out and do their dirty work for them."

The repeated demands for more policing, as well as the increased policing itself, sometimes produced racial tension. One CAPS beat group in Uptown developed a creative strategy of improving police response to their service calls. If the caller could identify the presumed troublemakers by name, the service request would appear more legitimate. After all, most of the individuals the residents called about were listed in the police database, including their arrest records, photographs, and gang affiliations. The calls would also become more "enforceable" because responding police officers would know who to look for rather than going by the vague descriptions callers could provide. Thus, at each beat meeting, the images of three notorious offenders were to be projected on a screen so that participants could learn their names. The group's facilitator, a white man named Eric, explained the strategy to me: "instead of saying 'They're wearing an oversized white T-shirt and dark jeans and white tennis shoes...' What good is that to a cop? It doesn't do any good! So, yeah, the idea was—say who it is! Say it by name!" Given the fact that a small number of repeat offenders were known to be responsible for the majority of shootings in the neighborhood, this CAPS group found it reasonable to focus on this inner circle.

I observed the first—and last—beat meeting at which this practice was implemented. As the meeting began, a revolving set of three pictures was projected on a large screen. They were mug shots of three black men and included the men's names, ages, and height. In this beat, CAPS meetings generally drew only whites, but coincidentally this time several black residents attended. The meeting began without anyone offering an explanation for the projection. A few minutes into the event, Phyllis, an African American woman of about fifty years, asked why these images were being shown. Eric answered that all three men had previously been arrested for weapons violations. I could see that he was blushing. He explained that the goal was to brief the locals about the most dangerous offenders in the area. Phyllis followed up: "Are any of them wanted by the police? Is there a warrant for their arrest?" Eric replied that this was currently not the case. Irritated, Phyllis commented that it didn't seem right to single out individuals in this way, and Eric did not continue to defend the strategy. In an interview, Eric told me that he thought Phyllis's response was ridiculous, particularly because he knew that she herself had lost a son through gang violence:

> Most likely one of those people on the screen knows who killed her son. And she's yelling and screaming and causing a big scene that we were putting innocent kids' pictures up on the screen. We weren't! Each of those kids has over 300 arrests! You know, one has 642! And he's been shot *four* times in the neighborhood! So we weren't doing anything that wasn't truthful.

Race remained just barely below the surface of the interaction between Eric and Phyllis, but their disagreement was certainly not only about the right to privacy and to be deemed innocent until proven guilty. The projection was provocative at least in part because it was informing whites about alleged black offenders. The CAPS group never repeated the practice of publicly projecting mug shots, because Eric felt that it had proven too controversial. Ironically, the practice of distributing the images continued, just in a more covert and hence less inflammatory way. Eric now emailed the images to those who asked for them.

At other times, racial discontent became more explicit. In 2012, there was a concerted push to reduce crime in Rogers Park's North of Howard area. This disadvantaged area, which housed many African American and West Indian residents, experienced significant problems with drug dealing and violence but was also showing signs of reinvestment. Several new businesses had opened on Howard Street, and the number of homeowners, many of them white, was increasing. These homeowners were growing more vocal in complaining about crime and disorder in the North of Howard area and demanding increased policing. The alderman and the police commander were thus under pressure to reduce crime. In order to achieve this, the commander wanted to raise the number of service requests. Of course, CAPS activists were already calling 911, but the commander sought to expand the pool of people doing so. Trying to rally residents to the cause, the commander and Alderman Moore held a series of widely advertised public safety meetings in the North of Howard area.

The second meeting, which took place in the auditorium of a local school, attracted around 250 people, about two-thirds of whom were white—even though whites still constituted a clear demographic minority in the area. At the meeting, the costs of intensified policing for black residents became quite clear. During the question-and-answer period, a middle-aged African American woman who was sitting in the row ahead of me stood up to address the police commander. Over the past couple of weeks, she said, she and her husband had been stopped by the police three times while circling the block in search of a parking spot. One time, an officer had issued a ticket for a missing front license plate after he heard how her husband had said to his friend, who was driving the car, that this was a case of "driving while black." While issuing the ticket, she reported, the officer said, "This is for your friend over there! This is for his comments!"

The auditorium grew very quiet as the woman described the incident in detail. She ended by saying that "something's got to be done instead of assuming everybody's a criminal." The commander was about to respond, but applause from the audience—from both black and white people, as far as I could see—forced him to wait. Rather than yielding the floor to the commander, the woman's husband then took the microphone, repeating parts of the story and adding his own perspective. His voice was shaking. He said that the officers, when asked to explain their stops, had justified them by stating that neighbors had been calling 911. He was exasperated. "Why would anybody call on me? I am just going home! I am not doing anything suspicious besides trying to find a parking spot!" The man clearly perceived a connection between public safety initiatives and the officers' behavior, because he went on to say: "I understand that the CAPS program, along with the police, have made a *huge* difference in the neighborhood. Which is a very positive thing! But just because a black man drives a nice vehicle, does not mean that he's into drugs!" Another round of applause ensued.

In his response, the commander tried to appease the couple. He thanked them for sharing their experience and acknowledged that this was a dilemma of what he called "proactive policing." "You're looking for a parking spot, but someone else sees somebody driving around the block numerous times looking for something." He said that because of the ongoing problems in the neighborhood, it was important for people to be on the lookout and to readily report suspicious activity to the police. When in doubt, he said, it was good to call the police, although he also added that once a police investigation had been requested, "*how* the officers conduct it is going to make all the difference in the world." He sounded sincerely empathetic in his response, but he ultimately did not yield on the main point: that police stops of this kind were simply necessary.

Later in the meeting, several community policing volunteers engaged the black couple, encouraging them to prevent tense encounters by taking personal initiative. One white man suggested that they should try to get to know their beat officers. "I apologize that it [the police stop] put a negative aspect on you, but try to be positive. Attend beat meetings. Attend, you know, things like this." Once again, the audience applauded. After the meeting, one of my fieldwork acquaintances, Linda, who was of Puerto Rican origin, also approached the couple. Linda attended CAPS meetings and sometimes went to positive loitering events. She said that she agreed with the white CAPS activist that it really was helpful to know the beat officers. "I walk my dog three times a day and I wave to the police officers whenever I see them. So they get to know you. Going to CAPS also helps. You get to know the sergeant and the beat officers." The couple seemed hesitant. The wife said she understood that police stops had to happen, but it was still her right to demand that those stops be conducted in a courteous and professional manner.

While the safety activists and the police commander expressed their sympathy with the couple, their fundamental view was that intensive policing had to continue. The last thing they wanted was to make Rogers Parkers feel racially self-conscious about calling the police. The number of calls had to increase to justify the allocation of additional police resources and to direct the police to where they were needed. Instead, the onus of fixing the problem was implicitly put on the couple. They were law-abiding citizens and needed to demonstrate this fact to the police by going to CAPS meetings, getting to know officers, and even waving to them on the street. The couple was thus given the choice between negative police encounters and investing time and energy to prevent these encounters by proving their upstanding character. Either way, reducing crime through increased policing imposed a severe burden on black residents that white people did not have to bear.[11] This fact remained undiscussed and unaddressed at this particular meeting but also at public safety events in general.

Naturally, antigentrification activists interpreted interactions of this kind in racial terms, arguing that they revealed the safety activists' cynical perspective toward racial justice. A few days after the North of Howard meeting, I spoke with Ben, a community organizer, who had also been at the meeting. He commented: "the white homeowners, they don't have any problem with that [police harassment] happening to black people. They don't mind. If you're trying to change the view of the people that pick up the phone to call 911—good luck!" No safety activist ever told me that they found police harassment acceptable, but Ben was certainly correct in saying that—whatever their feelings may have been—they continued to push for more intensive policing in Rogers Park and Uptown. The racial inequities this entailed the safety activists simply ignored.

Imposing Sentences: Court Advocacy

In addition to increasing policing, another concern of safety activists was how to make arrests "stick." Gang members were arrested frequently enough but were usually released very soon because they avoided carrying guns or substantial amounts of drugs so as to avoid serious charges. According to police officers, they gave the drugs to their youngest members to carry, boys who had no prior convictions and who, if arrested, would be released with "a slap on the wrist." Consequently, when "promising" arrests were made that might yield longer sentences—these usually resulted from undercover sting operations—safety activists did their best to help maximize these sentences. To do so, they attended court hearings as "court advocates."

Court advocates regularly met with a representative from the state's attorney's office at the district police station. There, the court advocates selected local cases that were currently negotiated in court and that seemed particularly important. They would then attend hearings for these cases. Sometimes, they did so in order to provide emotional support for victims who were scared to face perpetrators on their own. But the presence of court advocates at hearings also carried weight insofar as it communicated to the judge that the offense had a particularly detrimental impact on the neighborhood—since community members obviously cared enough about the hearings and their outcome to attend the proceedings.[12] I have no evidence that court advocacy had an effect on sentencing, but in a conversation a prosecutor confirmed this impact, and so did the court advocates. When Frank tried to recruit new court advocates at CAPS meetings, he always said, "I wouldn't do it if I didn't think it had an impact."

Court advocates also fulfilled an important function by relaying court proceedings to the wider community. In this context, it is important to remember that judges are elected public officials and periodically have to run for reelection. Court advocates had an opinion on which judges were lenient or strict, and on the basis of that opinion they made voting recommendations, although they usually followed the recommendations of the Chicago Bar Association. Given that turnout for judicial elections is notoriously low, however, it is likely that judges running for reelection considered the impressions they made on the court advocates.

Court advocacy was less contested than other practices of safety work. Left-leaning residents rarely talked about court advocacy, perhaps because they did not know very much about it. Nonetheless, court advocates proactively engaged in racial neutralization when I observed their meetings. At the first meeting of a court advocacy group I attended, the attendees—all four of them white—told me a story that neutralized court advocacy as a legitimate and nonracial practice. Steve, one of the court advocates, asked Frank: "do you remember the wheelchair guy?" Frank laughed, turned to me, and said, "This was the craziest case I've ever been to. The defendant was shouting at the judge and the judge was shouting at the defendant." Harry continued: "he was accusing him of being racist, right?" Frank confirmed this and Harry said to me: "and you know what the best thing was? The judge's wife was African American." Everyone laughed.

Later during the meeting, we talked about a recent uptick in gang violence. A woman in her forties, Esther, said that the shootings were related to turf war: "they fight because their turf is shrinking. Lakeview [the neighborhood south of Uptown] used to be a pretty rough area, but now that it is gentrified all the gangs have been pushed out." Frank frowned and said: "you know, on the South Side, they don't call that gentrification. They don't even use that word at all. They call it neighborhood rejuvenation. They think it's a good thing." Frank disapproved of the word "gentrification," at least in this context, because he thought it had unduly negative—and possibly racial—connotations. Struggling against gangs was not gentrification. If anything, it rejuvenated the neighborhood. The fact that South Siders—in Chicago, "South Side" serves as a synonym for "the black part of town"—celebrated this outcome and called it rejuvenation neutralized safety efforts.

I believe these interactions reveal that the court advocates wanted to teach me that their work constituted a race-neutral form of civic involvement. The "wheelchair guy" story had a clear moral—attributions of racism had to be taken with a grain of salt because they could be opportunistic attempts to deploy racial challenges for personal benefit. Since the judge had a black wife, the story suggested, he could not possibly have been a racist. Similarly, Frank made a case that attacking the gangs was legitimate because black South Siders did it, too. In support of my interpretation, I should note that the "wheelchair guy" story did not emerge from the natural flow of conversation. Steve initiated it without any context that would have called for it. Even if my interpretation is incorrect, however, the conversations at the meeting certainly show that the court advocates were highly cognizant that their efforts could be subjected to racial challenges.

"Reclaiming" Space: Positive Loitering and Other Spatial Interventions

One influential source of guidance for members of the public safety camp was George Kelling and Catherine Coles's (1996) book *Fixing Broken Windows*, which some had read and others had absorbed indirectly through conversations with neighbors and police officers. Broken windows theory was popular because it proposed simple steps people could take that would allegedly reduce crime. Just as littering and small infractions like public drinking could, according to the theory, initiate a vicious cycle of urban decline, residents hoped they could reverse urban decline by reclaiming public space. Thus block clubs, CAPS groups, and other safety organizations promoted such practices as litter patrols, graffiti removal, and urban gardening. They also tried to suppress loitering by pressing businesses to police their spaces (see figure 3.2). In doing these things, safety activists wanted to send a message that vigilant and organized citizens were monitoring the neighborhood, which might convince potential lawbreakers to move somewhere else. All of these practices, it was thought, would make public spaces more appealing, which would then encourage people to spend more time outside and thereby initiate a virtuous cycle.[13] Channeling the words of Jane Jacobs (1961), Uptown's Alderman Cappleman liked to say: "every pair of eyes on the street counts."

Figure 3.2. A strip mall in Uptown discourages loitering. Photo by the author.

The most explicit practice of "reclaiming" public space was positive loitering, a well-known type of safety intervention in Rogers Park and Uptown. Positive loitering was a kind of public neighborhood watch. Together in groups, neighbors loitered on street corners or conducted walks to deter crime. During the time of my fieldwork, a total of five groups conducted regular positive loitering events in Rogers Park and Uptown, and several more held sporadic events. As their primary locations, positive loiterers selected street corners across from "gang corners" in order to deter gang members from congregating. Occasionally, the police district would dispatch an officer to join the positive loiterers for part of an event. In addition to this preventive component, positive loiterers reported crime to the police and collected information about patterns in presumed criminal activity. For example, the loiterers tried to monitor the ways gang members conducted drug deals or where they would go to hide from the police.

By design, positive loitering was a highly visible form of safety work. In this context, the fact that the groups were primarily made up of whites often became a topic of debate. Some social justice critics derisively referred to positive loitering as "white people loitering." When I asked Ben, a community organizer from Rogers Park, whether he knew about positive loitering, he said: "yeah, I know about large groups of white homeowners standing on the corner. They are loitering the same way that young people do, only the police don't bother them. My black friends tell me 'When I stand on this corner, that shit ain't positive. It's only positive when they do it.' I don't even know what to say about that."

Just like the court advocates, positive loiterers tried to forestall any negative interpretations that might lead to racial challenges. The first night I joined one positive loitering group in Uptown, I was standing together with Greg and Henry, two white men in their sixties. Henry told me that the group had successfully ended drug dealing on this street, pushing the activity away from their residential area, where many of Uptown's wealthiest residents lived. The group now conducted positive loitering mostly to prevent drug dealers from returning. As a black woman walked past us on the sidewalk, Henry said, with a friendly and upbeat tone, "Hi, how you doing." He turned back to me. "This is another thing that we try to do. We don't intimidate people. I can't tell you how many black men and women have later walked up to us, thanking us for what we are doing, because they did not feel safe walking around here." Greg picked up this thread. "We are not racists. We could not even afford to be racist around here," he said, explaining that Uptown was incredibly diverse and that he appreciated this aspect of the neighborhood. "The problem is there are two kinds of people: people who have worked hard for their money all their lives and people who get their money for free. And you can imagine that sometimes leads to somewhat strange encounters."

Greeting the black pedestrian, Henry could demonstrate that the group took steps to avoid alienating black residents—the positive loiterers did not simply suspect all black people of being criminals. And in telling me about how black residents had thanked them for conducting positive loitering, he assured me that neighbors responded favorably to positive loitering, independent of their race. Greg underlined this claim by explicitly rejecting the label of racism. Again, I interpret this interaction as a strategic performance, for my benefit, of racial neutralization.

As a study site, positive loitering provided especially valuable insights into the detailed decisions involved in public safety work because the groups had to collectively interpret their urban environment. For instance, they had to discuss whether to call the police about a group of loiterers further down the block. Furthermore, because of their public visibility as safety activists, the positive loiterers occasionally encountered racial challenges from other pedestrians. For me, this made them great sites to conduct what Gary Fine (2003) calls "peopled ethnography": the study of social practices in group-based settings. Repeated observations of positive loitering revealed in great detail how participants understood safety activism, their urban environment, and the implications of race for their work. I discuss positive loitering in more detail in chapter 6.

The Specter of Racism and the Racial Neutralization of Public Safety Work

Racial inequality suffused the politics of street crime in Rogers Park and Uptown. When safety activists engaged crime, they almost inevitably also engaged racial inequality and at least sometimes exacerbated it—whether this was their intention or not. It was therefore easy to construe their work as racist. Safety activists called for more—and more invasive—policing, but this exposed African Americans and Latinos to increased scrutiny and harassment. Safety activists fought the presence of crime in low-income housing, but this accelerated gentrification. They assembled in groups to reclaim public space as positive loiterers, but this alienated those who interpreted positive loitering as a symbolic enactment of racial aggression.

The foregoing sections have demonstrated that this potential for racial conflict did not remain hypothetical. Opponents of anticrime initiatives, such as Ben, Elliot, and Janelle, used any opportunity to underscore what they considered evidence of racial bias. And not only the inner core of the antigentrification camp complained—sometimes otherwise uninvolved residents, like the black couple at the North of Howard public safety meeting, did so as well. The specter of racism thus haunted safety activists. It affected them strategically because they needed to refute attributions of racism to continue their work, but it also affected them personally. Most of them were college-educated members of the middle class and inhabited social circles in which a progressive cosmopolitanism was de rigueur. Most said that they had voted for Barack Obama and expressed great concern about the Tea Party, which was growing stronger during the period of my fieldwork. To the safety activists, rejecting and preventing charges of racism was not only a strategic imperative but also a necessity for maintaining cherished self-conceptions. In order to do so, they drew primarily on three strategies: recruiting minority participants, promoting favorable, race-neutral narratives, and making strategic retreats.

First, the safety activists tried to recruit more minority participants—and African Americans in particular—for their organizations. They were unhappy with the whiteness of safety work. Eileen, a block club president, lamented that her block club had always been "very white and we were always trying to make it not so white." She knew that this racial homogeneity affected how the block club was perceived. She said: "if you are together in a group, in a block club or whatever, and you see that you're just the same, then I feel it helps, but it's easy to become us-versus-them when you don't have any interaction with each other." Like other safety activists, Eileen reasoned that actual interpersonal contact would convince black residents that the block clubs were sincerely trying to improve the neighborhood for everyone. And being multiracial would also make the club less susceptible to charges of racism.[14]

For a variety of reasons, it was difficult to recruit African Americans, however. Distrust of the police and anticrime initiatives was certainly one reason, as I learned through interviews. Another reason was that many African Americans in Rogers Park and Uptown were working-class or poor. For those residents, the daily concerns of getting by tended to outweigh any form of community involvement. Nonetheless, there were some African American safety activists. (And they did not at all concur with the charges of racism that were brought against safety activists' initiatives—I describe their perspective

in more detail in chapter 7.) As a result of their strategic value, they were frequently wooed to take leadership positions. When I asked Alicia, who was
one of very few African American block club members, whether people ever
asked her to take on more responsibilities, she laughed and said: *"Always!*
And it's not that I mind, but sometimes you look around and it's like 'Am I the
only one, you all? Am I the only one? Really?' For *years!"*

Second, safety activists disseminated positive narratives about anticrime
initiatives that countered the racial portrayals their challengers broadcast.
At their core, these counter-narratives depicted the struggle against crime
as a race-neutral or even racially beneficial community process, because it
gave people an opportunity to come together. Since everyone wanted to be
safe, all residents could and indeed should unite against criminals. In 2011,
for example, Uptown's Alderman Cappleman, newly elected, set up an advisory committee to create a public safety "master plan" that was to guide
his approach to crime. The resulting document, which acknowledged "polarization" over the topic of crime in the neighborhood,[15] ended on the
following note, which can be taken as a prototypical attempt at racial neutralization: "while it remains a given that the City of Chicago is in need of
more police, the purpose of this [document] is to reinforce the need for the
entire community to work together to address crime and crime prevention.
No ethnic group or income class can be singled out for the causes of crime,
and the true causes of crime remain complex. It then stands to reason that
the many approaches to addressing crime, when done together, will have a
profound effect on making any community safer."[16] This passage reframes
crime as being, instead of a divisive issue, a unifying one. Using the adjective
"ethnic" rather than the more charged "racial," the statement proposes that
crime is not an ethnic problem—so *fighting* crime is not about ethnic identities either. The passage calls on all law-abiding Uptowners, "the entire community," to come together. Similar narratives of unity were performed across
a wide range of situations: opening words at block club or CAPS meetings,
campaign speeches, and even conversations between neighbors on the street.
Of course, it must be added that, this enlightened language notwithstanding,
the complaints one heard at CAPS and block club meetings revolved practically invariably around presumed offenders who were black or Latino.

Socially acceptable motives were important components of these positive counter-narratives.[17] When explaining safety work in public settings,
the community volunteers projected motives and attitudinal underpinnings
that made their work appear legitimate. Since their social justice rivals

frequently charged that anticrime interventions were simply a tool of gentri-fication, safety activists avoided talking about the connection between crime and property values. Doing so would have validated the narrative that "the homeowners" were doing all of this out of greed, not because they actually cared about crime. Not once did I hear any safety activist say that they were targeting crime in a low-income tenement in order to turn it into middle-class housing. Fighting crime was the only acceptable motive.

Finally, safety activists could make limited adjustments to prevent or de-fuse racial challenges—usually through a strategic retreat. As a case of this, Eric abandoned the practice of projecting mug shots at CAPS meetings but then continued to distribute the pictures in private. Similarly, when a black couple complained about police harassment at a North of Howard public safety meeting, participants placated the couple without putting the need for intensified policing up for debate. And when Alderman Cappleman and FLATS, the developer that bought Lawrence House, faced media scrutiny as a result of awkward charges of "re-segregation," they earmarked a small number of units as subsidized housing. In sum, safety activists and their allies made strategic efforts to neutralize their initiatives, which could allow them to prevent racial challenges and to maintain positive interpretations of their own civic involvement.

Conclusion: A Tug of War

Describing the forms of safety work as well as the persistent pushing and pulling of racial challenges and neutralizations, this chapter has begun to disentangle the racial politics of fighting crime in Rogers Park and Uptown. Whether deliberately or not, safety work fed the process of displacement and elicited complaints about racial marginalization. In showing how this occurred, these findings add to existing work on the reproduction of racial inequality in the city. Essentially, safety activists had learned how to wield the tools that community policing, the state's attorney's office, and city resources, for example housing inspectors, gave them. Safety activists' control over these tools should certainly not be exaggerated—complaints about unresponsive police officers, dismissive city employees, and the clogged-up court system were rampant—but at times the safety activists successfully exerted pressure to intensify policing and to close down or transform buildings and businesses they considered to be "problems." As a result, black and low-income residents faced more of the police harassment and housing precarity that Victor Rios (2011) and Matthew Desmond (2016) have described in great detail.

The anticrime initiatives thus certainly had racial effects. But since it was not entirely clear whether these racial effects were unintended byproducts or the true goals of the safety activists, a persistent tug of war resulted. Racial challenges served justice activists as a tool for contesting safety work as they rendered visible the racial disparities that permeated the fight against crime. Public safety volunteers, on the other hand, neutralized their own efforts and portrayed them as contributions to the public good. After all, there really were gang shootings and drug dealing. How could critics deny that addressing these problems was good for the neighborhood? Occasionally, journalists gave one of these two camps an advantage by publishing an article that boosted their narrative. In the case of Lawrence House, gentrification critics could build on an article in the *Chicago Tribune* to criticize "problem building" interventions. At other times, the safety camp received media support.[18] These narrative struggles reveal the fundamental importance of racial challenges and neutralizations in shaping urban change in Rogers Park and Uptown.

Studying the specific uses of racial or race-neutral narratives shows what activists, community organizations, and politicians *accomplished* in challenging and neutralizing anticrime initiatives. The following chapters address these practical outcomes in more detail. Chapter 5 homes in on conflict in Uptown's political field, examining how justice organizations tried to fight racial marginalization and gang violence at the same time. Racial challenges and neutralizations, as I will show, served as crucial weapons in struggles between community organizations as they vied for legitimacy, funding, members, and support from public officials. Chapter 6 provides an in-depth portrayal of two positive loitering groups that unravels how participants implemented this contested practice. The chapter offers more contextual detail than the relatively brief snapshots I could provide here.

But first, in chapter 4, I address how the politics of crime unfolded in the realm of electoral politics. Corresponding to just how profoundly crime was tied to neighborhood change, the issue deeply shaped local elections. Aldermen wielded significant influence over housing and law enforcement in their neighborhoods and hence represented crucial allies for the safety and the justice activists. The next chapter examines how aldermen and aldermanic candidates positioned themselves in the heated politics of crime and race.

4

"You've Got Reason to Be Afraid"

Crime and Race in Electoral Campaigning

Steeped in Saul Alinsky's style of mobilizing the poor, Uptown's longtime Alderwoman Helen Shiller was a local hero in Chicago's leftist circles.[1] On the city council, Shiller had advocated for gay rights, police reform, and public school funding and had backed many other progressive causes. Often, she had been the only one to vote against the business-friendly ordinances that were typically fielded in Chicago's council chamber. Locally, in Uptown's 46th Ward, Shiller had forcefully supported the development of subsidized housing and an unusually dense network of social services. She was therefore revered by antigentrification activists and many low-income residents who had benefited from her work.

On the other hand many who complained about rampant street crime and gun violence in Uptown vociferously derided Shiller. They charged that she had been ignoring these problems, refusing to attack the purported roots of crime in Uptown's subsidized housing for ideological reasons. Some went so far as to claim that she actively protected gang members from the police in order "to bring the gang element into the fold and build up her voting base."[2] These attacks against her had grown more and more vitriolic during the late 2000s. After having held the office for twenty-three years, Shiller finally announced in 2010 that she would not seek reelection in 2011, noting that the neighborhood had simply become too divided for her to remain in office. Her decision had caused quite a stir.

One of my earliest fieldwork excursions on the Far North Side was to an aldermanic candidate debate for the 2011 run-off in Uptown's 46th Ward. The debate was held on a frigid March night at Truman College, one of Chicago's community colleges. It was hosted by Shiller, the departing incumbent, and her city council colleague Tom Tunney of Lakeview's 44th Ward. Truman's bare foyer, where the candidate debate took place, was packed, and many audience members had to stand or sit on the floor. I estimated that about 400 Uptowners had braved the icy wind to attend. Uptown's block clubs

Us versus Them. Jan Doering, Oxford University Press (2020) © Oxford University Press.
DOI: 10.1093/oso/9780190066574.001.0001

Figure 4.1. 46th Ward Alderwoman Helen Shiller (right) is honored for her public service at a "Women and Leadership" event at Loyola University, 2011. Photo by the author.

had already hosted several debates, all of which had focused on how the candidates would fight the gang presence, evict repeat offenders, and make the neighborhood feel more secure.[3] But instead of the middle-class residents who had dominated those events, tonight's debate drew many of Shiller's core supporters—African Americans, leftist whites, rooming house dwellers. It was thus a difficult audience for James Cappleman and Molly Phelan, the two candidates who had made it into the run-off through a crowded field of eleven candidates.

Cappleman was a slight white man, openly gay. He had been president of the Uptown Chicago Commission—a prodevelopment organization that had been at odds with Shiller for decades—and had taken a leading role in the neighborhood's public safety camp. He had already run for alderman in 2007 and narrowly lost to Shiller after an acrimonious campaign. Phelan was known in Uptown primarily for spearheading the legal battle against one of Shiller's signature accomplishments: the construction of Wilson Yard, a mixed-use affordable housing project. Phelan had argued that the construction of Wilson Yard had to be prevented because it was going to become a crime-ridden housing project reminiscent of the infamous Robert Taylor Homes and Cabrini Green.[4] Phelan's court case had failed, but her candidacy illustrates the kind of credentials candidates appeared to need in order to succeed Shiller. Both Phelan and Cappleman had made it into the run-off first and foremost as antidotes to Shiller's purported legacy: violence, urban decay, fear.

As the debate began, it became clear that tonight's forum was not going to revolve around crime. Shiller, though not running for reelection, relished the opportunity to discredit her adversaries. She did not ask about gangs or how to make it easier to evict offenders. Instead, she rebuked Cappleman and Phelan for their opposition to Wilson Yard and demanded to know how they would prevent racial displacement and protect the interests of Uptown's working-class and minority residents. Knowing that the audience largely supported Shiller, Cappleman and Phelan did their best to placate her and her constituents, promising that their fight against crime was not going to constitute a fight against low-income residents and affordable housing. Nonetheless, after about thirty minutes, a black woman in her thirties who had been sitting in the first row got up from her chair and made her way toward the exit. As she did, she loudly proclaimed: "I am leaving. We're fucked either way."

This chapter investigates aldermanic politics, especially the roles race and crime played in electoral campaigning. Building on campaign documents, journalistic accounts, and fieldwork data, I provide insights into the dynamics and effects of electoral campaigning in Rogers Park and Uptown over the three decades 1990–2019. Recent scholarship in urban ethnography has begun to contextualize ethnographic observations in their local political contexts, but urban sociologists overall have neglected to study electoral politics and their consequences.[5] One influential analytic framework, John Logan and Harvey Molotch's (2007) growth machine theory, regards city politicians as little more than puppets of powerful development interests. But even if politicians have limited leeway, electoral politics still matters. For example, political discourse in the form of electoral campaigning influences how individuals think and feel about certain issues. Electoral campaigning shapes voters' perceptions of crime and even their racial attitudes, as studies of national and statewide elections have shown. For decades, politicians have mobilized white voters by invoking and thereby affirming stereotypes of black criminality.[6]

Tough-on-crime campaigning would appear to be a promising strategy in racially diverse neighborhoods. Given that crime is typically a fundamental concern, candidates could try to activate or strategically amplify elevated levels of fear—especially among whites—in order to use fear as a political resource. Since whites are already sensitive about street crime, they may prove receptive to shrill campaigning. At the same time, crime can also prove a risky issue to run on. Considering the type of tug of war I discussed in chapter 3 over the racial implications of combating crime, tough-on-crime campaigning can alienate black as well as left-leaning white residents who detest racial stereotyping, police harassment, and dislocation—especially if they can be convinced that a candidate's campaign exhibits a racist subtext.[7] The issue of crime therefore holds promise but also peril for political candidates in neighborhoods like Rogers Park and Uptown.

Given these contingencies, it is important to investigate the electoral politics up close. This chapter examines the positions incumbents and challengers adopted on crime and gentrification, how they communicated them, and what they could hope to accomplish in doing so. The chapter also investigates how candidates strategically framed certain policies by deploying racial challenges and neutralizations. And, of course, the chapter shows how candidates implemented their policies in office. In this way, I provide insights into the significant impact formal politics had on urban change in Rogers Park and Uptown.

But there is a second reason why electoral politics matter. Elections do not only distribute political offices and their attendant powers; they also contribute to the unity or dividedness of local communities.[8] This point has received much public attention since Donald Trump's presidential campaign, but of course *all* electoral campaigns leave lasting effects on the communities in which they take place. I will trace particularly how electoral politics shaped the relations between the two neighborhoods' social justice and public safety organizations. Aside from the aldermen, these organizations were the most important entities in the local political fields. Whether they were at peace or embroiled in conflict with one another had substantial consequences for community life and local activism.[9]

As I will show, the electoral politics of crime and race were quite similar in Rogers Park and Uptown up until 2007. In both neighborhoods, elections frequently revolved around crime, and campaigning incited a notable amount of racial strife. However, only in Uptown did these electoral conflicts translate into direct confrontations between the local social justice and public safety camps. This heightened and perpetuated tension over the politics of crime, enshrining it in the neighborhood's political field. In contrast, crime became a less contested theme in Rogers Park after 2007, which meant that residents and activists there felt less racially divided than in Uptown when I conducted fieldwork. Chapters 5 and 6 will specify the effects these different political contexts had on the ways community organizations and individuals engaged one another between 2011 and 2014.

Over the following pages, I describe the uses of crime and race in electoral politics separately for each neighborhood. This requires me to introduce a fair amount of contextual information. Impatient readers may jump to the chapter's final section, where I discuss the patterns that emerged from a condensed analytic perspective.

The Politics of Crime and Race in Uptown

Helen Shiller was first elected alderwoman of the 46th Ward in 1987 and remained in office until James Cappleman succeeded her in 2011. Although she had fierce critics from the day she took office, elections in Uptown until 1999 revolved more around her quarrels with Mayor Richard Daley than any neighborhood concern like crime or gentrification.[10] During the 1990s, Shiller was Daley's most outspoken critic on the city council, which led him to field and actively support electoral contenders in the 46th Ward who would replace her with another reliable "rubber stamp" alderman.[11] None of these candidates enjoyed much recognition or support in Uptown. And despite record-breaking crime rates throughout Chicago in the 1990s, crime played no detectable role in these contests.

Beginning in 1999, Shiller's electoral challengers began to emerge out of Uptown's public safety camp rather than Mayor Daley's anointed circle of allies. These candidates refocused local elections on the issue of crime, criticizing Shiller for her alleged unwillingness to rein in local problems ranging from disorder to gang violence. In terms of housing policy, they framed her uncompromising advocacy for subsidized housing as a factor that aggravated crime. Over the following years, debates about crime and the purportedly related topic of subsidized housing thus became increasingly impassioned and contentious.

In the 1999 general election, three candidates ran against Shiller and forced her into a run-off. Her opponent in the run-off was Sandra Reed, an African American woman who had gained political visibility in Uptown as a CAPS activist. Reed's campaign concentrated almost exclusively on crime. For example, her campaign volunteers denounced Shiller for endangering "the safety of children amid a growing population of shelters in the area that serve the homeless, drug addicts and sex offenders."[12] Reed also warned that Shiller's housing policies would eventually turn Uptown into "another ghetto."[13]

Sandra Reed had the advantage of being able to attack Shiller for her record on crime and invoke the looming threat of the "ghetto," including the attendant racial imagery and stereotypes, while being much less vulnerable to racial challenges than a white candidate would have been. As a black candidate, Reed was able to legitimize residents' fear of crime. In fact, her candidacy *itself* neutralized the issue. If Reed, as a black resident, fretted about crime and ghettoization, how could it be racist for white Uptowners to do so? Correspondingly, one political commentator called Reed a "trump card" for Shiller's opponents, suggesting that "they can now safely claim their opposition is not about race or class."[14]

Despite the fact that Shiller unmistakably represented the aggregate interests of Uptown's minority residents more than Reed did, it would have been difficult for Shiller to discredit Reed on racial grounds. Aggressive racial challenges against Reed could have even backfired, because they would have been culturally inconsistent with the typical thrust of racial conflict in America (white racism against black resistance). Accordingly, Shiller's campaign refrained from making full-out accusations of racism, which Reed's dire warnings about Uptown becoming a "ghetto" would have arguably permitted. Shiller's campaign instead insinuated racial bias only in a cautious, indirect way and focused much more heavily on denouncing Reed as "a puppet for [Mayor] Richard Daley and real estate speculators."[15]

Reed's promising position notwithstanding, Shiller won reelection with 56 percent of the vote. But despite this defeat, Reed's campaign successfully elevated crime into the key grievance Shiller would face throughout the rest of her tenure. Ever more loudly, her critics complained that she was an obstacle rather than a resource in the fight against street crime.

Shiller and her supporters insisted that her critics from the public safety camp were producing false perceptions in the interest of mobilizing residents through fear. In the aftermath of the 1999 election, Shiller withdrew her support from CAPS—through which Reed had emerged as a candidate. Shiller argued that CAPS had become a thinly veiled platform for attacking affordable housing, even though crime was actually decreasing. In an interview, she told me: "what they [the gentrifiers] realized, I think, was that, if you make it about crime—and they've made it about crime since the '99 election—then you create at least the perception that it's worse and that's all you need, politically." Shiller's assessment that CAPS had become a political platform may or may not have been correct, but her withdrawal almost certainly helped to make it one. Participants at CAPS meetings frequently voiced frustration about Shiller's lack of support, citing as evidence the fact that neither she nor her staff members attended the meetings.

In addition to Shiller, Uptown's social justice camp responded to the changes in the neighborhood's political field. Before the 1999 election, leading activists from the justice camp had simply considered CAPS a failed opportunity for establishing more community oversight over the police, but now CAPS seemed to threaten Shiller, their political ally. Justice activists thus began to attend CAPS meetings so as to contest them as a tool of racial marginalization. They charged that the safety activists did not actually care about crime and violence but merely wanted to use CAPS to harass and evict black residents. In an interview for a news story that was printed months after the 1999 election, one gentrification-critical resident commented on his experience at a recent CAPS meeting: "they talked about little kids like they were predators. . . . Man, it was crazy. It wasn't like anybody had gotten stabbed or anything. The bottom line is that they want to clean out poor people and black people so their property values will rise."[16]

Reed again challenged Shiller in 2003, continuing to focus on street crime.[17] Shiller did not change her position on crime but, in a surprise move, secured an endorsement from Mayor Daley, with whom she had recently made peace. Consequently, Reed now lacked the crucial funds, office space, and campaign staff Daley had still provided in 1999.[18] Shiller won the 2003 election relatively easily with 58 percent.

Meanwhile, crime continued to spark bitter conflicts among Uptown's community organizations as justice activists continued their campaign against CAPS.[19] In chapter 3 I described how Eric, a CAPS facilitator, abandoned the idea of projecting images of gang members during CAPS meetings after a black attendee questioned the practice. This was not Eric's first encounter with racial contestation. He complained that justice activists had disrupted his meetings for years. He said: "they would sit in the back and say 'Don't ever call 911! Every time you call 911 an innocent black kid goes to jail.' They guilt people into thinking 'Oh, yeah, maybe I shouldn't call 911.'"

Around the same time, the debate over the development of Wilson Yard, a former rail depot that had been destroyed by fire, further hardened the lines between Uptown's social justice and public safety camps. Shiller wanted the Wilson Yard redevelopment to contribute to the neighborhood's stock of subsidized housing, but her opponents rallied against these plans, demanding that the project include subsidized housing only in the form of "artist housing": combined work and living spaces for artists. Shiller's opponents argued that more conventional subsidized housing would produce "severely concentrated poverty" and thereby nurture crime.[20] Justice organizations responded with charges of racism. The director of ONE claimed that public safety activists used "coded" language that built on racial fears and stereotypes.[21] An editorial in the *Chicago Tribune* concurred that the call for artist housing (rather than regular subsidized housing) "seems to have a classist or even racist ring."[22] All of the longtime residents I asked about the Wilson Yard battle said that leading up to the 2007 election, Uptown had been more polarized over crime and gentrification than ever before.

In the 1999 and 2003 elections, Shiller and her supporters could not easily make racial challenges to oppose Reed's tough-on-crime campaigns, but things changed in 2007 when James Cappleman, a white CAPS activist, ran as Shiller's only challenger. In his campaign, Cappleman built on the widespread feeling that crime, especially gang violence, was getting worse. In bold letters, a series of Cappleman's campaign mailers featured the words "fear," "gangs," and "vacancy" (see figure 4.2). The "gangs" mailer included a map of gang territories in the ward and stated that "violent gangs and their major stock-in-trade—drug sales—flourish in many sections, jeopardizing the safety of all residents." A passage of the "fear" mailer asked: "afraid of walking home from the 'L' at night? Afraid of walking down trash-littered streets with empty stores and boarded-up windows? You've got reason to be—neglect breeds criminal activity." Like Reed before him, Cappleman reinforced the

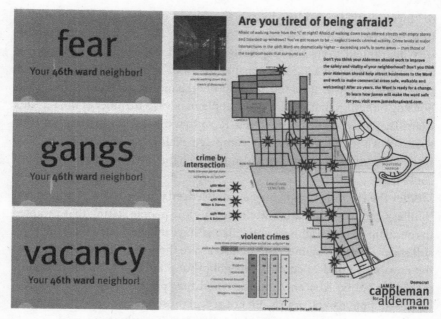

Figure 4.2. Cappleman campaign mailers, 2007, 46th Ward.

belief that street crime posed a significant threat and Uptowners had every reason to fear crime.

Shiller tried to dispel the notion that crime was rising. The cover of one of her campaign's mailers proclaimed: "crime reaches 40 year low in the 46th ward!" Inside, citing police data, Shiller's campaign claimed that Uptown's police beats were among the safest in Chicago. The mailer also featured a photograph of a black resident who was quoted as saying that when he and his neighbors "had trouble with gangs and drugs—Helen Shiller was there for us." In invoking support from a black Uptowner, Shiller could defend her record on crime without appearing to betray her core constituency of black and low-income voters.

The tug of war over racially challenging and neutralizing the fight against crime became the perhaps decisive factor in the election. Shiller accused Cappleman of "using polarizing language to rally higher-income, mostly white residents."[23] Conversely, Cappleman challenged Shiller for using race to silence legitimate concerns. He said that Shiller "regards the persistent street crime, gang-related murders and international drug trafficking as facts of urban life that residents should simply get used to, or, in her words, 'move to Lincoln Park' [a wealthy white neighborhood on Chicago's North Side]."[24] In a more blatant manifestation of this conflict, Shiller's supporters reportedly distributed flyers that explicitly portrayed Cappleman as a racist. As the former editor of a local newspaper told me: "a week before the election, some people went around the neighborhood handing out flyers at the public housing buildings that said . . . that Cappleman was a member of the Ku Klux Klan. They even spelled him with a 'K' so that it would fit in with 'Ku Klux Klan.'"[25] Although Cappleman's campaign plainly resembled Reed's 1999 and 2003 campaigns, Cappleman could be charged with racism while Reed could not.

After the election, Cappleman acknowledged the accusations, noting that "Shiller's campaign literature went out to some people stating that I wanted to round up all the neighborhood kids and have them arrested on sight. I will still speak up about crime, but I'm also aware there's a price to pay."[26] Given the racialized political conflict, "neighborhood kids" here almost certainly stands for young African Americans and the "price to pay" for charges of racism. Cappleman obviously did not accept those charges but credited them with having had an important and possibly decisive influence.

I cannot assess what impact the charges of racism had on the election's outcome, but Shiller narrowly prevailed with 53 percent of the vote, remaining in office for a final term. In light of Uptown's changing demographic composition, however, it seemed less and less likely that she could continue to win reelection this way. Acting on comparably low housing prices, middle-class residents continued to pour into Uptown, speculating that the gangs would eventually be pushed out. In conversations with neighbors, these newcomers were told that Shiller would have to go in order to further improve the neighborhood. In the summer of 2010, to the cheers of her detractors, Shiller announced that she would not seek reelection in 2011.

No fewer than eleven candidates ran for the office in 2011, and not one of them attempted to downplay crime and violence as a critical challenge for Uptown.[27] Two candidates promised to sustain Shiller's legacy of advocating for the poor, but even they acknowledged street crime as a major problem. Ultimately, two of Shiller's fiercest critics made the run-off: James Cappleman and Molly Phelan.

Cappleman portrayed himself as a seasoned community leader who had long been combating crime through CAPS and grassroots safety initiatives. One campaign mailer showed Cappleman standing in a gritty alley (see figure 4.3). The mailer claimed that Cappleman, through his

Figure 4.3. Cappleman campaign mailer, 2011, 46th Ward.

public safety work, had "cleaned up" what he dubbed "blood alley" for its pervasive muggings and violent altercations. The mailer concluded that he had "proven he is the leader we need to keep us safe." Phelan was known in Uptown primarily for leading the charge against Shiller's Wilson Yard project. She could not invoke safety accomplishments that matched Cappleman's but promised to hire more police officers and also touted an endorsement from the Fraternal Order of Police. In the run-off, Cappleman won 55 percent of the vote and was thereby elected alderman in his second attempt.

During his first term (2011–2015), as I was conducting fieldwork, Cappleman worked tirelessly to combat crime and Uptown's gang presence. The neighborhood's social justice activists felt severely threatened by Cappleman's efforts, which they regarded as covert efforts to promote racial displacement. They thus used any opportunity to denounce Cappleman's efforts by making racial challenges. Their resistance, which I describe in chapter 5, kept race, crime, and gentrification on the political agenda. In addition, crime remained an issue simply because expectations for Cappleman's tenure were sky-high—having hoped for even more drastic and immediate changes after ousting Shiller, some Uptowners remained dissatisfied.

Cappleman's main opponent in 2015, a white woman named Amy Crawford, tried to tap into both of these sources of discontent at the same time. Crawford vowed to fight crime more effectively while also challenging Cappleman for having divided residents along racial lines. At one campaign event, Crawford said that Cappleman had "not been effective at getting the things done that he has said were priorities [reducing street crime]. At the same time I think he's exacerbated some of the tensions that we have in our diverse community."[28] Regarding crime, Crawford's campaign broadcast rather dubious messages. One of her mailers charged that "last year [2014] alone, homicides increased 400%" under Cappleman's watch. Indeed, homicides *had* increased by that rate—but from one in 2013 (an unusually peaceful year) to five in 2014, an average year for Uptown.

Together with another candidate, Crawford forced Cappleman into a run-off. Ironically, having succeeded Shiller, it was now Cappleman's turn to downplay crime. He told a journalist that before he took office, "we had five gangs and they were selling drugs like a lemonade stand and we were seeing massive amounts of fighting in the middle of the street. We are now seeing gang members who feel threatened they will go extinct."[29] A campaign mailer depicted Cappleman shaking hands with a police officer and reported that he had "reduced crime by as much as 80% in crime hot-spots." Cappleman won the run-off with 54 percent of the vote.

In the most recent election, in 2019, Cappleman's opponents avoided the issue of crime and instead attacked the incumbent for his alleged failure to control gentrification and maintain affordable housing in the neighborhood.[30] Again, this race yielded a run-off, and again he won reelection, albeit by a mere thirty votes. Winning margins in Uptown's 46th Ward elections thus remain very small, which reflects the deep divisions between those who primarily want to see faster development and lower crime and those seeking to maintain affordability and racial diversity. Like Helen Shiller before him, James Cappleman cannot take his hold on the office for granted.

The Politics of Crime and Race in Rogers Park

In Rogers Park's 49th Ward, crime became a major electoral theme in 1991, much earlier than in Uptown. Concerns about peaking crime in Rogers Park in the early 1990s were compounded by alarm about the rapidly growing black population[31]—between 1980 and 1990, Rogers Park's share of black residents had increased from 9 to 27 percent. In 1991, no established incumbent was competing for reelection because David Orr, the longtime, left-leaning incumbent, had recently been elected to a county office. To serve out the remaining months of Orr's aldermanic term, Mayor Daley had appointed Robert Clarke, a white man who had formerly served as president of the Rogers Park Community Council. In the election, Clarke was challenged by Joe Moore (also white), who had worked closely with David Orr and promised to continue his leftist politics.

Since residents perceived Orr and Moore as supporters of racial integration rather than crime fighters, Robert Clarke tried to blame Orr and Moore for rising crime in Rogers Park. The *Chicago Reader* reported: "'Crime is the issue,' reads a flier distributed by Clarke's campaign. And wherever he goes, Clarke recites local crime statistics. 'Public safety is a legitimate issue in this campaign,' says Clarke. 'It's what's on people's minds.'"[32] Moore countered that inflated *perceptions* of crime were the real problem that he would tackle as alderman.[33] He also deployed a racial challenge against Clarke's "irresponsible" emphasis on crime that was fanning "these flames and these fears." Moore framed campaigning on crime as illegitimate because he claimed that it intensified fear and disrupted racial harmony. A prominent social justice activist named Elliot, who had volunteered for Moore, told me that outside the public spotlight, Moore's campaign made more forceful racial challenges, drawing on Clarke's tough-on-crime postures to portray him as a racist. Elliot recalled campaigners "going door to door and saying, 'Don't vote for this racist [Clarke].'" Moore narrowly beat Clarke in a run-off with 52 percent.

Moore served as alderman of the 49th Ward from 1991 until 2019. In accordance with his position in this first election, he pursued a cautious approach when addressing crime, supporting CAPS and safety initiatives,[34] but also warning against hyperbole that could produce racial division. Perhaps as a result, he never became quite as polarizing a figure as Uptown's Shiller, who reacted much more defiantly when challengers attacked her as soft on crime. In an interview, Moore told me that street crime "unfortunately stokes racial fears and encourages profiling, not only from police but from community residents. And so one of the things that I think is important is to address crime in a very responsible fashion."

Some Rogers Parkers interpreted this perspective as "liberal hand-wringing" and complained that Moore did not sufficiently support the fight against street crime. In the 1990s, his most adamant critic in this regard was a white woman named Karen Hoover, a CAPS activist. Hoover ran as Moore's main challenger in the 1995 and 1999 elections. Her campaigns resembled those of Sandra Reed in Uptown. Hoover argued that Moore had approved too many "group homes and halfway houses." She also warned of menacing street gangs: "our business districts are faltering. They're unsafe and congested. We have gangs you've never even heard of, one for each ethnic group."[35] Crime remained a major issue in Rogers Park's electoral politics throughout the 1990s, but Hoover's campaigns nevertheless faltered. Moore won the 1995 and 1999 elections with comfortable margins: 69 percent and 64 percent, respectively. When I asked Elliot to explain Hoover's lack of success, he said that "she was a terrible campaigner and she's the kind of campaigner that, when she campaigns, she turns people off." Hoover, Elliot held, was simply too blunt.

Unlike Helen Shiller, Joe Moore did not denounce or distance himself from CAPS after it had served as a springboard for a political opponent. One reason for this was that by no means all members of the public safety camp sided with Hoover. Several CAPS beat facilitators were self-identified Moore supporters; one of them even became Moore's chief of staff in 2015. Public safety initiatives thus did not turn into sites of political conflict. Some safety activists continued to voice discontent with Moore's record of improving security, but neither CAPS nor other safety organizations became a rallying ground against the alderman, as was happening in Uptown at the same time.

In the 2003 election, Hoover did not run again. Moore's strongest challenger that year was Michael Harrington, a gay African American man. According to residents I interviewed about the neighborhood's political history, crime played no significant role in this election. Instead, Harrington tried to beat Moore by claiming that he had abandoned his progressive roots and become too closely aligned with Mayor Daley's Democratic establishment. Nevertheless, Harrington's efforts proved just as unsuccessful as Hoover's campaigns. One of Harrington's problems was that Moore still maintained a solid degree of recognition as an independent, progressive alderman,[36] even though, as Ellen Berrey (2015) shows in her research, local antigentrification activists were increasingly dissatisfied with Moore. But Harrington failed to mobilize this discontent and lost with only a quarter of the vote.

The 2007 election constituted a more formidable challenge. In the general election, three candidates ran against Moore, two of them focusing heavily on crime. Moore barely missed the benchmark of 50 percent and faced a run-off against a white candidate named Don Gordon. The run-off became heavily contested, with both sides collecting and spending record-breaking amounts of campaign funds.[37]

Gordon's campaign revolved around crime as well as Moore's supposed disinterest in development and ward management. Most of Gordon's campaign material highlighted the threat of street crime in Rogers Park. One of his mailers quoted an Asian woman saying: "I want to feel safe walking alone on our streets." Another mailer alleged that Moore was "more concerned about the war in Iraq, which we all oppose, than the war on Howard Street." Moore had sponsored a city council resolution opposing the Iraq war, and Gordon used this as evidence of Moore's indifference to neighborhood problems. Howard Street, by contrast, was the main artery of the ward's only majority-black census tract and a well-known center of gang activity. In this context, the notion of a "war on Howard Street" suggested that gang violence was so rampant that it brought war-like conditions to the neighborhood. Yet another mailer criticized Moore's longtime effort of trying to calm voters by emphasizing decreases in the crime rate. The mailer stated: "Joe claims 'crime is down.' That's about all we get."

Indeed, Moore did emphasize continued decreases in crime. A campaign brochure proudly proclaimed that Rogers Park had "proven skeptics wrong" by showing that "economically and racially diverse communities like ours can be stable, safe, and prosperous." At the same time, Moore asserted that he took crime seriously. One mailer (see figure 4.4) depicted a black senior who stated that "Joe Moore drove the gangs and drug dealers out of this building. Now, senior citizens from our community call it home." Just like Helen Shiller in Uptown, Moore chose testimony from a black resident to signal that he was fighting crime *for* black voters, not against them.

Continuing the parallels to the 2007 election in Uptown, a fierce battle over the candidates' racial politics ensued. At one campaign event, Jesse Jackson Jr., son of civil rights leader Jesse Jackson Sr. and a member of the US House of Representatives at the time, reached for the most sweeping comparisons to endorse Joe Moore as a warrior for racial justice: "you might not have been there for Rosa Parks, you might not have had the chance to walk across Edmund Pettus Bridge [in Selma, Alabama], you might not have been there for Mandela when he went to jail, you might not have been in the grape fields

"Joe Moore drove the gangs and drug dealers out of this building. Now, senior citizens from our community call it home."

Rose Green
W. Morse

Real People.
Real Results.
Rogers Park.

Figure 4.4. Moore campaign mailer, 2007, 49th Ward.

with Cesar Chavez, but in 2007 you can be right here for Joe Moore in the 49th Ward."[38] At the same event, Moore charged that Gordon conspired with "those very same people who have been fighting the diversity in this neighborhood, who have been fighting against opening our doors to everyone."[39] As evidence, Moore invoked Gordon's focus on street crime, especially one of Gordon's campaign mailers that depicted a white woman walking alone in the neighborhood at night. The mailer ominously asked: "do you feel safe in the 49th ward?"[40] Moore interpreted this as a deliberate play on racial fears. In an interview, he told me that the mailer "had a photograph of a young white woman clutching her purse and there was this silhouette, a dark silhouette of someone there in the background. It was just pretty blatant of what that was referring to." Ben, a leftist community organizer who supported neither Gordon nor Moore, explained how Moore used this mailer to discredit Gordon's campaign:

> I watched as our Alderman [Joe Moore], you know, they robocalled every African American household in the ward with messages of "Don Gordon's a racist" and snipping quotes out of things that he said to make it sound that he said things he hadn't said. . . . So, if Don's campaign played the race card a little bit in one way, Joe matched him in every way, at every step, at every chance he got.

Toward the end of the campaign, Gordon officially responded to the charges of racism in an open letter: "you [Alderman Moore] attacked my character by suggesting that I am a racist. I certainly am not. . . . Let us celebrate our racial diversity by honoring and respecting it. Do not use our diversity as a weapon." Just like James Cappleman in Uptown, Gordon thus tried to neutralize his own campaign but also made a racial challenge in reverse, claiming that Moore was cynically using race as a weapon and inciting racial division. In the end, however, Moore narrowly prevailed in the run-off with 52 percent of the vote.

After nearly losing against Gordon, Moore substantially changed course to reduce grievances about crime. He replaced his chief of staff and improved his office's citizen responsiveness.[41] He also became more visibly involved in CAPS and hired a staff member who concentrated specifically on "problem buildings." Consequently, he tried to win back voters who had supported Gordon in 2007, which reduced the chance that future elections would again revolve around crime. Indeed, in the 2011 election, crime played no role at all. Instead, Moore was challenged by Brian White, a white candidate promising to defend Rogers Park's affordability and socioeconomic diversity.

White ran on an ambitious housing policy that would have used a portion of local property taxes to create and maintain subsidized housing in the neighborhood. Since Moore's advocacy for subsidized housing had waned and he had also adopted a tougher stance on crime since 2007, White's candidacy could have realigned the neighborhood's political field. A bold and effective campaign might have repainted Moore as a gentrifier and supporter of racist policing tactics. After discrediting prior electoral contenders with the help of racial challenges, Moore could have now himself become the target of such challenges. But White's campaign struggled because it did not receive crucial support from social justice organizations, which would have been instrumental in mobilizing the voters White was trying to target.

At the same time that Moore had worked more aggressively to combat crime, he had also taken steps to ensure the continued support of the social justice camp by helping to secure a state grant through Illinois's Neighborhood Recovery Initiative (NRI). Between 2010 and 2013, several million dollars were funneled through ONE, which redistributed the money among social service agencies in Rogers Park.[42] In procuring these funds, Moore placated ONE, the affiliated social service agencies, and their community organizers. In 2011 when I asked a ONE community organizer what she thought about Moore, she said: "well, he's not perfect, of course, but he just got us the NRI funding so that's pretty good." The NRI funds greatly benefited Moore's standing among the numerous Rogers Parkers who were linked to social service organizations as employees, clients, or volunteers.[43] As a result, White failed to rally left-leaning residents against Moore, who easily won reelection with 72 percent of the vote.

Unlike in Uptown, the politics of crime thus quickly quieted down in Rogers Park after the heated 2007 battle between Moore and Gordon. This trend continued through the 2011, 2015, and 2019 elections. After twenty-eight years in office, Moore actually lost the 2019 election to Maria Hadden, a black woman and political newcomer who faulted him for abandoning the ward's progressive voters. But neither Moore's victory in 2015 nor his defeat in 2019 had much to do with crime in Rogers Park.[44] For now, crime has all but disappeared from electoral politics in the 49th Ward—even though gang violence continues to take the lives of about five people each year, just as it did in the early 2000s.

Crime, Race, and Political Campaigning

Crime is a charged political issue—especially in racially heterogeneous neighborhoods. Candidates may hope to capitalize on voters' fear of crime but also run the risk of being charged with racist fearmongering. What decisions, then, did candidates make? Did they embrace crime as a campaign theme or avoid it for its potential pitfalls? And what factors led them to do so? Table 4.1 provides an overview of the electoral races discussed in this

Table 4.1 Summary of electoral contests in Rogers Park (49th Ward) and Uptown (46th Ward)

	Year	Run-off	Winner		Runner-up		Salience of crime in election	Homicides (prior year)
Rogers Park	1991	Yes	Moore	52%	Clarke	48%	Strong	N/A
	1995	No	Moore	69%	Hoover	20%	Strong	N/A
	1999	No	Moore	64%	Hoover	16%	Strong	12
	2003	No	Moore	55%	Harrington	27%	Weak	8
	2007	Yes	Moore	52%	Gordon	48%	Strong	4
	2011	No	Moore	72%	White	28%	Weak	3
	2015	No	Moore	67%	Gordon	33%	Weak	8
	2019	No	Hadden	63%	Moore	37%	Weak	6
Uptown	1991	Yes	Shiller	53%	Quigley	47%	Weak	N/A
	1995	No	Shiller	57%	Kuzas	43%	Weak	N/A
	1999	Yes	Shiller	56%	Reed	44%	Strong	4
	2003	No	Shiller	58%	Reed	42%	Strong	6
	2007	No	Shiller	53%	Cappleman	47%	Strong	3
	2011	Yes	Cappleman	55%	Phelan	45%	Strong	4
	2015	Yes	Cappleman	54%	Crawford	46%	Strong	5
	2019	Yes	Cappleman	50%	Lalonde	50%	Weak	2

Note: For reasons of simplicity, the table includes only the two most successful candidates. In cases in which a run-off took place, percentages reflect candidates' results in the run-off. Since the Chicago Police Department began to release neighborhood-level statistics only in 1998, homicide numbers for 1990 and 1994 are not available.

Sources[45]: *Chicago Tribune*, Chicago Board of Election Commissioners, Chicago Police Department, Chicago Data Portal.

chapter. It lists crime as a "strong" campaign issue if canvassing documents, newspaper coverage, records of candidate debates, and interviews with long-time residents indicated that at least one candidate in the race campaigned with a focus on street crime. This happened during nine out of sixteen of these electoral races.

The candidates who decided to push crime as a political issue were electoral challengers, not incumbents. The only exception to this pattern was the 1991 Rogers Park election, which was unusual in that it featured a recently appointed incumbent who ran against the legacy of the prior officeholder.

Generally, incumbents appeared content to deemphasize crime if their opponents allowed them to do so. After all, they had to worry that frightened voters might turn against them, holding them responsible for having failed to make the neighborhood safer during their time in office. Accordingly, incumbents were not interested in highlighting the dangers of street crime. To the best of their ability, they instead showcased how they had already reduced crime to more or less acceptable levels.

These findings suggest that discontent about crime was at least in part a political phenomenon that electoral challengers produced and exploited strategically in order to undercut incumbents. Of course, a plausible alternative explanation would be that candidates ran on crime when crime was rising or remained high. But this was not the case. As table 4.1 shows, the homicides tally during the years leading up to the elections does not correspond to the salience of crime as a campaign issue. And overall index crime rates declined steeply during the late 1990s and 2000s, but crime as a political theme persisted regardless, especially in Uptown. Despite falling index crime rates, electoral contenders forcefully charged that the incumbents had failed to protect law-abiding residents from allegedly ubiquitous gang shootings, muggings, and other kinds of threats. In fact, in Uptown, crime emerged as a major issue only in 1999, notwithstanding the fact that crime had actually been higher in 1991 and 1995. The political salience of crime was not simply a byproduct of crime rates.[46]

One factor that appears to shape the electoral salience of crime is whether candidates challenged incumbents "from the left," as potential allies of the antigentrification camp. When candidates ran on a platform of defending the neighborhood from full-out gentrification, they typically avoided the topic of crime. This happened in 2019 in Uptown as well as in Rogers Park's 2003, 2011, and 2019 elections. Knowing that many voters associated affordable housing with crime, these electoral contenders could have undermined their calls for protecting affordability if they had stressed the issue of crime. As one campaign volunteer for Moore said when I asked her why his leftist 2011 opponent, Brian White, had not discussed crime: "Brian's thing was housing, not crime. He would have shot himself in the foot if he had talked about crime."

When electoral challengers did run on crime, clashes about race generally ensued as well. Incumbents Helen Shiller and Joe Moore could build on suspicions about tough-on-crime messages, which, to some, smacked of racist stereotyping. Accordingly, the incumbents made a plethora of racial challenges. They condemned their opponents' spotlight on crime as inflammatory politicking that would cause racial rifts and aggravate racial inequality. During closely contested elections, they (or their supporters) also made full-fledged charges of racism. Thus, Moore's campaign interpreted the shadow looming over a white woman in Don Gordon's mailer as evidence that Gordon was invoking antiblack stereotypes. And Shiller's supporters in Uptown charged that "Ku Klux Kappleman," if elected, would summarily arrest young black men. As their challengers tried to tap fear of crime as a political resource, the incumbents conversely tried to tap alarm about gentrification and racism.

It should be noted that these charges were made without conclusive evidence, which suggests that Shiller and Moore expected a significant number of voters to nonetheless find them persuasive. Moore interpreted the shadow in Gordon's mailer as a "blatant" reference to stereotypes of black criminality, but white criminals also cast dark shadows. Shiller's campaign framed Cappleman's focus on crime as a sign of racism, although Sandra Reed, a black candidate, had previously run against Shiller on a nearly identical platform without facing such charges.

Tough-on-crime candidates were certainly aware that their campaigns could be challenged in racial terms. This awareness is reflected in their ubiquitous efforts to neutralize and hence justify crime as a campaign issue. For example, Moore's first opponent, Robert Clarke, stated that crime was a "legitimate issue" because "it's what's on people's minds." James Cappleman assured voters that they had good reasons to be "afraid of walking home from the 'L' at night." And Sandra Reed could validate fears of Uptown becoming "another ghetto" because, as a black candidate, she was uniquely invulnerable to accusations of racism. All of these statements endowed fear with an aura of legitimacy, which aimed to shield the campaigns against attributions of racism. In addition, these messages probably also were aimed at alleviating possible racial quandaries white voters might have about basing their votes on crime: being afraid was appropriate and thus not a sign of racism.

In addition to racially neutralizing their tough-on-crime campaigning, electoral challengers also deployed their own types of racial challenges. Essentially, these challenges sought to portray their attackers as "race-baiters" who allegedly made unfounded charges of racism in order to suppress necessary and important conversations about crime and how to address it. In doing so, tough-on-crime candidates charged, their opponents recklessly divided residents along racial lines and thereby damaged interracial community. In other words, electoral challengers attempted to use attributions of racism against those who were making them.

Finally, this chapter uncovered a relatively recent political divergence between Rogers Park and Uptown. While electoral dynamics in both neighborhoods were quite similar until 2007, crime then waned as a campaign topic in Rogers Park while remaining contentious in Uptown. This difference is particularly noteworthy because the two neighborhoods' crime rates largely mirrored each other.[47] Instead of different crime rates, the neighborhoods' political divergence attests to the importance of the local political fields. In Uptown, Shiller's perceived resistance to addressing crime increasingly polarized that neighborhood's political field. The tensions among residents and organizations that resulted all but ensured that crime would remain on the local political agenda. Chapter 5 describes how these tensions materialized during my ethnographic fieldwork.

In Rogers Park, the politics of crime never produced a similar degree of polarization, in part because neither the safety nor the justice camp became clearly aligned with specific aldermanic candidates. Neither camp had much to gain from confronting Moore by fielding a candidate who might challenge the incumbent. As a result, I found Rogers Park's political field much less polarized over the issue of crime than Uptown's. Notably, this relative peace prevailed despite the fact that Rogers Park's anticrime initiatives relied on the same tactics as did those in Uptown. For instance, activists in Rogers Park, like those in Uptown, also methodically called the police about specific buildings so as to bring in city inspectors, who might then initiate problem building interventions.[48] But the same practices engendered less opposition in Rogers Park.

Consequently, the two neighborhoods' divergent political fields had significant consequences for local racial contestation. As chapter 3 showed, public safety work was always vulnerable to racial challenges—in Uptown *and* Rogers Park. But neighborhood politics systematically raised or lowered the degree to which crime incited conflict. While the same connections between safety work, displacement, and racial marginalization could be drawn in both neighborhoods, justice activists less frequently acted on this potential in Rogers Park. Due in part to the absence of political conflict over the issue, crime had simply become less of a mobilizing force than it had been in the 1990s and the 2000s. Chapters 5 and 6 demonstrate the effects the two neighborhoods' political trajectories had on the relations between justice and safety organizations (chapter 5) and on how residents encountered each other in the context of positive loitering (chapter 6). This will further expose the profound impact politicians had on community conflict and especially the salience of race within it.[49]

5

Resisting Gentrification and Criminalization

According to most social scientists, community organizations are an une-quivocal benefit to urban neighborhoods and society as a whole. This eval-uation reaches back at least as far as Alexis de Tocqueville, who pointed to associations of citizens as the bedrock of American democracy in the early nineteenth century.[1] Tocqueville argued that it was in such groups that cit-izens would form political opinions in mutual deliberation, learn the ways of democratic governance, and create the social and political fabric that would integrate the nation. Over recent decades, Robert Putnam (2000) has been the most prominent exponent of this theory of democracy, fa-mously claiming that the decline of voluntary associations had gone so far that Americans were soon going to be bowling alone. According to Putnam, this decline threatened to weaken the foundations of American democracy. Without the social glue that organizations like neighborhood associations provided, Americans would drift apart.

Specifically in urban sociology, this favorable view of community organ-izations can also be traced to the Chicago School of urban sociology and its main theorists, Robert Park and Ernest Burgess (1925). Trying to under-stand the forces that integrated Chicago during a time of rapid growth and change, Park, Burgess, and their colleagues devoted great attention to com-munity organizations, including churches and ethnic associations, because they believed that these organizations provided a necessary source of social control for molding individual behavior in the city, especially the behavior of adolescents, who might otherwise descend into delinquency. As Park wrote, "delinquency is . . . in some sense the measure of the failure of our commu-nity organizations to function."[2]

The scholarly traditions of Tocquevillian and Chicago School sociology suggest that community organizations both reflect and produce cohesion. But while it is undoubtedly true that community organizations matter a great deal, I argue that there is no reason to assume that they necessarily

Us versus Them. Jan Doering, Oxford University Press (2020) © Oxford University Press.
DOI: 10.1093/oso/9780190066574.001.0001

create cohesion. Community organizations may pursue the goals of certain residents at the expense of others. They may be competing with other local organizations over members, resources, and political influence. They may even exist *primarily* to oppose the work other organizations are doing. A vibrant set of community organizations *can* be the sign of an unusually civic-minded community but might just as well point to significant local divisions.[3]

Especially in Uptown, organizational vibrancy indicated conflict rather than unity. As I discussed in chapter 4, electoral competition had engendered a persistent battle between social justice and public safety organizations. After Alderwoman Shiller's retirement in 2011, Uptown's social justice activists reinvigorated their resistance against the safety initiatives and newly elected Alderman Cappleman because they feared that an all-out push for racial displacement was about to begin. To resist this push, the justice activists developed an ambitious program of fighting gentrification, criminalization, and even gang violence.

Urban scholars like Japonica Brown-Saracino (2009) and Lance Freeman (2006) have shown that community conflict is not at all unusual in gentrifying neighborhoods. In consistency with their findings, the preceding chapters have already uncovered a sizable amount of tension among residents as well as political leaders, but the mesosociological level of community organizations was at least as important. In chapter 3, I uncovered the significant impact that public safety initiatives had on Rogers Park and Uptown's urban landscape, and I now turn to social justice organizations to examine how they resisted gentrification. Specifically, I examine the case of Resist Youth Criminalization and Harassment (RYCH), an Uptown-based, grassroots social movement organization. This organization used racial challenges as an effective weapon, securing a symbolic victory against racial marginalization and displacement. At the same time, sustained resistance proved difficult without funds, staff, and powerful allies. The organization's more encompassing goals thus remained unfulfilled.

In the process of fighting gentrification, RYCH and its allies underscored Uptown's racial and socioeconomic dividing lines. They did this so as to spotlight and publicize racial injustices as well as to rally potential supporters. But in doing so, they inevitably deepened those dividing lines even further. As the conflict in Uptown's political field continued, drawing public attention from throughout the Chicago region, discord over the politics of crime and housing grew. In 2011 and 2012, Uptown saw another spike in shootings,

but the safety and justice camps were too divided to face this problem together. Both camps made independent efforts to reduce the violence, but the
neighborhood's divisions stymied their work.

This chapter focuses only on the Uptown neighborhood. Conducting
fieldwork in Rogers Park, I observed very little interorganizational conflict.
During interviews, I usually asked community activists whether there was
anyone who made their work harder, who opposed their efforts. In Uptown,
interviewees readily pointed to the opposing camp in the political field, but
Rogers Parkers did not usually respond in this way. Instead, they talked about
broader challenges—funding cuts, the police department, apathetic residents,
and so on. This is not to say that there were no misgivings in Rogers Park's political field, but the activists there, unlike those in Uptown, were not actively
embroiled in interorganizational conflict.[4] The only exception was a particularly zealous positive loitering group that sparked outrage and accusations of
racism from social justice activists. I discuss that group in chapter 6.

Broncho Billy Park and Resist Youth Criminalization and Harassment

In May 2010, about nine months before the upcoming municipal elections,
Uptowners learned that Alderwoman Shiller would not run for reelection in
2011. Her enemies were elated. *Uptown Update*, a local blog that had persistently criticized Shiller for her alleged failure to address street crime, filled up
with disdainful commentaries about her tenure. One reader wrote: "Shiller
was worse than the gangbangers, drug dealers and criminals she allowed to
prosper and terrorize law abiding citizens in Uptown."[5]

Beginning with this day, a great sense of optimism washed over the many
residents who felt that Shiller had stifled development and efforts to quash
crime. Her critics thought that without her, Uptown would quickly improve.
They also anticipated that Uptown's political culture would change. Many
held her responsible for fueling racial strife and believed that tensions would
now dissipate. This was true especially for the safety activists, who hoped that
their organizations would no longer be attacked as the domain of "the white
gentrifiers." At a positive loitering event in 2011, Jim, a white man around
fifty, enthusiastically told me: "James [Cappleman] can create a neighborhood that is both diverse *and* safe!" To Jim, diversity and security were not
mutually exclusive goals, and once what he saw as Shiller's distorted rhetoric

went silent, Uptowners would no longer perceive them that way. No longer would the fight against street crime be framed as racial warfare.

These hopes did not pan out. Uptown's justice activists feared that racial dislocation would accelerate now that they could no longer count on Alderwoman Shiller to shape the direction and speed of urban change in Uptown. They expected that all the things Shiller had helped to establish in Uptown—the dense network of social services, the subsidized housing, a social-justice-themed high school—were going to come under attack. In his electoral campaign, Cappleman had stated that the service providers would need to become "better neighbors" and that there was "service duplication" in Uptown, which was taken to mean that undesired methadone clinics and homeless shelters would be shut down. Cappleman had also stated that as a long-term goal, affordable housing needed to be distributed more evenly across Chicago. Obviously, this suggested that he wanted to close down low-income housing. The justice activists' wary hostility toward Cappleman turned into open conflict when, soon after taking office, he ordered a set of basketball hoops to be removed from a local park—a seemingly minor urban intervention that proved symbolically potent.

Broncho Billy Park (see figure 5.1) was a small recreational space that was located along Magnolia Avenue in Uptown's Sheridan Park, an area of verdant residential boulevards with pleasantly limited car traffic. Named in honor of a silent film persona, Broncho Billy Park consisted of a play lot area with a water spray feature for children and an adjacent basketball court. During the warm months, the playground teemed with families and small children in the mornings and afternoons. Many families would leave once teenagers, most of them black, began using the basketball court in the late afternoon.

Broncho Billy Park and the surrounding blocks were a constant topic of discussion at CAPS and block club meetings in Uptown because Magnolia Avenue between Montrose and Wilson was one of the neighborhood's gang hotspots. The housing in the area consisted of nicely refurbished townhouses and low-rise apartment buildings, some of which contained project-based public housing. Residents believed that one of these buildings contained the local "headquarters" of the Black P. Stones. At one CAPS meeting, a board member of the area's block club vented her rage about the situation:

> They have grown *bolder* and *bolder*, day by day, week by week, and year by year. My street should be renamed "Black P. Stone Way!" The Black P. Stone

Figure 5.1. Broncho Billy Park, Uptown. Photo by the author.

headquarter is right across the street from me. Until the landlords get rid of, of the *crap* that lives in their buildings and all of these little . . . *punks*, they rule our streets!

The evictions the safety activists desired proved hard to attain because the buildings in question were public housing, so tenants' leases could not simply be terminated. A court had to order their evictions. Securing the necessary evidence and institutional support from the housing provider was difficult for the safety activists, but they hoped that they could at least contain the gang's public presence by closing the basketball court in Broncho Billy Park. They regarded the court as a space that the Black P. Stones used to recruit vulnerable teenagers.

After Cappleman took office as alderman in 2011, he granted the safety activists' request and instructed the Chicago Park District to remove the basketball hoops from the park. This meant not only that one could not play basketball but also that people without children were no longer allowed to spend time in the park because they did not have a justification for loitering there. The park had essentially been converted into a play lot.

In response to this intervention, justice activists formed RYCH to demand that the basketball hoops be reinstalled and, more important, to oppose the agenda of gentrification and racist criminalization that they perceived beneath the surface of their opponents' demands to tackle the gang presence. To the justice activists, Broncho Billy Park was a prime example of criminalization. Removing the facilities that permitted and enticed black teenagers to frequent the park made their presence conspicuous and ultimately enforceable for the police, because they were now spending time in a play lot rather than a park that welcomed all. Thus, criminalization and gentrification went hand in hand: the gentrifiers were using the police to banish black residents from public spaces in order to make the area more attractive for white middle-class buyers, who would then displace even more black renters.[6] To oppose this process, RYCH developed an ambitious program of racial justice for Uptown, including an initiative to reduce gang violence.

RYCH's core group consisted of about ten people, evenly made up of whites and African Americans. Almost all of them were affiliated with other justice organizations, such as NA4J or ONE. They were seasoned activists with a long history of political involvement in Uptown. Some of them worked or had worked as professional community organizers. In addition to this core group, RYCH meetings and events sometimes also mobilized a wider set of residents, who participated not so much with an interest in neighborhood politics as out of concern over the gang violence. Most of these participants were mothers and grandmothers with personal ties to members of the core group.

Wes, Kareem, and Robert directed RYCH. They were longtime friends in their late thirties who had grown up together in Uptown. All of them were strongly committed to the cause of racial justice. Robert was white. He worked for the nonprofit agency where RYCH held its meetings. He had long brown hair that he wore in a ponytail. Wes and Kareem were African American and worked low-paying service jobs. They were serious men—I rarely saw them laugh. Kareem wore long dreadlocks and large earrings. Wes had short braided hair and a stubbly beard. Wes and Kareem both identified with the tradition of black nationalism. Once, as the RYCH activists were discussing gang violence, Wes noted that one cause of violence was that young black men lacked a positive identity. He said: "they need to know where they are coming from. They don't know who they are." Kareem agreed and said that it was important for African Americans to reconnect with their African roots. "The powerful thing about Africans is they know their culture: they know their tribe, their language, their symbols. We [African Americans] have lost all that. We are the only people without a flag!" Kareem concluded that this showed just how disempowered African Americans really were.

Resist Youth Criminalization and Harassment met every Saturday morning in a stuffy, windowless conference room in an aging office building. The room was packed with social justice paraphernalia. Posters denounced gentrification and referenced icons of African American politics, including Martin Luther King Jr. and Malcolm X. A shelf at the head of the conference table contained a small library of documentaries and political feature films, such as Spike Lee's *Do The Right Thing*. The office's other room, where several computer workstations were located, contained shelves filled with political writings and scholarly works on race, the labor movement, feminist thought, and Chicago history.

Despite the rapidly depleted air in the conference room, the activists often spent hours decrying their opponents' perceived vision of a homogeneously white and wealthy Uptown. They argued that removing the basketball hoops was merely the first sign of the things that were soon to come. The hoops mattered, but more because of their symbolic than their practical implications. At a small fundraising event for RYCH, Wes explained: "I want more than the rims to go back up. I want that too! But I also want the alderman to understand *why* the rims need to be put back up." He said that the fight over Broncho Billy Park was just one example of how racial displacement was reshaping Uptown. The alderman needed to learn that this process was morally wrong and would be opposed at every turn. Robert said: "with Shiller in office, it was a little bit like we were all comfortably numb." But, he added, the removal of the hoops had awakened and united Uptown's justice activists and could serve as the initial step in a much larger struggle.

Seeking to prove their point that concerns about crime and violence served simply as a pretext for racial oppression, RYCH filed a Freedom of Information request to find out about the incidents of crime that had been reported in Broncho Billy Park. The report showed that the police had indeed documented very few. Technically, that did not contradict the justification for removing the hoops—gang loitering and recruitment could be happening on the basketball court without people calling the police. But RYCH used the low crime rate as substantiating evidence when framing

Cappleman's decision to remove the hoops in racial terms. Since crime could not have been the reason, they argued, the closing of the court revealed a racist agenda: the goal had been to empty the park of young black men so that anxious white parents could take their children there.

The activists contacted a journalist from the *Chicago Reader*, who decided to pursue the story and thereby handed RYCH a significant victory. The *Chicago Reader*, a weekly magazine available free of charge throughout Chicago, was widely read as a source of political commentary, and its influence in this regard rivaled that of the city's main newspapers, the *Tribune* and the *Sun-Times*. In September 2011, the *Chicago Reader* featured a piece on "basketball controversies" as its cover story, focusing primarily on Uptown's Broncho Billy Park, as well as two similar cases from other Chicago neighborhoods and examining the ways "residents and elected officials are wrangling over questions of safety, race, and public space."[7]

All but explicitly, the journalists sided with Alderman Cappleman's enemies. They invoked the low crime rate in the park and the broader context of gentrification and incorporated the racial conflict narrative RYCH disseminated. The authors cited one justice activist as saying that closing the basketball court was "clearly an attack on low-income and black families."[8] Cappleman was depicted as an ominous political leader. The journalists wrote that removing the hoops "wasn't out of character for Cappleman, who was elected in a runoff in April after campaigning for more than four years to attack crime and clean up the ward, one of the most diverse in the city."[9] They also quoted Cappleman himself, who in an interview with the journalists tried to racially neutralize his decision but—unwisely—requested that the journalists do the same thing: "Cappleman bristles when asked how the rim removals were helping reduce violence. 'If you can show me research showing a benefit from basketball in an unsupervised setting where gang recruitment is going on, I'll reconsider.' He also insists that his decision on the rims had nothing to do with race, though we didn't ask. 'If you play the race card, I will not talk to you again,' he informed us." Cappleman's opponents in the political field—and probably many readers—interpreted especially this final statement, Cappleman's warning against "playing the race card," as a smoking gun. If the alderman's decision had nothing to do with race, as he claimed, why would he bring it up? Why would he threaten the journalists? Thus, the article in the *Chicago Reader* became an additional warrant for denouncing the removal of the basketball hoops. The RYCH activists could draw on it as evidence that this was an instance of racist tough-on-crime politics. The article also helped to discredit racial neutralization as a clumsy and transparent political move to silence critics. In time, the article became a widely known point of reference among gentrification critics in Uptown. Many residents had read it.

Fighting for Peace, Resisting Gentrification

As part of its fight against displacement, RYCH launched its own initiative to reduce crime in the form of gang violence. Wes, Kareem, and the others were sincerely committed to saving lives, but they also saw violence reduction as a necessary component of their political struggle because violence played into the hands of their rivals, who could point to shootings as a justification for evicting and marginalizing more African Americans. Whether crime really was just an excuse or not, RYCH's understanding of what their rivals were doing was entirely accurate. At one of the weekly meetings, Kareem talked about the safety camp's practice of targeting "problem buildings." He said: "I know that gentrification has advanced a lot. The only thing I can think of is to keep on doing what we are doing. That's why I'm doing all this! Every time there is a shooting, it gives those people more reasons to close down buildings for low-income folks!" He explained how the safety activists called the police to get the city's inspectors to shut down entire buildings. His eyes open wide, Kareem exclaimed: "that's total bull! If I live in a building and I commit a crime, that's *my* problem! What does that have to do with the *building*!"

Another reason for reducing gang violence was that RYCH's members believed that the violence suppressed black political dissent. Shootings kept African American youth divided and effectively prevented them from joining hands to collectively demand social reforms that might improve their situation. Complicit in this process, the police were not even trying to stop the violence. One Sunday morning, Kareem and Wes discussed several shootings that had taken place in Uptown the night before. Kareem had been on the scene during the first shooting. He was trying to help a young man who had been shot when the police arrived. Kareem said that the first thing the officer had said to him was: "there's no use in talking to them." Wes was not surprised and commented: "the police just don't give a crap." Despite the heavy police presence in the neighborhood, two more shootouts occurred later that night—even though the police, according to Kareem, knew full well where retaliation would take place. He concluded: "the police, they let that shit *happen!*" Kareem and the others argued that only a united and self-conscious black movement could overcome this cycle of institutional racism and violence—as long as gang violence continued, low-income African Americans would remain powerless. Resist Youth Criminalization and Harassment needed to create peace and unity among black youth, who could then become allies in the battle for racial justice in Uptown and possibly beyond.

In trying to reduce gang violence, RYCH drew on support from CeaseFire, a violence prevention program that ONE had recently implemented in Uptown and Rogers Park with the help of a grant from the state. Even before CeaseFire, several of RYCH's core members had done violence prevention work. Wes, Kareem, and Leticia, another core member, spent time with gang-involved youth and spoke to them about their role in the larger system of racial oppression, as well as their rights when facing the police. Consequently, RYCH was a natural ally for CeaseFire, although, as I will discuss further, this alliance also came at a price for CeaseFire.

Together, RYCH and CeaseFire organized a number of events to reduce violence. In the summer of 2011, they held three barbeques, one in each of Uptown's gang territories. They invited gang members and their parents to learn what they thought was needed to create peace.[10] Later that year, CeaseFire, RYCH, ONE, NA4J, and several other social justice organizations held a "march for peace and unity," which drew hundreds of people. As Robert told me after the event, the march had permitted some African Americans to walk through parts of Uptown they had not seen in years because, even if they were not affiliated with a gang, they could not cross gang boundaries without fear of reprisals. However, the peace march was also a showcase of Uptown's political rifts, insofar as almost no safety activists participated. After all, the peace march was clearly associated with the justice organizations. A flyer for the event advertised the march as an effort not only to "push for peace" and "stop the violence" but also to "stop criminalization." Speeches made by RYCH, ONE, and NA4J activists at the end of the march condemned violence as well as gentrification. This combination reflected the prevalent view among social justice activists that crime and gentrification were inherently related to each other.

After the peace march, in the fall of 2011, RYCH planned to hold a series of "speak-outs" for Uptown's youth—moderated encounters and discussions that aimed to unite the attendees around the goals of peace and fighting racial marginalization. There was to be one speak-out for each gang territory, and one final overarching event for the neighborhood at large. Essentially, RYCH wanted to use these speak-outs to end territorial rivalries among Uptown's young black and Latino residents. Once this had been accomplished, they hoped, young people of color would join the struggle against gentrification and displacement.

In tandem with these efforts at youth mobilization, RYCH fought their opponents in the political field by racially challenging safety initiatives to disrupt what Robert called their "negativity." At one CAPS meeting I attended together with Wes and Kareem, a middle-aged white woman complained about the gang presence and the shootings on Magnolia Avenue and claimed that the "financial ramifications" for home values were threatening to "displace" her and other homeowners. This was actually the only time that I ever witnessed an attendee at an Uptown CAPS meeting frame concerns about crime in terms of home values. As I noted in chapter 3, safety activists saw their financial interests as a taboo topic because it could confirm suspicions that their work was really just about making money, not about neighborhood safety. Nevertheless, after the meeting, the RYCH activists expressed surprise about how "tame" the meeting had been and attributed this fact to their presence. Wes said: "we got PG13 tonight. As long as we come to these meetings, they are going to keep a low profile." Kareem agreed: "that was the front, what we saw tonight. These motherfuckers, they are not going to say anything because they see that there's a few black people from the community in the room." As this conversation shows, Wes and Kareem were convinced that race and class interests underpinned CAPS meetings. Unsurprisingly, they therefore also untiringly denounced CAPS and other safety organizations when talking with neighbors and friends.

Resist Youth Criminalization and Harassment did not accomplish all of its ambitious goals, but it did succeed in getting the basketball hoops reinstalled in Broncho Billy Park. The activists had collected hundreds of petition signatures and obtained letters of support from former Alderwoman Shiller and the principal of a nearby school. Armed with this material, as well as copies of the *Chicago Reader* article, RYCH and ONE procured several school buses and transported about fifty protesters to a public board meeting of the Chicago Park District. The protesters had prepared speeches to address the board, but this turned out to be unnecessary. Before the meeting even began, the board sent a delegate who informed the protesters that their complaint was reasonable and the board had decided to reinstall the hoops. The board's decision reveals the substantial public pressure RYCH and the article in the *Chicago Reader* had produced. Quite apparently, the board was unwilling to become embroiled in this racial controversy, even if it meant going against a sitting alderman. The hoops were reinstalled the next day.[11]

Reducing Violence in a Divided Neighborhood

Despite the Broncho Billy Park victory, RYCH fizzled after about six months. The sweeping project of fighting for the basketball hoops, monitoring CAPS meetings, and organizing Uptown's black youth had simply exhausted the members. A first youth speak-out failed when practically no young people showed up for the event. This frustrated the activists, who had toiled to secure a free location, convince businesses to supply them with food and other needed items, and created a program for the event. But they learned from the experience and decided to hold a second speak-out in conjunction with a popular afterschool program, where an audience would already be present. As it turned out, however, the afterschool program consisted mostly of students from outside Uptown—they commuted to participate in the program. Wes, Kareem, Robert, and the students had a sincere and deeply emotional discussion about violence and its toll on young people's lives, but of course it was impossible to discuss Uptown's specific issues, much less mobilize a neighborhood-based youth movement, because most of the participants did not live there. After the second speak-out thus proved only moderately successful, the activists were simply worn out. Attendance at the weekly meetings had already declined and by the end of 2011 RYCH stopped meeting altogether.

Probably the single most important reason for RYCH's decline was the organization's lack of resources. CeaseFire staff sometimes helped with essential things like photocopying flyers, but CeaseFire could not contribute the much-needed work hours to help plan, promote, and implement events. Successfully mobilizing Uptown youth for the speak-out events, for example, would have required support staff (or a large group of devoted volunteers) that RYCH did not have. The organization did not even have the money to buy food and other basic necessities. As Kareem said when I met him again in 2012: "we couldn't even feed them [the youth at the speak-outs]! How can we get the youth together if we can't even feed them?" Kareem recounted how, every time an event was organized, the group had struggled to assemble even the most basic necessities.

Access to resources from Alderman Cappleman's office and CAPS was blocked because RYCH and these organizations were opponents in the local political field. But in a less divided neighborhood than Uptown, RYCH's antiviolence work could well have received support from these actors. Cappleman was under immense pressure to contain the uptick in shootings that shook Uptown in late 2011. While he would not have agreed to abandon his efforts to address the gang problem through arrests and evictions, he did not oppose preventive interventions. In principle, the same applied to CAPS groups, which had a small budget for holding community events. But RYCH members, even those who cared more about peace than gentrification, did not see any overlap because they thought that an agenda of racial oppression lurked behind the calls for safety.

After the fight over Broncho Billy Park, any cooperation across these boundaries was unthinkable anyway. Many public safety activists were now convinced that RYCH had no actual interest in reducing violence and was merely another vehicle for continuing the long tradition of discrediting public safety initiatives. Some safety activists went so far as to attribute the uptick in violence to RYCH, because that uptick harmed Alderman Cappleman's credibility as an effective political leader. When I asked Eric, a CAPS volunteer, about RYCH, he said:

> It was backlash. Political backlash. That's not to say that they didn't have some legitimate concerns [about Broncho Billy Park]. . . . But I do think the RYCH group, they agitated and got those kids to act up. Yeah, I think they agitated and brought everything to a frenzy.

For Alderman Cappleman on the other hand the Broncho Billy Park controversy remained a sore issue that made it harder to work with African American residents, some of whom still remembered the Shiller campaign's "Ku Klux Kappleman" charges, which seemed to be confirmed by Cappleman's actions. He now refused to discuss Broncho Billy Park entirely. In 2012, a resident complained at a CAPS meeting about physical altercations he had recently witnessed on the basketball court. Cappleman defensively raised both of his hands and ended the discussion, saying that he would not engage in the subject of that park again. The same applied to his staff. I knew one of Cappleman's ward office staffers—we occasionally went for drinks after attending the same community meetings. He was a personable and seemingly confident young man. I tried to interview him about Broncho Billy Park, but he became so flustered that I broke off the interview. After I stopped the recorder, he said: "I just don't want to get in trouble saying something wrong. I don't want my words to get twisted."

In some ways, RYCH had therefore been quite successful. In choosing Broncho Billy Park to take a stand, Uptown's social justice camp had demonstrated that the battle over Uptown would not end with Alderwoman Shiller leaving the office. The activists also lastingly discredited Alderman Cappleman in the eyes of those who accepted as true RYCH's racial challenges about the hoop removal and the safety initiatives in general. In doing so, they reinforced Uptown's divisions over the politics of crime and specifically underlined race as a dividing line. However, they also further reduced the possibility of joining forces across these boundaries to mutually reduce crime and violence. Safety activists felt reassured in their resentment toward the social justice camp after the Broncho Billy Park controversy. I also spoke with several African Americans who shied away from CAPS, block clubs, and positive loitering, because the recent incidents had convinced them that these were racist groups for white homeowners. They did not expect to be welcomed. Conversely, the efficacy of the justice activists' violence prevention efforts suffered because they could not receive support from Cappleman and the safety initiatives. This was true obviously for RYCH but also for CeaseFire, which I address now.

CeaseFire: Trapped between the Battle Lines

As I mentioned, it made sense for CeaseFire to collaborate with RYCH, and so CeaseFire's director for Uptown, an African American man named Eddie, frequently attended RYCH events. Eddie was an experienced community organizer, sociable and charismatic. He could talk with practically anybody. In contrast to other RYCH members, Eddie hoped to separate violence prevention from Uptown politics, instead foregrounding Uptowners' shared interest in peace and safety. Accordingly, he also tried to neutralize the issue as nonracial. At a RYCH planning meeting for the first youth speak-out, Eddie said: "we don't want to make this a black thing. We don't want to make this a poor thing. We want to make it the right thing. It's a crime issue. We need to get the community together on this." Eddie wanted to involve as many residents and community groups as possible. He knew that this was an organizational imperative for CeaseFire—each year, CeaseFire had to lobby the state for renewed funding, and this required vocal support from the neighborhood and elected officials.

CeaseFire held several community meetings that were intended to increase the organization's reach in Uptown. At one such meeting, held at a field house, Eddie introduced the idea of mobilizing a wider set of residents through "community patrols" that would escort students after school to prevent them from being harassed or possibly recruited by gang members. Eddie emphasized that the patrols should bring together a wide cross-section of residents, not just African American parents, whose children were usually the victims of gang violence. "A lot of people think it's just an issue for low-income people or for people of color," Eddie said; "but a stray bullet has no color." An African American woman agreed and proposed that CeaseFire should reach out to the block clubs and "the condo buildings"— her shorthand for the white middle class. The idea received enthusiastic support from Somer, a middle-aged white woman, who was representing Alderman Cappleman's office at the meeting. Somer said: "people realize that there is violence, but they think they can't do anything about it, or they think it's a low-income thing or people-of-color thing. But they complain a lot. So maybe this could be a way to get them more involved." The community patrols, it seemed at that moment, had the potential to bridge some of Uptown's rifts.

The mood turned, however, when Craig and Paul began to criticize the idea. Craig and Paul were white antigentrification activists. Both of them had campaigned against Alderman Cappleman during the recent election; Craig was also one of RYCH's core members. Craig noted that the patrols would need an "educational component" in order to distinguish them from positive loitering groups, which revolved around "animosity and mistrust for certain people." Only white people participated in these groups, he said. Somewhat hesitantly, Eddie conceded: "the racial component is definitely an undertow." Paul then further accentuated what Craig had said. "If I were a young black man and saw this group of white people standing on the corner, I'd get the message. *I* am other. *I* am the one they want to get rid of." With Craig and Paul's objections, the initial excitement about the community patrols as an initiative to unite Uptown evaporated. Deploying this racial challenge against positive loitering, Craig and Paul undermined the idea that white safety activists should participate in Eddie's community patrol.

This interaction shows how CeaseFire was entangled in the dynamics of Uptown's political field. Alderman Cappleman's office, represented by Somer, was interested in transcending racial barriers and demonstrating that Cappleman cared about his black constituents, no matter what his opponents claimed. Collaborating with CeaseFire would have been a great way to show this. Conversely, Eddie could use a good working relationship with Cappleman to secure his support when the time came to renew CeaseFire's funding. Craig and Paul, however, were not interested in seeing Eddie and Somer build this coalition. As members of the social justice camp, they wanted to keep CeaseFire on *their* side of the political field. In fact, at the next RYCH meeting, Craig told Wes about Eddie's idea of launching community patrols and suggested that RYCH should use these events to recruit new members. Ultimately, this did not happen because Eddie did not follow through with the project—at least in part because it had become clear to him that the patrols would not achieve the outreach effect he had hoped for.

In short, it was next to impossible for CeaseFire to remain neutral, despite Eddie's aspirations. For his part, Alderman Cappleman did not fail to notice CeaseFire's close affiliation with RYCH and the social justice camp. Unsurprisingly, he thus never publicly endorsed CeaseFire's Uptown operation. When I interviewed Eddie in early 2013, he claimed that Cappleman's lack of support limited CeaseFire's efficacy and also hampered the organization's efforts to obtain new funding. Eddie said:

> The alderman should, you know, definitely align with our program because our program is aligned with trying to keep the community safe. I think that if the alderman came out and publicly endorsed what we are trying to do, it would make it easier for us to go to businesses and even the block clubs, you know, and we know those are his main supporters. And I think that, you know, with any community-run project or organization, when you have the elected officials saying that your program's worthwhile, that does go a long way with people who fund the program. It's a no-brainer.

Frustrated by Cappleman's lack of support, Eddie abandoned his prior strategy of framing violence as a race-neutral issue and instead embraced a more confrontational approach. In Uptown, CeaseFire staff now formally participated in protests against the alderman's housing policies. At one event, the organization's violence interrupters, wearing their CeaseFire jackets, carried a coffin with the inscription "Diversity Of the 46th Ward"

Figure 5.2. CeaseFire Uptown participates in a 2013 protest against Alderman Cappleman's housing policies. Photo by the author.

to Cappleman's office (see figure 5.2). A corresponding flyer that ONE distributed in the neighborhood read: "our communities are plagued by violence. Harassment of poor community members and people of color is not the answer. We expect you [Cappleman] to work closely with and support CeaseFire Uptown to help curb the violence in our community." Eddie thus attempted to force—rather than persuade—Cappleman to support CeaseFire. When Eddie explained to me why this new approach was necessary, he contrasted CeaseFire's situation in Uptown with the one in Rogers Park, where Alderman Moore often spoke at CeaseFire events and vocally supported the organization's work as well as its efforts to renew its funding. Eddie said:

> I think it's a little more open [in Rogers Park] with the political officials. I never got the sense that it was a racial thing. I never got that sense of, you know, it's a poor-rich thing. . . . You get a different sense in Uptown. It's a real difference. . . . I mean, Rogers Park is, like, less divided. And I think the Alderman [Moore], on some days [laughs], makes an effort to support that. Not that he [Moore] is, you know, a rose in the garden, but I think he does a better job as opposed to what's going down in Uptown.

Eddie hoped that public pressure would push Alderman Cappleman to endorse CeaseFire, but Cappleman did not budge. Eventually, ONE had to shut down the CeaseFire program in both Rogers Park and Uptown because sufficient funding could not be obtained. I cannot assess whether Cappleman's advocacy would have made a difference. What I can say is that Uptown's justice activists *blamed* Cappleman for CeaseFire's demise, and I never heard similar complaints against Rogers Park's Alderman Moore. The termination of the CeaseFire program became yet another controversy that pitted people and organizations against one another in Uptown. The political field exhibited a polarizing force that proved hard to overcome.

The Prospects of Grassroots Resistance Against Gentrification

Members of Rogers Park and Uptown's social justice camps recognized that safety initiatives wielded a substantial amount of local influence. To the social justice activists, these initiatives were an essential component of a creeping displacement process. At least in part, police officers harassed, arrested, or evicted black residents in response to the safety activists' incessant prodding. Galvanized by the election of a tough-on-crime alderman, justice activists in Uptown thus formed RYCH to fight back. What does the case of RYCH reveal about the potential of antigentrification activism?

The closing of the basketball court in Broncho Billy Park provided the justice activists with a symbolically powerful opportunity to publicly challenge and thereby resist criminalization and racial marginalization. The hoop removal was an incident that handily demonstrated these larger problems. It illustrated the literal racial displacement of working-class African Americans from neighborhood space. It also allowed the justice activists to identify a culprit and his purportedly racist motives. The park's low crime rate as well as Cappleman's warning against "playing the race card" suggested that racism was indeed at play. The media began to take an interest; public pressure increased. Eventually, this won RYCH the symbolic victory of reversing this specific instance of racial displacement. Resist Youth Criminalization and Harassment also managed to durably blemish Alderman Cappleman's reputation among black, low-income, and left-leaning residents.

Grassroots resistance against racial marginalization in gentrifying neighborhoods can thus accomplish hard-fought victories. In this case, the activists' strongest asset was their ability to make plausible charges of racism that aroused public attention throughout the neighborhood and indeed Chicago overall. Under these conditions, racial challenges effectively pressure political actors and may engender corrective moves. In the case of Broncho Billy Park, the Chicago Park District decided that backing Alderman Cappleman's order to close the basketball court was not worth the public relations cost this might entail.

On the other hand RYCH could not sustain its project of resisting gentrification and criminalization on a larger scale. The RYCH activists had hoped to unite the factionalized black youth and ignite a movement that would fight for racial justice within Uptown and beyond. This goal eluded the activists, first and foremost due to their lack of resources. Without money and support staff, they could not implement their ambitious racial justice program.

Can these findings be generalized to other neighborhoods? Uptown's social context was certainly unique, but it is likely that the factors shaping RYCH's struggle were not. Examining first its main victory, one can easily find cases in gentrifying neighborhoods that resemble the Broncho Billy Park controversy. In the Shaw neighborhood in Washington, DC, for example, a wave of protest erupted in 2019 after a longtime business owner was forced to mute the go-go music he had played outside his T-Mobile franchise for years.[12] Like the basketball hoops in Uptown, this issue turned out to be symbolically potent. The store's go-go music served as a symbol of the neighborhood's black, working-class heritage. And the complaints about the music were attributed to new wealthy white residents inhabiting an upscale development nearby. Local leaders and activists, politicians, and journalists rallied to the cause. Ultimately, T-Mobile's chief executive personally announced that the music at the store would return. As in Uptown, a symbolic victory was thus celebrated in Shaw. But *also* as in Uptown, it appears that resistance against the larger process of gentrification faltered. According to one journalist: "you could hear a lot of activists expressing a little bit of frustration" that most of the advocates for the store's go-go music disappeared as quickly as they had emerged, failing to support the broader struggle for affordable housing in the neighborhood.[13]

Effectively battling gentrification requires more than a core group of committed volunteers. With a hint of sarcasm, Patrick Sharkey (2018:174) has noted that organizations "that rely on residents' time and effort tend to run out of steam, and we wonder why." These limitations apply all the more to groups who primarily rely on low-income residents of color, who face everyday challenges that may preclude intensive, prolonged community activism. When seen against this backdrop, the prospects of grassroots organizations to resist gentrification without access to funds and other resources appear bleak. In a comparative study of community organizing, Kristina Smock (2004) concludes that long-term success requires effective fundraising and durable organizational structures as well as vibrant grassroots activism and consciousness-raising. Mark Warren's (2001) research on the Industrial Areas Foundation in Texas and Nicole Marwell's (2007) work on activist organizations in Brooklyn suggest the same conclusions.

Finally, it is important to note that vibrant activism and mobilization may entail costs that no party desires. As Robert Sampson and his colleagues have argued extensively, community-based crime prevention requires social trust, ties, and shared values.[14] According to Tocquevillian and Chicago School urban sociologists, community organizations should produce exactly those social goods. But Uptown's community organizations instead appeared to deepen social fissures, drawing together residents who felt closely tied to those who shared their local priorities but alienating them from those who pursued allegedly incompatible goals.

Uptown's divided political field, it seems, made all actors less effective in their efforts to reduce crime and violence. The public safety camp found it harder to mobilize a broad cross-section of the community because many black and low-income residents perceived community policing and grassroots safety initiatives as sites of racial aggression. On the other side of the divide, CeaseFire and RYCH's violence prevention efforts suffered because they could not draw on support from the neighborhood's power brokers and wealthier residents. During a period of peaking violence in 2011 and 2012, Uptown's community organizations were thus too polarized to effectively reduce shootings. These findings about the negative effects of political division are consistent with Robert Vargas's (2016) study of Chicago's East Little Village, an area politicians left so gerrymandered that gangs could thrive unfettered. While not as gerrymandered, Uptown as a community was too divided for organizations to collaborate. The effect was similar to the one Vargas observed: a lack of trust that made it harder to contain crime and violence.

At the same time, however, it is important to note that this chapter could produce an exaggerated image of community polarization because it focuses on activists. The degree to which divisions between activists and their organizations are matched by division among less politicized residents remains to be assessed. As Lance Freeman (2006:18) writes in his study of gentrification in Harlem: "a focus on the political conflict stemming from gentrification . . . does not provide a complete picture of how residents are impacted or experience the changes taking place in their neighborhoods. For one thing, the most active and vocal residents are not necessarily representative of the entire neighborhood and are likely different, perhaps being most concerned about the changes taking place—hence their activism. Moreover, political combat does not lend itself to nuanced positions. Rather the protagonists must stake out a position and fight for it." The following chapter demonstrates that conflict in the political field did complicate public safety work, but the dynamics of racial division were not as straightforward as one might expect.

6

"White Vigilantes?"

Two Case Studies of Positive Loitering

The politics of crime in Rogers Park and Uptown engendered clashes on various levels of community life. Struggles to frame the fight against street crime as racist or race-neutral shaped electoral campaigning and—at least in Uptown—the relations between community organizations who were vying for competing directions of neighborhood change. This chapter returns to the level of grassroots safety activism—specifically positive loitering. Chapter 3 provided an overview of anticrime initiatives and their racial entanglements, but I now delve in deeper, tracing the micropolitics of race in the context of social groups who developed unique cultural styles of negotiating race.[1] These fine-grained data afford insights into the negotiation of racial meanings, showing how residents clashed over this racially contested practice. In addition, however, the findings illustrate the possibility of interracial cooperation in public safety initiatives, because the two positive loitering groups I discuss in this chapter attracted not only white but also African American and Latino residents. Sometimes, lasting interracial relationships were formed; sometimes, residents met only to discover that incompatible views precluded collaboration.

Positive loiterers tried to reclaim public space by assembling in areas that were troubled by street crime. They reported suspicious activity to the police and thereby served as what one police commander described as the police's "eyes and ears." But perhaps more important, positive loiterers wanted to send a message that the local community was vigilant and watchful. This message, the positive loiterers hoped, would discourage criminal activity by convincing gang members and other potential offenders that the risk of detection was simply too high to operate there.

Given this goal of sending a message, positive loitering had to occur outdoors and in public, where everyone could see it. Occasionally, participants even carried signs or wore T-shirts that identified them as positive loiterers. But the publicness of positive loitering also exposed these volunteers to

Us versus Them. Jan Doering, Oxford University Press (2020) © Oxford University Press.
DOI: 10.1093/oso/9780190066574.001.0001

critical scrutiny. The fact that positive loiterers explicitly attempted to exercise social control endowed the practice with a visibility and symbolic weight that other, more discreet forms of safety activism did not have. In this context, the loiterers' whiteness became highly contestable.

The feminist scholar Ruth Frankenberg (1993) has argued that whiteness tends to be "invisible" to whites since they typically do not experience their racial category as a meaningful factor that shapes their experiences, actions, and perspectives.[2] Instead, whiteness is taken as an implicit point of reference for what is normal in America. This means that most whites exhibit a very low degree of racial self-awareness, whereas nonwhites may be forced to continually consider how race shapes their lives, especially if they work in the white-dominated professional and commercial environments that, for example, Elijah Anderson (2011) has described. Nevertheless, whiteness too can become marked in certain contexts, as ethnographic work by John Hartigan (1999) and Monica McDermott (2006) reveals: in majority-black Detroit and Atlanta, whites cannot take for granted their status as the implicit point of reference. Instead, they and their actions may stand out. The same occurs when whites engage in behavior that appears problematic in relation to their racial category. Under these circumstances, whiteness may become politically marked.

Positive loitering in Rogers Park and Uptown was precisely such a context. If one believed, as the majority of justice activists did, that whites' idea of "combating crime" really meant harassing black residents, here one could actually observe this kind of racial aggression in practice. Positive loitering was therefore a prime target for racial challenges. And this potential became even more tangible after the widely discussed 2012 shooting of black teenager Trayvon Martin by a neighborhood watch volunteer in Sanford, Florida. Unlike Trayvon Martin's shooter, the positive loiterers I observed did not carry guns,[3] and they usually did not directly engage with individuals they considered suspicious. But since most of the positive loiterers were white and the "negative" loiterers they suspected of being criminals were invariably black, the charge of racial vigilantism simply suggested itself. Positive loitering prompted more racial challenges and also more protective neutralization than any other form of safety activism in Uptown and Rogers Park.

At the same time, I discovered that positive loitering groups were not *only* sites of tense interracial contact. In fact, most of the African American safety activists I met I first encountered at positive loitering events. Positive loitering was a site of racial conflict but also of occasional interracial collaboration. This complicates any unqualified interpretation of anticrime initiatives as unifying or divisive and points to an important divergence between how political leaders and politicized activists *framed* public safety work and how it actually *unfolded*. As Rogers Brubaker and his colleagues (2006:12) have cautioned, leaders and activists can have "organizationally entrenched" interests in framing ethnoracial relations in specific ways, and their descriptions need not match the ways the people in question feel about one another.[4] Depending on their position in the political field, Rogers Park and Uptown's aldermanic candidates and leading activists had clear strategic incentives for emphasizing or downplaying the racial divisiveness of anticrime initiatives. But the racial dynamics of positive loitering, as one example of safety initiatives, matched neither the unambiguously negative nor the rather rosy narratives that community leaders typically promulgated. Furthermore, there was important variation, because the micropolitics of race could play out differently across groups.

Focusing on two groups that I call the "Northtowners" and the "Lakesiders,"[5] this chapter describes the ways safety activists navigated local racial politics and how they responded when they were faced with racial challenges. These two cases add an interesting layer to politics in Rogers Park and Uptown. Due to ongoing conflict in the neighborhood's political field, the politics of crime were more contested in Uptown than in Rogers Park. But ironically, Uptown's Northtowners became a microcosm of racial harmony in a rather divided neighborhood, while the Lakesiders emerged as a paragon of safety activism's divisive potential despite operating in a less contested environment. These counterintuitive outcomes were no coincidence, however, but reflected the priorities the positive loiterers set in the context of their neighborhoods' political fields. Consequently, as micro sites of racial politics, these two groups shed additional light on the strategic negotiation of race. I return to this point toward the end of the chapter.

The Northtowners

The Northtowners were launched in Clarendon Park, a dense urban area in Uptown's southeastern corner. The local housing stock consisted of renovated condo buildings, low-income rental towers, and subsidized townhouses. Before the onset of the 2007 recession, real estate boomed here, and many whites moved into the neighborhood. A street gang had been active in the area for years, but its presence was cyclical. Occasional police stings temporarily suppressed gang activity, but the gang rebounded once its members returned from jail or new members were recruited. Gang activity spiked once again one summer during the time of my fieldwork. In addition to an increase in drug dealing and loitering, shootings erupted in the area as a result of long-standing gang rivalries.

In response to the worsening situation, several frequent CAPS meeting participants decided to form a positive loitering group. Nina, a white woman and longtime Uptowner, organized the group. She had already been working with the local CAPS group for several years. She was also involved in the block club, as were Sarah and Eric, a married, white couple in their fifties. Two additional participants were Mimi and Mahandra, whom I introduced in chapter 2 and who lived across from a corner where the gang members regularly hung out. They were in their thirties and new to the neighborhood. In addition to these five, all of whom were condo dwellers, the group included two middle-aged African American women, Wanda and Erica. Both of them were already attending CAPS meetings when they helped launch the Northtowners. Wanda and her preteen daughter lived in a subsidized townhouse that Wanda rented. It was located in a row of buildings in which gang members had established a stash house. Erica lived by herself in a small unit in a nearby apartment tower.

The Northtowners convened once a week on the corner of a busy neighborhood thoroughfare. The bright streetlights and steady stream of cars made it a bad location for dealing drugs and other kinds of illicit activity. Nevertheless, from this location the positive loiterers could monitor an area down the block where the gang members frequently congregated. In terms of their self presentation, the Northtowners were sociable and communicative. They often brought baked goods that they shared with each other and passersby. Some homeless people became so used to their presence that one would occasionally walk up and ask for food. However, the Northtowners still regarded themselves as a public safety group. They hoped that the loitering events would discourage gang activity and called the police when they saw groups of teenagers they believed to be gang members. They also worked with the alderman and the police to support arrests and evictions.

A Racially Delicate Practice

The Northtowners considered positive loitering a racially delicate practice. I learned this even as I negotiated my access as a researcher. The first Northtowners I met were Sarah and Eric. After introducing myself to them during a community bike ride, I called Sarah about the possibility of joining the Northtowners. But Sarah was skeptical. She told me that she did not want to deal with people who had an "agenda." By way of explanation, she invoked a work-related experience of holding a job readiness seminar for the tenants of one of Chicago's infamous public housing projects. In this context, a journalist had challenged her. "And she was just so rude! 'What are you white people doing here, coming into this neighborhood?'" In telling me this, Sarah informed me that she did not want me around if I was simply out to frame her as a bigot. Sarah and Eric eventually accepted my presence, but they remained suspicious. Eric declined my request for an interview. And during one community event I observed, Sarah reached for my field notes in order to browse through them. I made sure to let her—the notebook did not contain any sensitive or revealing information.

The other Northtowners were less defensive but nonetheless concerned about how they and the group might be perceived. In an interview, Nina, the organizer, told me that positive loitering ran the risk of amplifying discord in the neighborhood if the groups did not have black participants. She said:

> I think that [having an all-white group] is a huge risk, especially in a neighborhood like Uptown that's always been just a little divided and defensive about that stuff [anticrime initiatives]. Yeah, I think about it all the time. I think it's a big concern. And, like, I've joked about it to Wanda and Erica and they totally acknowledge that it's an issue, and I say to them all the time, you know: "I don't want this to be just a bunch of worried white people standing on the corner."

For Nina, positive loitering presented an opportunity to have Uptowners come together and build relationships. Being "just a bunch of worried white people" in this context would have simply reinforced the prevalent narrative that the politics of crime pitted whites and African Americans against one another. Instead, Nina and the Northtowners thought the group should unite residents around the goal of safety. Erica and Wanda, the black participants, agreed with these goals. They appreciated the opportunity to connect with other residents to fight crime, even if the impact might be small. As Erica explained to me: "we're not a threat to anybody, but at least they [the gang members] see that we're walking the streets as a collective group. And then, you know, it's another way to meet up with people in the neighborhood." Erica and Wanda's participation in the group helped the Northtowners reach a wider set of people. Sometimes, black pedestrians who recognized Wanda or Erica stopped to talk to the positive loiterers and joined them for the night.

In addition to the shared interest in building community, Erica and Wanda also vocally agreed with the white Northtowners about what it would take to make the neighborhood safer: the gang members would have to be arrested or evicted. Once Rita, a black woman of around forty-five years, joined the Northtowners for an evening together with her daughter, who was ten. Rita said that she could frequently see gang members loitering outside her apartment. Like Wanda, Rita worried about her daughter's security. She said that she called the police when she saw the gang members loitering but it did not seem to solve the problem. Nina explained that Rita should also call the district's CAPS sergeant and, more important, Alderman Cappleman. The best strategy for fixing the problem, Nina said, was to evict the gang members, and the alderman could help her do so. Wanda agreed and said that residents needed to use all the tools they had at their disposal. She warned: "don't think it'll just take a little social therapy to turn these people around. These people don't change!" Nina concurred: "it's true. Some people will just have to move away."

While the Northtowners insisted that only evictions and arrests could resolve the gang problem, they were willing to work with organizations pursuing different approaches. Perhaps most important, the Northtowners created a tie to CeaseFire. Among safety activists in Uptown, CeaseFire was unpopular because the organization participated in protests against gentrification and Alderman Cappleman's policies. And the fact that CeaseFire worked *with* rather than *against* the gangs to reduce violence did not help to improve the safety activists' views. The Northtowners became the only safety group in Uptown to develop a positive relationship with CeaseFire, making them an exception in the neighborhood's polarized political field.

One night, two of CeaseFire's violence interrupters—Deon and Hector, who were African American and Latino, respectively—came across the Northtowners, and the two groups started talking about the gang problem, CeaseFire, and positive loitering. That evening, a white man named Jim had joined the Northtowners for the first time. Jim told Deon: "this is actually my first time here. The group I usually go to is actually all-white, for some reason." Deon said he believed that positive loitering could be a good thing and, after a short pause, added: "and it probably works better when it's a little diverse." The Northtowners and the CeaseFire workers then talked about the importance of overcoming racial disunity in Uptown. Referencing Uptown's long history of acrimonious battles over the issue of crime, Nina said: "you know, it's actually just the past few years that we've gotten people to accept that there's a [gang] problem. That this is not just a bunch of white people pointing fingers." Deon and Hector agreed that Uptown had a serious gang problem that needed to be addressed.

Deon then told the Northtowners that Eddie, CeaseFire's supervisor, was looking for ways to connect with the white middle-class population. Sarah invited the violence interrupters to set up an info table at an upcoming party the local block club was organizing. Deon and Hector conveyed the offer to Eddie, who gladly accepted it and sent Deon to join the party. I spent a good part of that day with Deon to see how residents would respond. Deon was in fact able to introduce the program to a substantial number of white residents, including some who at first seemed skeptical about CeaseFire's approach of working with the gangs to prevent violence. CeaseFire appreciated the Northtowners' support, and Deon and Hector occasionally returned to participate in the loitering events, which further increased the group's racial diversity and also differentiated the Northtowners from other safety groups in the eyes of antigentrification activists. After spending one evening with the Northtowners, Craig, one of the core members of RYCH, told me that he would never join the other positive loitering groups in Uptown but the Northtowners seemed different. He said: "Nina, I think she has a good heart."

Navigating Neighborhood Division and Racial Challenges

Although the Northtowners were multiracial, they could not entirely avoid racial challenges. When their safety work became contested, however, the white group members willingly discussed their critics' complaints. For example, Mimi described a situation in which she was volunteering in the kitchen of a homeless shelter. When talking with an African American covolunteer, Mimi's involvement in positive loitering came up. The woman told Mimi that positive loitering merely "drives a bigger wedge." According to Mimi, the volunteer said: "what good can a group of white people standing around do? What could they possibly know, when so many of the neighborhood's problems are rooted in race and poverty?" Although she had not actually met the Northtowners, the volunteer believed that they *had* to be a group of white people because to her, positive loitering was a white practice. Although the charge was incorrect, Mimi maintained that her covolunteer "had a strong point." Mimi agreed that after all, the Northtowners were still *mostly* white and might therefore be perceived simply as a group of white people. She tried to convince the woman to join the positive loiterers and eventually "agreed to disagree" with her—rather than dismissing her challenge as unfounded, which she could have done instead.

The Northtowners encountered another challenge in the aftermath of a shooting that, once again, killed a young black man. In collaboration with CeaseFire, several African Americans organized a vigil in Clarendon Park, but the police disrupted the event and told the gathered crowd to disperse. Among those present was Leticia, an active member of RYCH and NA4J. Leticia told me that the vigil's participants interpreted the police response as "a race thing. Because we were black, you know." Leticia decided to go to the Clarendon Park CAPS meeting to complain about the police response. At that meeting, Nina had just advertised the Northtowners' positive loitering events when Leticia spoke up, sounding angry: "to piggyback on what she [Nina] said about positive loitering. There's been a couple of shootings, so we were out there last Wednesday in response to that. The police pulled up and told us we had to leave. So, can you tell us what would be the difference between responding to a shooting in your community, and trying to take back your streets and positive loitering?" Leticia's question constituted a problem for the Northtowners. Given her interpretation of the police response as a "race thing," she insinuated that the police had interrupted the vigil but did not interrupt positive loitering because vigils were for black and positive loitering for white residents. Responding to Leticia first, the CAPS sergeant said that the officers had probably worried about gang members targeting the vigil. After some back-and-forth and an assurance from the sergeant that Leticia and her group had the right to reject the "request" to disperse, Leticia accepted this explanation. Nina then told Leticia that she supported holding vigils in the aftermath of shooting deaths. She asked to be informed about future events so that the Northtowners could participate. She also invited Leticia to join the Northtowners.

Indeed, Leticia joined the Northtowners for their next positive loitering event, which surprised me because RYCH and NA4J activists usually depicted positive loitering as a strategy of criminalization and displacement. I interviewed Leticia to find out how she experienced the CAPS meeting and the positive loitering event. Leticia said that she had to overcome the warnings of fellow antigentrification activists before going to the CAPS meeting.

> I was warned not to—I was told not to go to beat meetings. Because they are very polarizing, they are not really about peace, they are about criminalizing the young guys. You know: "you're going to be yelled down! You are going to be shouted down." And, so I decided to go! To see, you know? And ... I wasn't shouted down [laughs], you know! And I just—you know, there it is again, that miscommunication! No one's talking to each other. You just assume. So, that was the first meeting I went to, but I kept going after that. It's going to take *everybody* [stretches word], *everybody* [stretches word] to work together.

About her subsequent evening with the Northtowners, Leticia said:

> I expected to get there and sort of feel like an outsider, or sort of get like "What is *she* doing here?" You know, and actually I didn't get that at all. I got: "Thank god, we need more diversity out here!" I think they know they are being perceived as us-against-them. And I think they appreciate other people, you know, bringing diversity to the group so they won't be perceived that way.

The racial framing of safety initiatives made particularly black and left-leaning Uptowners apprehensive about these initiatives, even when they had not had any first-hand encounters with them. Like Mimi's covolunteer at the homeless shelter, Leticia had perceived CAPS and the Northtowners as racially divisive, but Leticia's personal experience convinced her that this perspective was incorrect. She agreed with the Northtowners that discord between black and white residents had to be overcome and it would take interracial unity to make the neighborhood safer. She even became sympathetic to the racial awkwardness that positive loitering entailed for the white Northtowners. She understood that the Northtowners wanted black residents to attend positive loitering so that their safety work would not be criticized as racially divisive.

Mimi's interaction with her covolunteer and Nina's efforts to accommodate Leticia show that the Northtowners were willing to discuss race and its implications for safety initiatives, even when critics approached them with a certain degree of hostility. Rather than simply attempting to racially neutralize their public safety work, the Northtowners used these situations as opportunities for interracial dialogue and creating new ties with nonwhites. In Leticia's case, these efforts proved successful; in the case of Mimi's covolunteer, they did not. Overall, however, the Northtowners case shows that safety initiatives *could* bring black and white residents together. They did not inevitably aggravate racial disunity.

The Lakesiders

The members of the Lakesiders lived along two blocks of a residential side street in Rogers Park. The houses, most of them typical Chicago "six-flat" buildings, were well maintained, and the sidewalks and fenced yards free from litter. The Lakesiders had considered their area a quiet and peaceful space; longtime inhabitants said that it had steadily grown safer over the past decade. One summer, however, gang activity peaked. According to the police as well as CeaseFire staff, several gang members moved into nearby units and started dealing drugs from one of the units as well as nearby corners. Because of a gang conflict, several shootings occurred in the area over the following months. In the aftermath of one shooting, which killed a black man whom the police identified as an uninvolved bystander, several residents formed a positive loitering group, the Lakesiders. The core group consisted of eight members—all of them white, but heterogeneous in terms of age, gender, and class. Bob, a retired working-class man in his midfifties, organized the group together with Steve, a young professional. For most of the Lakesiders, positive loitering was the first time they became involved in neighborhood activism.

Bob arranged the group's first meeting through an Internet forum on which residents had debated the uptick in drug dealing and shootings. Initially, the group scheduled two or three loitering events per week, which lasted between two and five hours. A few times, the Lakesiders even began their events at midnight and continued into the early morning. This reflected their sense of alarm: they felt that the neighborhood was deteriorating rapidly and that only quick and forceful resistance could save it. Much of their conversation revolved around how often they called 911 to report suspicious activity. In the interest of gaining attention from the police and the alderman, they encouraged each other to call the police as frequently as possible.

Corresponding to their anxiety, the Lakesiders created an aggressive style of positive loitering. First and foremost, they developed a practice they called "cat and mouse." When playing cat and mouse, the Lakesiders would stand across from groups of adolescent black loiterers and stare at them. If that group then moved to a different corner, the Lakesiders would follow them to continue with the game. This practice came to define the group—it was what the Lakesiders expected to do together. In playing cat and mouse, the Lakesiders aimed to disrupt drug deals and other illicit activity.

The Lakesiders knew that their style of positive loitering was risky, but participants also felt exhilarated by the power the group conferred. One night, six of the Lakesiders were loitering after a shooting had occurred. Anticipating trouble, the Lakesiders had repeatedly called the police about groups of teenagers wandering through the area. As two black teenagers approached the group on the sidewalk, one of them asked: "Are these the people that are calling the police?" The other answered: "Yeah, that's them bitches." As he walked past us, he looked at us and loudly imitated the sound of gunshots—"pow, pow, pow." The Lakesiders remained silent until the two had disappeared but were visibly shaken by the experience. A few minutes later, an unmarked police car stopped by in response to the group's earlier 911 calls. Rita, an older white woman, told the officers about the threat and asked whether the Lakesiders had to worry about retaliation. One officer said: "I don't want to say that nothing could ever happen to you. But if something were to happen to any one of you, it would be over for them and they know it." The Lakesiders seemed reassured. The officer also said that he could arrest and hold the two teenagers overnight if one of the positive loiterers were to file a complaint. Steve volunteered, and the officers drove off in search of the teenagers. I do not know whether they found and arrested them, but the incident shows that the Lakesiders wielded a certain amount of power, especially through the support they received from the police.

Facing Racial Challenges

Unlike the Northtowners, the Lakesiders showed little concern about the possibility of being accused of racism. This is not to say that they were unaware of race. The positive loiterers certainly recognized that their cat and mouse game opposed racially homogeneous "teams," the white positive loiterers and the groups of presumed gang members they were observing. Once, as a group the Lakesiders were watching left its location across the street, Britney, a woman in her thirties, said: "they must be so confused by us just standing here." Rita laughed and responded: "I know! 'What are all those white people doing out there?!' " While this conversation reveals that Rita and Britney recognized positive loitering as a racially meaningful practice, the group never discussed the potential of facing resistance from anyone but the purported gang members. And when such resistance began to emerge, the Lakesiders were both surprised and exasperated. Perhaps the clearest evidence for their initial lack of racial concern is that I did not have to overcome any reservations in order to gain access. As I noted, at least two Northtowners, Sarah and Eric, never became very comfortable with my presence, even though their group was multiracial. By contrast, the Lakesiders, who were all white and much more aggressive, simply accepted me.

The Lakesiders encouraged racial challenges via their practices, especially in trying to disperse groups of black loiterers. Bob and the others knew that the attributions of criminality this practice entailed could be wrong. The Lakesiders could not tell with definitive certainty whether loiterers were gang members or not. But the danger of false attributions did not deter them; they considered the goal of fighting crime more important than the risk of offending black residents. For example, in a discussion of gang activity on a neighborhood blog, one person argued that gang involvement had to be addressed by reducing poverty, which she called the "root cause" of crime. In the meantime, Rogers Parkers needed to build community and respect each other, she wrote. Chris, one of the Lakesiders, responded: "the social welfare stuff like creating respect and understanding is a very low priority item until we can begin reducing crime in the first place. We do community safety before we do public charity." Racial harmony was a luxury the Lakesiders felt they could not currently afford.

The Lakesiders also withstood direct interpersonal confrontations on the street. In chapter 1, I described the encounter between the Lakesiders and a group of young black residents in which one of them shouted "Trayvon Martin" at the Lakesiders to protest their aggressive scrutiny, framing them as racist vigilantes. As I noted, the Lakesiders did not respond, and Bob later neutralized the racial challenge, suggesting that the young people had in fact been "gangbangers," which also implied that their attribution of racism did not have to be taken seriously. This was one case in which the actual victims of harassment fought back, but more frequently those confronting the Lakesiders were white.

Once, the Lakesiders hosted an afternoon sidewalk barbeque—they called it a "smoke-out"—outside a building they suspected housed gang members. Steve and I were chatting and eating potato salad when a skinny white man of around thirty stopped his bike next to us. He wore a mustache and tight-fitting pants that terminated above his ankles. He asked me who was in charge of the event. I pointed over to Bob, who was standing next to a fold-able table and sweating heavily even in the shade. The young man hesitated. Perhaps he was unsure whether he should walk over to Bob or not, but then he decided to talk to Steve and me instead. His voice was hoarse with tension.

The young man told us that he wanted to discuss positive loitering, be-cause he found the group "confrontational." "Have you been to any of the positive loitering events?" Steve calmly asked. The young man replied that he had not, because he felt that it was exclusionary. He said: "I look at this group and it's all white. And this is a gentrifying neighborhood so I think it's really problematic what you are doing." Steve replied: "well, it seems like you have made up your mind." "No, I have done the *math!*" the man snapped. "You have to take into account how you will be perceived." He charged that the white positive loitering group would appear racially aggressive to black residents. Steve said: "it's not exclusionary. Anyone can join us. Mostly, posi-tive loitering is just about getting neighbors out so they can get to meet each other. Part of the reason I moved to Rogers Park is *because* of the diversity." Steve's controlled response eventually calmed the young man down. The con-versation felt a bit less volatile now. The young man even introduced himself; his name was Kyle.

Kyle told us that he worked at a bike shop in the North of Howard area, a part of the neighborhood where many of Rogers Park's low-income African Americans lived. When they opened the shop, Kyle said, he and the other bike mechanics worried that it might encourage gentrification. But they did not simply want to create a space—and by extension, a magnet—for "white hipsters," as Kyle put it. In order to address this problem, the mechanics de-cided to reach out and involve kids and teenagers in their bike repair pro-gram. However, building bridges to their black neighbors had proven difficult. "When you go inside [the bike shop], it'll look a lot like when you look around here in this group," Kyle said. But just like the bike mechanics, Kyle insisted, the positive loiterers needed to try and make their group more diverse. He pointed out that this was particularly important for the positive loiterers, because they were tackling the sensitive issue of street crime. In particular, Kyle urged us to work with organizations like CeaseFire, which fought not only crime but more specifically to reduce violence and to eradicate its "root causes." Steve nodded and said: "that's an ongoing issue." Steve then invited Kyle to help himself to some food, but Kyle rejected the offer, saying that he was going to eat at home. He got back on his bike and rode off. Once he had left, Steve turned to me and said: "phew! That could have gone either way! It seemed like it was going one way, so I decided to try and take it the other way."

Steve thus felt that he had defused the situation successfully. To do so, he relied on one of the strategies of defending public safety activism I discussed in chapter 3. Against Kyle's challenge of racial exclusion, Steve provided a nonracial counter-narrative of positive loitering as an open forum where neighbors could meet and connect. Everyone was welcome to join, Steve claimed. He emphasized this aspect of community building over the group's staunch commitment to reduce crime. He also accepted Kyle's demand that the positive loiterers seek out ties to organizations like CeaseFire. Staying calm and presenting an alternative interpretation of the group from the one Kyle had in mind, Steve neutralized the situation.

However, Steve's counter-narrative was not accurate. As I will discuss further, the Lakesiders did *not* actually welcome everyone. Nor did the group sincerely attempt to build connections to groups like CeaseFire. At first, some community organizations from the social justice camp did in fact express interest in working with the Lakesiders. However, all attempts to engage the positive loiterers failed. As the Lakesiders became more widely known throughout Rogers Park, the group's reputation among justice activists and their organizations continually deteriorated.

Shortly after the Lakesiders began positive loitering, Jaime, a community organizer for ONE, invited Bob to a coffee shop to talk about positive loitering and its goals. However, Jaime was irritated by Bob's frequent use of the term "gangbanger." He tried to convince Bob that the people he was talking about were "disenfranchised black youth." Bob dismissed this as phony political correctness. He said: "I am not going to call gangbangers and drug dealers disenfranchised youth. I call it what it is. And if you don't like that, the door is right there!" As Bob explained to me after the meeting:

There [are] a lot of disadvantaged youth out there that are not drug dealers, not gangbangers, that have very successful lives, and that are doing good. So don't hand me that crap! My background was not that good. But I'm not out on the street corners selling drugs. I never have, I never will.

Another time, an umbrella group of social workers invited Steve and Bob to one of their meetings to talk about their safety work. I did not attend the meeting, but I witnessed Steve and Bob's report back to the group. Steve said: "I felt—and Bob agrees with me—that we were being cross-examined." Bob said that after he and Steve had introduced the Lakesiders and their efforts, the meeting's facilitator, an older black man, commented: "so, you are basically a group of white vigilantes!" Bob continued: "Steve and I looked at each other and we got up and left!" The Lakesiders summarily dismissed the charge of vigilantism and the attribution of racial resentment, refusing to discuss the group on those terms.

As the situations I've described in this section show, the Lakesiders' critics relied first and foremost on the group's racial composition as evidence when making racial challenges. Kyle confronted Steve about the Lakesiders' all-white racial composition at their smoke-out. Similarly, the charge of "white vigilantism" made sense only when wielded against a white group. And even shouting "Trayvon Martin" at the Lakesiders would have been less compelling if the Lakesiders had been multiracial.[6] The Lakesiders responded to critiques of this kind by claiming that their group was open to all. When a resident wrote on a local blog that she had seen the Lakesiders in the neighborhood one night and criticized them for their racial composition, Bob responded: "race is not a part of it [positive loitering]! We will welcome anyone that wants to join us." However, African Americans and Latinos did not *feel* welcome when they joined the group.

Fractured Ties

The Lakesiders started out as an all-white group, but they organically encountered opportunities for adding nonwhite participants. When their immediate neighborhood quieted down after several arrests and evictions had been made, the Lakesiders temporarily moved their events to Rogers Park's majority-black North of Howard area. There, the Lakesiders were joined by several black residents and also encountered CeaseFire. Working with CeaseFire could have been a promising strategy for attracting nonwhite members to the group, since CeaseFire was highly regarded among African American and Latino Rogers Parkers. However, all of those ties eventually dissolved because the Lakesiders rejected the concerns their new contacts brought to the group.

One person who joined the Lakesiders in the North of Howard area was Linda, a low-income woman of Puerto Rican origin. She hoped that positive loitering might help to deter violence in her neighborhood. She heard about the Lakesiders online and began attending events when they came to the North of Howard area. One night, before a loitering event she could not attend, Linda sent an email to the Lakesiders asking the loiterers not to bother a group of black car mechanics who worked out of an alley close to her house. She wrote that the mechanics were upstanding residents and established in the community. Writing back, Bob refused the request, reminding Linda that alley car repair was illegal. He wrote that he would call the police if he saw them. Other Lakesiders responded and uttered approval for Bob's position.

This incident marked the end of Linda's work with the Lakesiders. At a subsequent positive loitering event, Bob and Chris discussed her decision to leave the group. Laughing, Chris reassured Bob that her reaction had been "so petty." When I interviewed Linda to find out more about her position, she said:

> There are people out there shooting each other. And you are going to worry about these guys [alley car mechanics] trying to make a living? They keep an eye out on things, you know? They help keep the neighborhood safe. Plus, they are making a living. Maybe it is illegal and they are not supposed to be doing it, but, from what I understand, the cops haven't been harassing them. They've been leaving them alone. Because, you know, you've got to weigh out the risks and benefits and I think leaving them alone is a greater benefit than hassling them. And for Bob, who doesn't even live in my neighborhood, to say, "Well, we are going to do it! Meh, meh, meh, meh, meh [makes childlike, sneering sounds]." Fuck you, you know? I was pissed! But I don't—I try not to be confrontational so it's easier for me just to step back.

Establishing a lasting relationship with Linda would have required the Lakesiders to consider shades of gray in their thinking about crime and order. Linda supported the idea of positive loitering in order to discourage violence, but she did not want it used against the car mechanics—in part because she felt that the car mechanics actually made the neighborhood safer. Since the Lakesiders proved unwilling to compromise, she left the group.

The Lakesiders' contact with CeaseFire represented an opportunity for improving the visibility and reputation of positive loitering especially among African American residents. In principle, Rogers Park's political field made a partnership between the positive loiterers and CeaseFire easier than in Uptown, because CeaseFire in Rogers Park was less embroiled in antigentrification politics, and therefore also less critical of CAPS and other safety initiatives. After CeaseFire staff and the Lakesiders met each other during a positive loitering event one night, Steve and Bob set up a meeting with Pete, CeaseFire's Rogers Park supervisor.

Pete told me that he saw working with the Lakesiders as a chance to introduce white Rogers Parkers to the local youth. He wanted white residents to understand that most of the teenagers were not involved in gangs, even if their clothing and style might make them look that way to untrained eyes. Pete thought that whites felt unnecessarily unsafe because they overestimated the presence of gang members on the streets. He said: "if you have, in this community, only fifty, sixty, seventy recognized gang members, that means that every kid in this community could not be a gang member." Consequently, Pete believed that it might help the positive loiterers to get to know young black residents and learn about their perspective.

However, when Pete suggested that the Lakesiders adopt a more communicative approach in order to, with Pete's help, engage some teenagers in dialogue, the group refused. There were no more conversations between CeaseFire and the Lakesiders after this disagreement. While the Lakesiders had initially expressed appreciation for the work CeaseFire was doing, the positive loiterers now began to talk about CeaseFire as a waste of tax dollars. When a black man was shot and killed on the Lakesiders' home turf, ONE and CeaseFire organized a prayer vigil against violence in order to appeal to the dead man's associates not to retaliate. The Lakesiders decided that they did not want to endorse CeaseFire by participating, and none of them attended the vigil.

At the vigil, I ran into Margaret, an African American senior living in subsidized housing, who, like Linda, had joined the Lakesiders as they held positive loitering events in the North of Howard area. Margaret seemed like a natural fit for the Lakesiders—she was very committed to safety and public order, and she already worked with CAPS and grassroots safety initiatives in her part of the neighborhood. I had not seen Margaret in a while and talked with her after the vigil to catch up. Margaret told me that she and Bob had spoken on the phone about the vigil earlier that day but Bob had said that he and the Lakesiders would not participate, in protest against CeaseFire. Margaret was as perplexed as she was annoyed. She said:

> See, sometimes I don't understand those guys. We have to fight *together*! [Bob] didn't even want to come over and do this prayer vigil! So what I'm saying: if you're going to do all this stuff, have walks and try to keep the community safe, you got to get rid of that racism.

Margaret did not find positive loitering racially objectionable and largely agreed with the Lakesiders' perspective on the gang problem. She supported tough-on-crime policing but also thought that the gang problem needed to be addressed from all possible angles. This, she believed, required that all law-abiding Rogers Parkers work together on all fronts. Selectively rejecting CeaseFire was racist. By refusing to attend the vigil, the Lakesiders therefore alienated even Margaret, despite their shared goals and views.

Conclusion

Positive loitering was the most visible form of safety activism in Rogers Park and Uptown. Indeed, the *point* of positive loitering was for safety activists to be publicly seen. The positive loiterers wanted to warn gang members and drug dealers that residents were organized and ready to call the police. This very publicness, however, also raised the symbolic stakes of positive loitering, because it highlighted the whiteness of safety activism. The groups consisted predominantly—and sometimes entirely—of whites. In addition, positive loitering entailed direct efforts to monitor and control black residents, whom the positive loiterers suspected of gang involvement primarily on the basis of their race. Positive loitering therefore invited racial challenges. At the same time, the growing national awareness of the killings of unarmed black men further encouraged people to think about the stark differences in the ways black and white Americans were perceived and treated in public settings. This awareness made it all the more likely for residents to vocalize racial concerns or complaints about positive loitering. By participating in positive loitering, therefore, white residents were forced to confront their whiteness, an experience that is unusual and uncomfortable for most whites.[7]

The loaded context of positive loitering constrained both groups, but the Northtowners and the Lakesiders reacted to it in different ways. The Lakesiders fought to assert positive loitering as a color-blind practice, fiercely resisting each and every racial challenge. However, they encouraged such challenges through their aggressive practices, their all-white composition, and, relatedly, their failure to build ties with nonwhites. The Northtowners, by contrast, were multiracial and avoided practices that could be perceived as aggressive. They were therefore less susceptible to racial challenges than the Lakesiders. They also tried to create new relationships with black residents and, by inviting CeaseFire to their block party, even Uptown's social justice camp. The racial challenges the Northtowners nonetheless encountered were rooted in the general perception among some Uptowners that positive loitering was inherently racist. Unlike the Lakesiders, the Northtowners did not immediately reject accusations in these situations but acknowledged race as an important dividing line. They argued that positive loitering could ease rather than aggravate racial tensions, as long as the group was multiracial. The Northtowners' willingness to discuss race helped them create new ties between African American, white, and Latino residents. These different racial micropolitics had nontrivial effects on trust and community in Rogers Park and Uptown. The Northtowners succeeded in fostering interracial collaboration in Uptown, a place where bitter and longstanding struggles about the politics of crime and race made this difficult, while the Lakesiders sparked racial alienation in Rogers Park, even though it was a less contested place for conducting safety activism.

In part, the groups' divergent modes of dealing with race reflected their different leaderships. As the groups' organizers, Nina and Bob could have hardly been more different—Nina was egalitarian and flexible, while Bob was rather autocratic and stubborn. But the groups' styles also echoed the political fields in which they operated. Given the ongoing conflict over Broncho Billy Park and Alderman Cappleman in Uptown, the Northtowners were careful to avoid controversy. Nina and the other Northtowners anticipated racial challenges; race would almost certainly come up because experience showed that it usually did. Thus, the Northtowners engaged with critics, even when those critics approached them somewhat belligerently. Since the Northtowners did not want to be categorized as racist gentrifiers, they had to self-consciously navigate Uptown's political field and the associated racial divisions. As Nina said to me: "okay, there's like this crime-fighting element to it [positive loitering], but I also just feel like making those connections between blacks and whites—I feel that's pretty much all that we got. Because then everybody can trust each other a little more."

Since the politics of crime had recently been less contested in Rogers Park, the Lakesiders did not expect to face racial challenges. At least initially, they operated without the sense of whiteness as a marked identity that was so pervasive among safety activists in Uptown. Given their grave concerns about growing levels of crime and violence, they developed a bold style of positive loitering that Uptowners would have probably avoided for fear of political backlash. When the Lakesiders then faced charges of racism, they felt wronged and remained defiant. After all, they were volunteering their time to combat crime. They thought that their critics, although surprisingly numerous, were flat-out wrong: positive loitering had nothing to do with race. After a series of failed encounters, Rogers Park's justice organizations, which initially approached positive loitering more open-mindedly than did those in Uptown, converged toward classifying the Lakesiders as white vigilantes.

The two groups had very different effects on racial unity and division, but in principle both cases demonstrate a potential for interracial cooperation in the battle against street crime. The Northtowners succeeded in creating and strengthening social ties across racial and even additional political boundaries. While the Lakesiders did not, this was not for want of opportunities— Linda, Margaret, CeaseFire, ONE, and other residents and organizations *were* interested in working with the Lakesiders. Positive loitering was certainly not the harmless community building that leading safety activists made it out to be, but neither did it inevitably spark racial discord, as antigentrification activists claimed.

Sociologists regard crime as a key site of racial conflict, and, from this perspective, the fact that residents collaborated across racial boundaries to reduce crime is surprising. Confronted with gentrification, pervasive stereotypes of black criminality, and police harassment, scholars of racism would generally expect to find conflict, not collaboration. But while some African Americans and Latinos accused the Lakesiders and the Northtowners of racism, others joined them—or, in the case of the Lakesiders, *tried* to. The issue of crime produced racial strife but also united diverse residents. This finding warrants an investigation into how the politics of crime actually corresponded to racial categories. In the next chapter, I analyze the range of views I found among whites and blacks, and also take stock of the divisions and alliances that crime engendered both within and across racial boundaries. As I will show, it would be incorrect to assume a simple correspondence between racial categories and political views.

7

Racial Identities and Political Standpoints

Expected and Unexpected Alignments

The preceding chapters have unearthed community conflict on several levels—the levels of electoral politics and of relations between community organizations as well as the street level of public safety work in the form of positive loitering. The conflicts I have described were *racial* conflicts insofar as they revolved around accusations of bias and bigotry and of racial divisiveness or, conversely, around efforts to defend certain urban interventions with the help of racial neutralizations. Nevertheless, it is important to emphasize that these racial conflicts did not always—not even most of the time—pit African Americans and whites against one another. Perhaps as a simple reflection of neighborhood demographics, perhaps as a reflection of class privilege, most of the active participants in the two neighborhoods' political fields were white. The antigentrification camp boasted more African American and Latino activists than the public safety camp, but even within the former, whites often constituted a majority at events and meetings. This meant that racial conflict often unfolded not between black and white residents but *among* white ones.

Thinking about neighborhood conflict from the structural perspective of modern theories of racism—including the writings of Lawrence Bobo (1999), Eduardo Bonilla-Silva (1997), and Joe Feagin (2006)—clashes among whites are not something one would expect to find in Rogers Park and Uptown.[1] Regarding whites' political behavior, these theories assert that whites seek to maintain or improve their privileged standing in American society. One important aspect of this privilege is that whites expect to be shielded from the symptoms of racialized poverty—ranging from underperforming public schools to criminal street gangs. As Ruth Peterson and Lauren Krivo (2010) have shown, residential segregation ensures that the vast majority of white Americans live well isolated from poor black neighborhoods, which are often riddled with crime. But whites in Rogers Park and Uptown—especially those living within the neighborhoods' centers of gang activity—did not enjoy

Us versus Them. Jan Doering, Oxford University Press (2020) © Oxford University Press.
DOI: 10.1093/oso/9780190066574.001.0001

this privilege as much as whites generally do. These white residents found themselves confronted with shootings and other forms of violent crime that endangered their physical safety, even though residents of color were much more likely to be injured or killed. Furthermore, they incurred financial losses because street crime undoubtedly reduced their property values—although crime had probably also made homeownership more attainable to them in the first place. Under such circumstances, racism scholars argue, one can expect white Americans to abandon any progressive racial views they might hold and instead demand an aggressive program of punishment and control—no matter what costs such measures might impose on the majority of law-abiding black residents.

But I found that not all whites reacted to crime in this way. In fact, many of the most vocal critics of invasive policing and gentrification were white. Nor did African Americans form one cohesive political unit against the criminal justice system.[2] Some black residents worked together with white safety activists to combat crime and in this process formed relationships that linked previously disjointed communities. The Northtowners, for example, brought together whites and blacks in spite of Uptown's tense political climate, even drawing in Leticia, a deeply committed gentrification critic. The Northtowners stood out as an unusually successful case of interracial collaboration, but they were by no means alone. In both neighborhoods, the public safety and antigentrification camps were polarized, but this division did not always correspond to racial boundaries.

To fully understand racial politics in Rogers Park and Uptown, it is necessary to examine additional political standpoints that sociologists might overlook if they approached politics exclusively through the lens of dominant theories of racism and racial conflict. Accordingly, this chapter portrays black and white individuals whose views and activism put them at opposite poles of the politics of crime and gentrification. Investigating their experiences and perspectives uncovers axes of conflict and collaboration that are rarely acknowledged in race scholarship. Race influenced all of these activists' views but did not always influence them in predictable or expected ways. As Corey Fields (2016:204) writes in a study of black Republicans, any "social identity . . . can be channeled into a broad range of political actions and strategies."

These findings certainly do not refute general theories of racism but add a microscopic lens to a perspective that—for good reasons—largely focuses on the broad landscape of racial conflict. Applying such a microscopic lens reveals important complications and unexpected position-takings, which make up a nontrivial part of racial politics but which the macro relations of power and privilege can easily eclipse. A more comprehensive understanding of race, however, should incorporate such political alignments. Those who do not fit the typical patterns of racial politics may have much to tell us about the relationship between racial categories and political behavior.

African Americans and the Politics of Crime and Gentrification

A light-skinned woman in her late forties with thin, long dreadlocks, Chloe was a radiantly friendly person, despite a biography filled with hardship. I interviewed her in 2012 at a coffee shop in an Uptown department store she liked to visit. Looking around, she smiled and said: "it's like a wonderland for me. You know, on the second floor, where they have all the television screens set up next to each other? I love that. It makes me feel better." She lived in subsidized housing and was receiving Supplemental Security Income after having undergone several cancer surgeries.

It was a stormy journey that brought Chloe to Uptown. After leaving her parents' home at the age of fifteen, she lived and worked in several majority-black neighborhoods on Chicago's South Side—alone at first and later with her son, Dante. Shortly after Dante entered high school, she found that he exhibited a growing level of anxiety. She discovered that he was being pressured to join a gang and had received an ultimatum to do so. Realizing this, she took him out of school and left the South Side in a rush. She recounted: "I told him: 'Pack your bag, we're leaving. We're getting out of here.'" She did not even have the money to pay for the train ride and vividly recalls asking commuters for help with the fare at the station. Chloe and Dante took the "L" train to the North Side, where they were directed to an Uptown shelter.

After staying at the shelter for several weeks, Chloe and Dante moved into a subsidized apartment in Rogers Park. She liked the neighborhood at first but soon learned that gangs were active in this area as well. She told of this period of her life with palpable horror. "At night, the gangs took over and the gangbangers would terrorize the people," she said. Eventually, several gang members found out that Chloe and Dante lived by themselves and began to prey on them. She said: "they basically took over my apartment. They pretty much held us hostage. I was staying in my bedroom pretty much all day."[3] After a month and a half, she and Dante "literally ran" back to the Uptown shelter, as she put it. With help from the shelter, she found a different subsidized apartment—this time in Uptown. She was still residing there when I met her. Dante now lived in a group home where he received professional care for schizophrenia, but the separation had been liberating for Chloe. It had given her the time to attend to her own mental health—she had been diagnosed as suicidal after her cancer diagnosis. The separation had also enabled her to pursue her political passion, which was to defend affordable housing in Uptown.

Chloe volunteered for ONE, which advocated for social services and affordable housing on the Far North Side. In that capacity, Chloe served as a low-income tenant representative when ONE held meetings with landlords or political officials. She also helped organize tenants threatened by bad housing conditions or displacement. She summed up her vision for housing in Uptown in three words: "clean, affordable, and safe." Given her experience—seeing her son pressured to join a gang and being victimized in Rogers Park—it was not surprising that she put a premium on housing that was not only affordable and clean but also safe. Nonetheless, she did not work with Uptown's safety initiatives or the police. Nor did she believe that the relentless calls to get tough on crime were in the interest of residents like her.

When I asked Chloe how she felt about CAPS, she took a big breath and said: "I am *trying* to be positive about it. But the average person on the street you don't see at CAPS, because they don't want to hear your ideas unless you are a condo owner." Chloe felt that the police in Uptown were "over the top" and were engaging in racial stereotyping because safety activists constantly called on them to crack down on crime. In addition, she believed that the gentrifiers' solution to the gang problem was to simply close down affordable buildings and displace their tenants. She said: "the idea of CAPS is: 'We are with the condo owners. Let's just get rid of those low-income buildings!'" She thought that this approach was not only unjust but also ineffective, since the gang members were not going to abandon their Uptown territories. Rather, she suggested that gang activity in Uptown would subside only if the neighborhood began to offer young people more opportunities for personal growth. She said: "the more exposure [to culture and new experiences] we offer the mobbers, the less of them we'll have." She concluded: "so, with CAPS, I want to be positive about it, but they are making it *really* hard for me."

Compare Chloe to Margaret, a fifty-nine-year-old black nurse. I first met Margaret when she joined the Lakesiders' positive loitering events in the North of Howard area, where she lived. Speaking with her at these events, I realized that a lot of common ground connected her with the sternly order-oriented Lakesiders. When we walked the neighborhood, she would often make disapproving comments about things she observed around her—from people congregating on the corner to rambunctious pre-teens playing in the park without adult supervision. She would shake her head and say, with quiet resoluteness: "this is unacceptable behavior!" After one of these comments, I asked her whether she would like to move out of the neighborhood. She turned her head, looked at me in disbelief for a moment, and then said: "Honey, I *can't!*" As I got to know her better, I learned what she meant.

Margaret had moved to Rogers Park in 1993 when a subsidized apartment became available for herself and her son, who had just returned to Chicago after serving in the navy. She had previously lived on Chicago's West Side. Rogers Park was not the first place where she had encountered gangs and street crime, but she found the situation in North of Howard shocking. She felt that the police had largely given up on the area and left law-abiding residents to fend for themselves. She began to regret moving there, but her decision was irreversible. Her apartment was located in project-based sub-sidized housing, which meant that her housing voucher was tied to this specific building; it would not transfer to a new apartment if she moved. Either way, she did not have the money to pay for another move. She would have to stay put for the time being. But rather than despair about her situation or lock herself in her apartment, Margaret became a passionate community activist. She insisted on her right to feel safe in her neighborhood, while most of her neighbors and acquaintances simply chose to stay indoors.[4]

> They say: "Oh, I don't come out when it's dark." And I don't go out because I'm feeling like nothing's going to happen. I go out because this is where I live and I want a safe neighborhood where I can go out if I feel like it. When I want to walk up to the corner, to the little store and get some snacks, I want to feel comfortable. I don't want to feel in fear walking from my building and walking up Howard Street and I got to almost run there and run back.

Margaret held an unusual social position in the North of Howard community, bridging two sets of residents that rarely interacted—at least not on amicable terms. Her daughter-in-law was a professional community organizer who fought for social services, high-quality public schools, and affordable housing in the neighborhood and throughout the metropolitan area. Margaret actively supported her daughter-in-law's work. She herself had rallied neighbors to demand that their housing provider renovate its buildings and improve tenants' living conditions. But Margaret was also very vocal about her desire to purge North of Howard of the gangs. She attended CAPS meetings together with white and a handful of black neighbors. Since she had found Alderman Moore's record of addressing crime disappointing, she had aided various political challengers over the years, from Karen Hoover to Don Gordon. And Margaret lobbied for increased policing, calling on her neighbors and acquaintances to support the police and CAPS. She realized that many of her black neighbors distrusted the police but criticized their perspective:

> Yeah, they say they don't trust the police. That's another thing I tell them. If you go to a CAPS meeting then you'll meet them! But you can't just say "Well, I don't trust the police." Because if you haven't dealt with them then what trust are you looking for? But you have to go to CAPS. Not even just CAPS, they'll be around your house. You need to . . . wave at them, talk to them, see. A lot of them be like: "What are the police always riding around here for?" Well, you should be glad! Honey, that's a good thing!

Along several key dimensions, Margaret's circumstances and experiences strikingly resembled Chloe's. Their socioeconomic conditions were quite similar, although Margaret worked whereas Chloe received social security support. Both were low-income, single parents with grown children and lived in subsidized housing. Both were active in the struggle for tenants' rights and decent housing conditions. And both had come into first-hand contact with the gangs and street crime. Nevertheless, their views about crime and what to do about it could hardly have been more different.

For Chloe, the safety initiatives were quite clearly about race. White middle-class people were using the gangs as a pretext to close down low-income housing and thereby rid Uptown of some criminal as well as many law-abiding black tenants. And the police willingly executed the safety activists' plans, harassing black residents whenever and wherever they could. Ultimately, for Chloe, the issue of crime was therefore really a question of racial justice. If crime was to be reduced, it had to be done through prevention, not aggressive policing that aided displacement. Margaret, by contrast, believed that the police could not be proactive enough. She had herself been one of the safety activists who had insisted that the police stop neglecting the North of Howard area. Residents needed to welcome the police and any additional police service they received. If they felt mistreated or distrustful, they could and should take action to create better relationships with the officers. She also saw no necessary connection between public safety initiatives and gentrification. For her, fighting the gangs had nothing to do with race or class but everything to do with creating a livable neighborhood.

Comparing Chloe and Margaret's positions on the street gangs reveals two distinct political standpoints despite a similar lived experience. Scholars often explain diverging standpoints by invoking different social identities that shape political decision-making, especially race, class, and gender. But Chloe and Margaret, notwithstanding their shared social identities and circumstances, arrived at fundamentally different conclusions when pondering questions of neighborhood change. I certainly encountered more black women on the Far North Side whose views approximated Chloe's social justice perspective more closely than Margaret's propolice position. Nonetheless, I observed a nontrivial amount of conflict among African Americans over the politics of crime.

To examine this, one does not need to leave the North of Howard area. At the time of my research, the three most committed safety activists in this part of Rogers Park were Margaret, Kay (who was also black), and Gayle, a white woman who was well-known—some of my social justice acquaintances would have said infamous—in Rogers Park. I describe Gayle's position in more detail in the next section. Here, it suffices to say that Gayle was staunchly and unapologetically conservative, which was rare even among the most fervent public safety activists. I repeatedly witnessed Gayle talk herself into a frenzy about single-parent motherhood, lax parenting among low-income people, and the way welfare "enabled" a "lifestyle of dependency." For Margaret and Kay, being closely connected with Gayle as well as the police meant that they sometimes faced racial challenges from their black neighbors.

Margaret did not share all of Gayle's views but nonetheless worked with her because she respected Gayle's unwavering commitment to lowering crime. When Margaret went to CAPS meetings and positive loitering events, she would occasionally bring along one or two acquaintances. After coming once, however, these neighbors usually dropped out, which Margaret attributed to Gayle's conservative rhetoric. This put Margaret in an awkward position: "people say, 'How you be around her?' And I say, 'Because I found out how she is. She's bold. She's got a voice.'" Margaret was frustrated by Gayle alienating potential community volunteers, but she also found it frustrating that they would forgo the opportunity to help reduce crime. She said:

> People be mad when me and Gayle be together. I say, well, it shouldn't matter to you, because we're not here about the color. Whatever we do in the neighborhood, we're supposed to be all coming together. Our differences, put them to the side and then we get things worked out. I don't have time for that.

Margaret's justification for working with Gayle—"we're not here about the color"—reveals that Margaret interpreted complaints about this collaboration specifically as racial challenges. She argued that the shared struggle for safety should override differences of race or ideology. The gangs, according to her, did not care about race, only about money. She said: "you know exactly how the gangs operate. It ain't just blacks. It's all colors!" A divided community could not successfully stand up to the gangs, she believed.

The racial challenges Margaret faced from black Rogers Parkers were probably alleviated by her working-class status and, furthermore, her simultaneous activism on behalf of low-income tenants and their housing conditions. Middle-class African Americans could not necessarily rely on this, as was demonstrated by the case of Kay, a middle-aged, college-educated woman who worked in education. Kay had moved into the North of Howard area as a college student. Although she felt that the neighborhood had steadily declined until recently, she had bought a house there in the early 1990s, simply because it was affordable to do so. Together with Margaret, Gayle, and several others, Kay had worked to demand increased police attention. She believed that the police and Alderman Moore had ignored crime in the area because they assumed that people living North of Howard did not really want an orderly neighborhood. She fiercely contested this assumption. When I asked her for an example, she recounted a conversation she had had with a police officer during her early tenure in the neighborhood.

> He said: "Why should we care what happens? The rest of the community doesn't care. Why should we do anything about it if they're not doing anything about it?" And it's like: "That is not why you are here. Your job is to serve and protect, okay?" It's like: "I care! I care! There are other neighbors

who care. They may be more afraid than I am. I'm not afraid to confront these knuckleheads out here, but, yes, they care. And, yes, you need to do something about it. You know, as many times as you may see gangs and drug dealers and shootings go on out here—that's still a *minority* and it's the *majority* that needs protection."

Kay said that the police had become more responsive over the years but Alderman Moore had not—perhaps because he was concerned about offending black voters if he aggressively combated crime in this majority-black part of the neighborhood. As a result of her dissatisfaction with Moore, Kay had campaigned for Don Gordon in 2007. I asked her what she thought about the charges of racism against him. My question led her to talk about her experience as a black middle-class person living in a low-income area.

KAY (SOUNDING UPSET): [Don Gordon's campaign] was not race-coded. Don is not a racist. *They* [Gordon's opponents] were!
JAN: I wasn't fishing for that, I was just interested in what you think about that.
KAY (QUIETLY): No, I . . . I guess you're also talking to a person, I've been called racist. By other black people, so, it's, I don't know.
JAN: Is this part of that name-calling component of working with CAPS?
KAY: That's part of it, yes, and part of it is just because of the way I look and the way I talk. I don't look like what I guess they consider the average black person should look like, and I also don't talk like the way they expect the average person to talk. And I can't help it. I'm sorry. . . . No, I'm *not* sorry! I like the way I look and I like the way I talk, actually. But I've had people say, "You must think you're white!"

More explicitly than Margaret's statements, this excerpt from my interview with Kay demonstrates how working with the police—in combination with certain personal features—could expose African Americans to racial challenges. In the North of Howard area, Kay stood out in multiple ways: as a black woman who was middle-class, as a property owner, and as a public safety activist. She believed that her activism served the interests of all upstanding citizens. Indeed, she told me that black residents sometimes thanked her for her efforts. However, in combination with her personal demeanor, her activism—which could be interpreted as antiblack—led some to accuse her of abandoning her racial identity and trying to be white. Racial challenges, this shows, materialize not only as charges of white racism but also as critiques of black identities. In such cases, racial challenges and neutralizations revolve around the question of what it means to be "authentically" black.[5] And Kay's account vividly conveys the pain and tension these charges incited, making her so defensive that she briefly—before correcting herself—went so far as apologizing for the way she dressed and spoke.

In sum, African Americans in Rogers Park and Uptown were not united against the criminal justice system and its civic collaborators. There was a substantial amount of disagreement and even conflict among African Americans. I should add, however, that there was also a core of agreement. First, all African Americans I spoke with concurred that investing in prevention was key. Children and teenagers needed good schools, afterschool programs, summer jobs, and opportunities for cultural enrichment that would keep them away from gangs. Second, there was widespread support for the notion that the community should not simply give up on those who had run into trouble. For example, support for CeaseFire was strong even among those who worked with the police. That is, all African Americans I encountered maintained a basic level of empathy for gang members and their situation, which was not always the case among whites.

Whites and the Politics of Crime and Gentrification

The majority of white community activists in Rogers Park and Uptown were involved in some type of public safety work, but there were also many white antigentrification activists. Even direct exposure to crime and violence did not necessarily turn whites into advocates of tough-on-crime policies. Twenty-four-year-old Jessica lived in a co-op building that was affiliated with a Rogers Park church. In addition to various arts and urban agriculture programs, she worked with Hope for Youth, a social justice initiative that offered a police- and gentrification-critical mentoring program for black and Latino teenagers. Between 2011 and 2014, several people were shot and killed on Jessica's block. One time, a bullet pierced the window of a nearby shop where Jessica worked part-time.

When I asked Jessica about her worst experience in Rogers Park, she did not talk about shootings—she talked about the police. She said that she played a game with her coresidents they called "count the cops . . . because they just drive by a lot and there's a lot of harassment. One time we tried to ask what they're doing and they started yelling at us and it made me really angry and feel kind of powerless about the larger system, the policing system." She and her community never called the police, not even when a shooting occurred. They did not see a point in having shooters arrested and locked away. Instead they called one of CeaseFire's violence interrupters. They certainly did not call the police about drug dealing, which sometimes happened right outside their house because they felt that the fight against drug dealing was "a bit of a conspiracy to target different racial groups," as she put it. In support of that interpretation, she referenced the book *The New Jim Crow* (Alexander 2010), which we had both recently read for a social justice book club that Hope for Youth hosted.

Unsurprisingly, Jessica also regarded public safety work from a critical standpoint. She said: "we [the co-op tenants] see it as largely a racial issue, because most of the people in that community [the safety activists] are white and they have this very 'other' approach to the violence in the neighborhood as people who . . . need to be gotten rid of." She even maintained that there was an upside to shootings—although not shooting *deaths*, of course— since shootings presumably kept gentrification in check. She said: "I like to think that [the shootings] keep people who are not open-minded out" of the neighborhood.

From the perspective of structural theories of race and racism, immediate experiences of gang violence and crime constitute disruptions of white privilege that one can expect will make whites significantly more hostile toward racial minorities, but Jessica resisted any impetus in this direction. Crime should also have a strong effect on the political views of homeowners, because homeownership ties residents to the fortunes of the neighborhood through property values. These theories would thus predict that homeowners will support measures that hasten gentrification, regardless of the process's racial impact. But homeowners did not cohesively endorse tough-on-crime policies either.

Consider the case of Phil, a martial arts instructor in Rogers Park who instructed low-income teenagers to, he said, support their development and self-confidence. In 2011, he and his wife bought a house off Morse Street after living close by for about a decade. The area saw occasional bouts of gun violence, but when I asked him how he felt about crime in Rogers Park, he said: "I think as a white middle-class property owner, the crime that I have to be concerned about is graffiti on my garage. And maybe rarely a mugging or someone trying to hold me up for money." He said that this had never happened to him, although it had happened to acquaintances and members of his church community. He then connected his perspective to his class and racial category.

> Most of the crime is happening within a race and class dynamic that I'm not a part of. So it affects me only in a secondary fashion. It affects the mood of the neighborhood. I think there are conditions in Rogers Park that help facilitate some of the violence that we have and I'm more inclined to address those conditions than I am to blame it on the perpetrators.

Phil believed that white Rogers Parkers had little reason to fear crime because violence unfolded almost entirely between the rival gang factions. To him, the fact that whites nonetheless called for getting tough on crime had less to do with any immediate physical danger than with homeowners pushing to increase property values, which he regarded as its own form of turf war. Consequently, he held a negative view of public safety initiatives. He said: "it tends to be all white folks, they have police protection . . . and they reclaim the neighborhood as if it's been taken from them." After explaining his stance on these dividing lines, he hinted with dry humor at the ostensible irony of holding these views against the backdrop of his socioeconomic standing: "I guess I'm a bad property owner." The joke articulated the general connection between homeownership and tough-on-crime views and, naturally, his desire to distance himself from this social position.

Jessica and Phil can serve as examples of those whites who rejected the criminal justice system as a tool for addressing street crime. Like other whites from the social justice camp, they discounted the risks that crime personally entailed for them and instead prioritized their commitment to affordability and racial diversity. They did so even when they were exposed to a nontrivial amount of physical danger and when they had material stakes in controlling crime, as Phil did as a homeowner. In addition, they forcefully criticized their white neighbors for calling the police. Jessica even welcomed shootings in the sense that they might lead some white middle-class people to leave the neighborhood or to avoid moving there in the first place.

Most white residents preferred a very different approach and enthusiastically supported a heavier police presence, promises to vigorously crack down on crime in subsidized housing, and other interventions that might potentially decrease crime. Almost all of them—I will discuss one exception—avoided racial terminology and instead engaged in careful racial neutralization work. As a strong and thus clear example, I will return to Gayle, the safety activist who worked closely with Kay and Margaret.

About sixty years old, Gayle was a small, pale-skinned woman, wiry and energetic. Drawn by the location near both the lake and the "L" train, she had bought an apartment in North of Howard in 2002. As she said, she saw herself as an "urban pioneer," buying in the hope that the neighborhood was going to improve. She was disappointed when, shortly after her move, the low-income housing providers who dominated North of Howard's housing market renewed their contracts with the Department of Housing and Urban Development, locking in their buildings as subsidized housing for another thirty years. She told me that she would have probably moved somewhere else if she had known this in 2002.

Gayle argued that all residents were harmed by the way the services and housing providers in the North of Howard area operated. More specifically, she claimed that the social service agencies gave low-income people too many "free things" without holding them accountable, which, she said, set them up for failure. In return for receiving services like subsidized housing, she thought, the tenants should do everything in their power to put their children on the right track in life, keeping them out of gangs and empowering them to become self-sufficient members of society. She said: "you have to take your child and make sure your child sits in that classroom all day. If you don't understand the homework, get help for the child so the child can understand it and maybe get out of this cycle." In addition to failed parenting, she held that the presence of criminal offenders in subsidized housing drew children into gangs and prevented low-income residents from improving their lives. She explained how she thought offenders could live in the neighborhood in the first place:

> Poor, unfortunate women . . . apply for the apartment. The waitlist opens up. So they have the clean record, they pass the good credit check, they get the apartment. They should cherish it because it's for them and their little kids. Get on with your life, get on with your job, things will fall into place. Get your GED, keep going. That's what the hand-up should be about. But instead, pretty soon there will be a boyfriend or two and his friends. And maybe she is going to work but they'll be in there with their ankle bracelets on and drinking and drugging and partying.

Gayle blamed the women for allegedly taking in these men, but first and foremost she blamed the lack of oversight in affordable housing. After all, the rules prohibited tenants from giving shelter to people who were not listed on the lease. But Alderman Moore, she charged, did not put enough pressure on the housing providers, who in turn did not pressure their building managers to enforce the rules. She claimed that if the rules *were* actually enforced, the situation North of Howard would drastically improve, but she did not expect this to happen because the "hand-wringing liberals"—including Alderman Moore—simply did not want the situation to change. Instead, she suggested that they were content to discredit safety activists as racist gentrifiers, because they ultimately profited from having a disempowered population at their disposal, which could then be mobilized on Election Day and kept the tax dollars rolling in. Consequently, she described charges of racism she had encountered as a result of her work with CAPS as hollow.

> They want to call me a racist for wanting things fixed. It's not about selling my condo at a higher price as much as it is, I want to be able to walk down the street. Or if I want to take off and go to a movie at 10 o'clock at night or if I want to garden, I don't want to have to worry about bullets whizzing through my hair, or people jumping the fence that don't belong there.

One can take Gayle's statements as prime examples of the rhetoric of color-blind racism as discussed by Eduardo Bonilla-Silva (2003): barely deracialized speech that nonetheless evokes and reinforces racial stereotypes. For example, her reference to low-income women taking in "a boyfriend or two" (rather than focusing on their work and children) can easily be interpreted as a stereotypical narrative of black poverty resulting from cultural pathologies that prevent upward mobility. In order to avoid an overly simplistic portrait, however, I should add that Gayle also engaged in community activism on behalf of low-income children in the neighborhood.[6] And whatever her true stance toward low-income and black residents may have been, she rejected any notion that she sought to advance racial marginalization through her safety work. Since low-income housing in the North of Howard area was project-based and locked in as such for decades, any resident who might be evicted for criminal involvement would simply be replaced with a law-abiding resident. "That's all I want," Gayle said.

Gayle was somewhat of an outlier in the public safety camp, because she seemed relatively unconcerned with what other residents and especially social justice activists might say about her. She was also unusual in that she freely attributed pathological behavior to black, low-income residents; the safety activists generally avoided negative commentary about anyone except for the gang members.

I found only one case in which a resident explicitly embraced a racist position in my presence, that of Andy, a sixty-four-year-old Uptowner. Andy had bought a condo in Uptown's Sheridan Park area without realizing that most of the buildings on his street were subsidized housing and that he was relocating into the core territory of the Black P. Stones. He said that, after moving into his condo on a Saturday, on Monday morning he encountered a "massive pool of blood" as he left his house to walk to the train. A trail of bloody footprints accompanied him part of the way to the train station. Living in Uptown had a stark political impact on Andy, who had previously considered himself a liberal. This passage from my interview with him is worth quoting in its entirety, because it details the self-conscious transformation he underwent upon moving to Uptown.

> Every night, for approximately three months, there was a riot on the corner. One night I came home and there were eleven police cars in front of my building. And then night after night, constant police, because, the—and I'm going to use the word—the niggers went crazy. The niggers—I'm, all my life I've been a liberal, been a Democrat, I've been equal rights for everybody. But after I moved in there, I hate them! Because they've broken the social contract! There's trash everywhere! When I walked out tonight: garbage everywhere. Because the niggers, excuse the expression, whatever they have in their mouths they throw on the ground. So it's Coke cans, McDonald's bags, potato chips, condoms, everything just thrown and usually in our yard. They attacked the yard one night when I wasn't home. They jumped over the fence, they broke all the furniture, the patio furniture, they broke it all, tore everything apart. They break into cars. They jump up and down on the car roofs until they're dented. They smash the windows. Night after night after night after night.... I have thought many times that I would burn down the [subsidized] building across the street. Like, in the middle of the day, when nobody is home. Burn it down! I don't want to get anybody killed. But get them the fuck out of the neighborhood!

As this passage shows quite vividly, Andy quickly discarded his liberal self-identification as well as the rhetorical conventions of a society that formally embraces racial equality.[7] Andy's political transformation is consistent with modern theories of racism, which suggest that whites' liberal views dissolve as soon as their racial privilege comes under threat.[8] In this case, it seems that Andy's experience of threat was so intense that it not only engendered severe racial hostility but even made him abandon any efforts to hide his racist views from me. Using more cautious language, however, other whites also described how moving to Rogers Park and Uptown had put their liberal beliefs in question. For example, Frank, one leader of Uptown's public safety camp, once said to me that before moving to Uptown, he had "totally believed all that liberal bullshit they taught us in college."

Considering the immense differences between antigentrification activists like Jessica and Phil and anticrime activists like Gayle and Andy, clashes among whites over the politics of crime and race naturally happened with some regularity. In the previous chapter, for instance, I described the way a young white Rogers Parker confronted the Lakesiders over the racial implications of positive loitering. Just as among African American residents, the politics of crime also materialized as *intraracial* conflict among whites. Going even further, however, the following section uncovers an additional line of conflict that fully reverses the conventional line of conflict one would expect to find in a gentrifying neighborhood.

Black-White Conflict, Reversed

Let me return to Wanda, a member of the Northtowners, an Uptown positive loitering group. Wanda was a single parent and worked as a cashier at a local supermarket. She and her daughter lived in a subsidized townhouse in close proximity to one of Uptown's gang hotspots. Wanda sent her daughter to a middle school far across town because she felt that many of the students at the neighborhood school lacked discipline and would have a negative influence on her daughter. Regarding the gang presence, Wanda first and foremost feared for her daughter's safety. A while back, when a group of gang members had moved into a unit in her row of townhouses, Wanda had started going to CAPS meetings and working with the police to have the gang members arrested or evicted. While she believed that the most crucial help she needed would have to come from the police and the alderman, she thought that any intervention might help. She thus also attended one of the outreach meetings that the violence prevention organization CeaseFire held in Uptown.

At the CeaseFire meeting, participants were split up into discussion groups; Wanda and I joined the same one. The task assigned to our group was to find strategies for being "proactive about violence." The group was facilitated by Jaime, a white ONE community organizer in his thirties. Aside from Wanda, Jaime, and myself, there were Craig, an activist with RYCH, and Janelle, a black woman I had not met before. After introductions, Wanda told the group that she lived in close proximity to a group of gang members. She said that she found it hard to conceive of proactive strategies because the gang members would not listen to her. All she could do was to call 911 when she saw them causing trouble. Jaime began his response by saying: "I really hear what you are saying" but then proceeded to argue that the police could not really resolve a complex issue like gang activity. The criminal justice system, he explained, could only lock people away. Once they were released from prison they were sure to resume their previous activities. "That's why," he concluded, "it is important to be proactive rather than reactive." Janelle then revealed that she had spent some time in jail. She found it unfathomable that Wanda simply called the police when she had safety concerns. Wanda remained unfazed, however, and insisted that there was no alternative because the gang members were not going to be impressed by talk. To illustrate the point, she told us a story of something that had happened to her "just yesterday."

As she was walking home, she said, she had passed a group of girls who were often hanging out with the gang members. She imitated one of the girls, making her voice sound belligerent. "What are *you* looking at?!" She reenacted her response: "Nothing? . . . Nothing? Cause that's what I'm looking at, right? Isn't that what you want to be? Nothing?" Wanda's eyes were blazing with anger, and after she had finished we sat in awkward silence. Trying to refocus the group, Jaime asked if anyone had any ideas for how to proactively address violence. Craig suggested a gun buy-back event at which Uptowners would receive gift cards in exchange for handing their guns over to the police, but Wanda commented that she found the idea implausible, pointing out that those who needed to be disarmed were surely not going to turn in their guns voluntarily. Again, silence ensued, now without anyone willing to take the initiative. Jaime turned around on his chair to ask the other group facilitators whether we should end the small group session.

The interaction between Jaime and Wanda reveals an ironic reversal of the lines of conflict one might expect to find in Rogers Park and Uptown. Working-class and black, Wanda sided with the police and the safety activists, dismissing the idea of reducing violent crime through interpersonal engagement and gun buy-back events as leftist fantasies. Jaime, who was white and college-educated, took the racial justice perspective. He tried to convince Wanda that incarcerating gang members would not sustainably solve her problems. What he ignored, of course, was that her main priority was to create a safe environment for her daughter *right away*. Wanda knew that jail would not make the gang members change their ways. That was precisely why they needed to be sent to jail in the first place—they were not going to change.

Wanda's story meshes with Margaret's case and shows just how fervently some low-income African Americans supported the criminal justice system. Examining their social circumstances illuminates that they did so not so much despite but rather *because* of being black and low-income. Since they depended on their subsidized housing units, they saw no alternative to having the gang members arrested in order to live in safety. They supported the idea of preventive interventions, but they did not believe that they could forgo the tools the criminal justice system gave them to possibly achieve a more just society at some distant point in the future. They needed safety *now*. This distinguished them from many whites, including some gentrification critics, who generally had the worst-case option of moving away if things were to get out of hand, even if it meant having to sell a condo or house at a loss.

Conclusion

The politics of crime and gentrification produced a complex tangle of divisions and alliances in Rogers Park and Uptown. All of the relationships within this tangle were in some way related to race, but the groups and organizations that formed did not always align with racial boundaries. Instead, neighborhood activism produced interracial as well as intraracial conflict and collaboration along at least six axes (see figure 7.1).[9] Of course, the most important axis, which overshadowed all others, was black-white conflict (bottom-left to top-right axis in figure 7.1). Since most of the newcomers to Rogers Park and Uptown were white and middle-class while many of those having to fear displacement were black, gentrification was suffused with black-white tension. However, this tension frequently materialized in forms other than black-white conflict, such as internal divisions among blacks or as collaboration among gentrification-critical blacks and whites. In one way

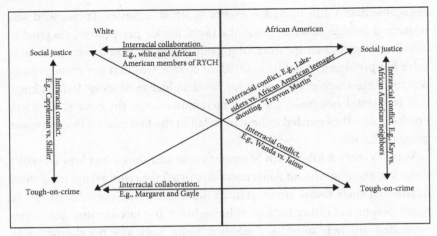

Figure 7.1. Axes of collaboration and conflict between whites and African Americans.

or another, all of these social forms still revolved around the central axis of black-white conflict. Like pain radiating outward from its source, black-white conflict percolated through residents' interactions and relationships. Frequently, it drove them apart. Sometimes, it brought them closer together.

In a nutshell, all of this is to say simply that race shaped but did not *determine* residents' political standpoints and relationships—nor did specific combinations of race, class, and gender. Drawing on the intersectionality framework pioneered by scholars like Kimberlé Crenshaw (1989) and Patricia Hill Collins (2000), I explored whether considering other identities in combination with residents' racial categories could account for the political heterogeneity I encountered. For explaining divergent politics among African Americans, Michael Dawson (1994) and William Julius Wilson (1978) have pointed to class, but I found no clear-cut pattern in this regard. Middle- and working-class blacks could be found in both the safety and the justice camps. I also looked specifically at gender. After noticing that many of the black safety activists were single mothers, I considered protective concern for their children as an explanation for why they worked with the police and the white safety activists. But I also found contrasting cases of single black mothers living in high-violence areas who decried police harassment and gentrification rather than the gang threat. Among whites, class and gender did not determine political standpoints either.[10]

In principle, the indeterminacy of social identities should come as no surprise to sociologists. Building on the work of the classic scholars George Herbert Mead (1934), Alfred Schütz (1967 [1932]), and Max Weber (1978 [1922]), most sociologists acknowledge the importance of meaning-making and must therefore allow for the possibility that similar people in similar circumstances will sometimes reach different political conclusions. This indeterminacy applies to race as well as other identities that inform meaning-making. Specifically for the case of black politics, Stuart Hall (2017:78) writes: "there is no way of limiting or trying to fix the varieties of subjects that black people will become." Hall's argument, of course, holds true not just for black people but for all racial groups.

If one accepts this line of reasoning, political heterogeneity among similarly situated individuals cannot come as a shock. Especially in the study of race and racial conflict, however, scholars frequently construe racial groups as more or less homogeneous entities and thus often discount within-group variation.[11] This may be appropriate for establishing a parsimonious and therefore powerful understanding of America's social landscape—sketching the general contours of racial conflict necessitates abstracting from the messy nuances that individual lives frequently exhibit. Nevertheless, the types of conflict and collaboration I have discussed in this chapter should not be overlooked. Scholars must beware of reducing social action to a mechanical enactment of identity categories. If they do reduce it this way, they overlook a host of important positions and constellations, including the intraracial friction and interracial cooperation that can exist even in the context of exorbitant racial inequality, enduring racism, and salient intergroup conflict. A comprehensive approach to race should thus incorporate unusual political alignments—white anti-racists like Jessica and Phil but also Margaret and Kay, who found themselves on the awkward margins of black politics in Rogers Park.

8

Crime and Gentrification beyond Black and White

The most heavily contested intergroup axis in the politics of crime and gentrification in Rogers Park and Uptown was the fraught relationship between African Americans and whites. But both neighborhoods were hyperdiverse, serving as metropolitan hubs for several immigrant ethnic communities.[1] Uptown's Argyle area was known as a destination for Southeast Asian cuisine and shopping throughout the Chicago metropolitan area. Rogers Park housed a great number of Latinos and Caribbeans. And the Far North Side overall contained large Sub-Saharan African communities with well-established religious institutions, businesses, and community associations.[2]

The accounts of activism and politics in the preceding chapters have mentioned these ethnic communities only in passing. The reason for this is that, surprisingly, members of these communities hardly ever became involved in the political debates about crime and affordability that were raging in Rogers Park and Uptown. I neither observed a substantial immigrant presence in the related forms of activism, nor did I register serious efforts to elect an alderman who was neither African American nor non-Hispanic white. In Rogers Park, I found no such candidate over the entire period between 1991 and 2019. In Uptown's 46th Ward, three candidates with immigrant backgrounds ran in 2011 to succeed Alderwoman Shiller—but with very limited success.[3]

Nevertheless, the immigrants' absence from the neighborhoods' political fields raises new questions. Why did these residents so rarely participate in community activism? Were they not affected by street crime and gentrification? In addition, notwithstanding their limited participation, how did they perceive the challenges and changes the neighborhoods were facing?

This chapter portrays the perspectives of three additional ethnoracial communities: East and Southeast Asians inhabiting Uptown's Argyle enclave,

Us versus Them. Jan Doering, Oxford University Press (2020) © Oxford University Press.
DOI: 10.1093/oso/9780190066574.001.0001

Latinos living on and around Clark Street in Rogers Park, and Sub-Saharan Africans residing in either neighborhood. Other ethnic contexts could also be investigated. And for all of the communities I discuss, more nuanced experiences might certainly be uncovered.[4] Nonetheless, the purpose of this chapter is not to strive for a comprehensive description of all local groups, which research in the community studies tradition would aim to accomplish. Instead, the goal here is to trace the ways the contested questions of urban change this book explores presented themselves to members of other ethnoracial communities. As the chapter will show, crime and gentrification affected each community quite differently and not always in the ways one might expect.

African Immigrants, Caught in the Middle

While immigrants rarely participated in the politics of crime and gentrification, Sub-Saharan Africans,[5] who formed sizable communities in both neighborhoods, sometimes became entangled in the attendant conflicts. Many Africans inhabited exactly those low-income apartment buildings that safety activists and the aldermen singled out as "problem buildings." Just like working-class African Americans, these immigrants were therefore directly exposed to gang violence and related problems but were also subjected to invasive policing and security measures. This put African immigrants in an awkward intermediate position in the debates about gentrification and crime.

Interviewing Sebele, a youth worker for the Ethiopian Community Association, I discovered that she had a lot to say about Africans' experience of crime. The Ethiopian Community Association operated out of a building just off Clark Street in Rogers Park but had previously been located at the intersection of Sheridan and Lawrence in Uptown, across from Lawrence House. Many of the organization's clients lived in the affordable rental towers close to that intersection. Sebele said:

> Some of [the clients], they live in low-income housing. We used to get a lot of violence. You know, we even had people shooting when our kids were playing in the playground. And we would see fights all the time.... We have kids in the program, who have seen, like, dead bodies and things like that. It does affect them.

The community association's current Rogers Park location was safer, but Sebele thought that street crime nonetheless continued to constrain the daily routines and options of African children and teenagers. She said:

> Like Pottawattomie Park [in Rogers Park]—I would never take the kids. I know what goes on there. I live right in front of it. What kind of teens hang out there and stuff. . . . And [our kids] are lacking [a safe park], because if their families are in a low-income building, they never see the outside. They never go outside. Everything they do: they come, they go to school, they go to the building, they go to school, they go to the building. But they need a place where they're really safe, a park, or have a chance to play. And this is the only place they have to do it, when they come here [to the community association's building].

One concern that is already implicit in Sebele's statement is that, in addition to facing potential stray bullets, African teenagers could also be at risk of becoming involved in crime themselves.[6] Sebele told me that a gang had recruited one Ethiopian high school student a few years ago. She said that African students "are easily targeted, because they don't know what a gang is." Consequently, Sebele's youth program as well as other African community organizations offered gang awareness seminars.

Some Africans were also painfully familiar with criminalization. I met a young African man, Ademola, at Hope for Youth, an intensive mentoring and consciousness-raising program for "at risk" youth that was run out of a Rogers Park church. I cannot say anything specific about Ademola's prior interactions with the criminal justice system—one rule for me in observing Hope for Youth events was that I did not ask questions about criminal backgrounds or gang affiliations. But Hope for Youth only worked with teenagers who had been in serious trouble and, in most cases, had been expelled from school. One time, during a social justice book club that Hope for Youth hosted, the participants—four young black men and a few white social justice activists—discussed personal experiences with criminalization and police harassment after reading excerpts from Michelle Alexander's (2010) *The New Jim Crow*. The unique details of those encounters aside, Ademola had undergone the same ordeals as the African American participants—incessant police stops, seemingly random interrogations, repeated charges of wrongdoing and stigmatization in school, and more.

Consequently, at least some Africans shared with African Americans disturbing experiences of racial marginalization that would indicate a basis for mutual political activism. I did not see this potential materialize, however, and actually heard more about conflict between these ethnoracial groups. For instance, Darrel and Wes, the two African American leaders of Uptown's RYCH, said that there was quite a bit of tension between Africans and African Americans about the issues of crime and gentrification in Uptown. Darrel and Wes found this distressing because they treasured their African roots, which they had studied and explored. Darrel explicitly bemoaned this tension: "to me, that's like brothers fighting." But he explained that it was important for immigrants to recognize that African Americans had come to the United States under fundamentally different circumstances than what voluntary immigrants experienced. Darrel said that African Americans deserved solidarity and recognition from African immigrants due to their shared heritage, but he did not feel that support.

Judging from the occasional conversations I had with Africans, it indeed seemed that there was more of an emphasis on distancing African communities from African Americans than on racial solidarity. Sebele, the Ethiopian youth worker, acknowledged that black teenagers faced police harassment, but she commented that not only the officers were to blame. She believed that there was "a certain way of dressing or putting your hair up" that encouraged the officers to stop teenagers. Her program participants, she said, "know I will not allow them, they'll put their pants up. Once they leave this building, they might pull them down. I have no control over that." But according to Sebele, Africans could and should limit police harassment by dressing differently from the way (some of) the African American teenagers did. The question whether to embrace African American styles of dress or not resembles the difficult identity challenges Mary Waters (1999) describes in her work on black Caribbeans.[7] But for people like Sebele, who were doing their utmost to support the teenagers' success in school and college, the choice was clear: African teenagers had to distance themselves from African Americans.

As a further sign of division, in shared housing environments, African tenants sometimes consented to security measures that some African Americans found unacceptably punitive. This difference could then pit Africans and African Americans against one another. I observed such a conflict at a subsidized rental tower located in one of Uptown's gang territories.[8] The building was indexed on Alderman Cappleman's problem building list; his office consistently urged the building management to reduce crime in and around the building. There certainly were problems. One time, I attended a CeaseFire shooting vigil just outside the building after a man had been shot in the chest upon leaving it.

The building was governed by a residents' association, and the association's elected chair, Mr. Jakande, was an African immigrant. Facing pressure from Alderman Cappleman, Mr. Jakande and the association made aggressive strides to thwart crime. A comprehensive CCTV system, which monitored the elevators, corridors, and outside spaces, had been installed. Security staff had been instructed to admit no visitors who could or would not present an ID. Evictions were also forcefully pursued. At a public safety steering committee meeting with Alderman Cappleman, Mr. Jakande promised: "I have been living in this building for thirty-five years, but now we are turning this building around. We have finally made a dent."

The stringent measures Mr. Jakande embraced alienated some African American tenants. Erica, whom I knew through the Northtowners' positive loitering events, was one; she believed that the residents' association had specifically ordered African Americans to be evicted. Erica was a kindhearted woman around fifty and formerly homeless. In October 2012, she invited me for lunch to show me her apartment and tell me about the building. At 11 a.m. that day, she called me, crying, to tell me that one of her friends had just received an eviction notice because he had fallen behind on his rent. Erica said that over the last two weeks, "they have put fifteen people out of the building. And they are all black Americans. I am just so worried because he's the only friend I have in the building. And he is the only African American; all the others are Africans." She said that she did not trust the African tenants because they were "flighty." And since she had distributed brochures about free legal support for residents facing eviction, she thought that the residents' association now wanted to see her evicted, too. While this did not happen, her impression that African American tenants were systematically targeted did not change. Leticia, another fieldwork acquaintance living in the building, said that she also felt targeted. She complained that her son's friends, most of whom were African American, were treated harshly by security staff and sometimes prevented from entering the building, while other visitors were admitted without scrutiny.

I cannot assess their accuracy, but the claims Darrel, Wes, Erica, and Leticia made about Africans reveal that at least some African Americans perceived intergroup conflict rather than racial solidarity. Despite shared concerns and experiences, strain between Africans and African Americans thus appeared to be more salient than a mutual politics of resisting gentrification and police harassment.

Apathy in "Asia on Argyle"

Uptown's ethnoracial character changed noticeably as one approached Argyle Street in Uptown's northeastern section, the commercial artery of a vibrant Asian enclave. Bounded approximately by Ainslie Street, Foster Avenue, Broadway, and Sheridan Road, this enclave went by various names: Little Saigon and New Chinatown as well as "Asia on Argyle," an appropriately panethnic moniker featured on a large sign that had recently been installed next to the Chicago Transit Authority train station. In the late 1960s and early 1970s, Chinese Chicagoans had bought a considerable part of the real estate in the area, much of which was then sitting empty, to create a "Chinatown North" that was to complement Chicago's well-established Chinatown on the city's Near South Side. In order to anchor this community, the investors had established a commercial row along Argyle Street. Several years later, the Chinese residents had been joined by hundreds of Vietnamese, Laotian, and Cambodian refugees who had fled Southeast Asia in the aftermath of the Communist victory in Vietnam.[9]

In 2014, the area still boasted a distinctly Asian flavor and continued to serve as a shopping destination especially for Southeast Asians living throughout the metropolitan area. Those residents who attained middle-class status tended to leave Uptown for the suburbs while often keeping their jobs and businesses in the Argyle enclave. Nevertheless, enough immigrants from East and Southeast Asia had continued to arrive to keep the area Asian-dominated. In addition to them, several subsidized housing buildings and residential hotels appeared to house mostly African Americans. To the east of Sheridan Road—and thus outside the Asian enclave—a string of city blocks running along the lakefront was occupied by expensive mansions and condominiums mostly inhabited by white Uptowners.

The Asian enclave had limited clout in urban politics. While the various Asian groups coexisted peacefully, they nonetheless formed more or less detached communities. In addition to separate religious institutions, there were separate ethnic associations, the Chinese Mutual Aid Association and the Vietnamese Association of Illinois. Obviously, this split made it difficult to advocate for the area when communicating with aldermen and the city administration. To gain a sense of the area's lack of political cohesion, it suffices to consider Andy Lam's 2011 aldermanic campaign. A Chinese American and member of the Chinese Mutual Aid Association's board of directors, Lam competed for the open seat in the 46th Ward to succeed Alderwoman Shiller. But Lam received only 187 votes, putting him second to last in a field of eleven candidates. I should add that in 2011, the Argyle enclave was still divided between Wards 46 and 48 (Edgewater), which certainly made it harder for the enclave's residents to assert their political voice.[10] But even after taking this into account, Lam's tally was quite low, and it stands to reason that a result of this kind would not help to increase the attention the aldermen paid to the Argyle community.

A public safety meeting Alderman Osterman (48th Ward) held for the Argyle area in 2013 neatly illustrated these complications. An Asian American police officer who both worked and lived in the Argyle area— and one of the only Asians I ever saw at a public safety meeting—charged that residents and organizations felt neglected and were unsure whether the aldermen would help them if they reached out. Osterman promised improvements but, for his part, bemoaned that the Asian community was "fractured" and that it was difficult to secure the cooperation of business owners and local ethnic organizations. Nonetheless, at Osterman's request, the local police district eventually assigned a foot patrol officer to Argyle Street in order to build connections with residents and to help address their concerns.

In terms of crime and disorder, Argyle residents complained about several different issues. There were occasional muggings. Sex workers sometimes walked the area in search of customers. Residents also criticized the residential hotels and subsidized housing providers for allegedly failing to control their residents. Groups of men drinking from paper-bagged bottles could frequently be seen on and off Argyle Street. A more serious concern was that the area, in its southwestern corner, abutted the Gangster Disciples territory around the intersection of Lawrence Avenue and Sheridan Road, where Lawrence House was located. Gang loitering, drug dealing, and violence thus sometimes spilled over into the Argyle area.

The Argyle community's limited political influence and internal divisions made dealing with crime more difficult. But another issue was that many of the Asian residents apparently hesitated to call the police or participate in public safety initiatives. I hardly ever saw any Asian Americans at CAPS meetings, positive loitering, or block club events—even in this

Asian-dominated area. The Chinese Mutual Aid Association employed a staff member, Paul Wong, who sometimes served as an intermediary for residents who had been victimized. He said that he did this especially when residents had been robbed or when drug dealing outside their businesses kept customers away. He explained: "we are like a lighthouse for them. They come over here, I call the police for them, and I do some follow up for them." In addition to language barriers and a lack of familiarity with the American criminal justice system, Mr. Wong pointed out that residents believed that nothing good could come from interacting with the police. He said: "in some Asian countries, the police . . . means trouble. Like the Chinese police. [The residents] say, 'If you are alive, don't go to the cops. If you are dead, don't go to hell.'" Insofar as Mr. Wong's assessment was correct, it would certainly be difficult to imagine the enclave's residents participating in safety initiatives that necessarily entailed contact with police officers. But Mr. Wong did what he could to encourage the residents to be proactive. He kept a stash of CAPS informational brochures that had been translated to make them accessible for the Asian residents. The Chinese Mutual Aid Association had also held seminars on street safety and burglary prevention.

Argyle's public safety activists certainly perceived a need to mobilize more Asian Americans in order to more effectively reduce crime and disorder. In 2012, newly elected Alderman Osterman launched a public safety steering committee for the 48th Ward. One of its objectives was to identify strategies for tackling problems in the Argyle area. In its final report, the committee—which contained white and black but no Asian residents—outlined three goals: to reduce the number of "problem buildings," to shrink the gang territory, and to "solicit and encourage immigrant and minority populations to become more involved in public safety efforts." The action steps the committee recommended for attaining these goals were utterly pedestrian, however, and basically revolved around creating relationships with ethnic community organizations.

I do not think that the CAPS and block club activists living in the area actually believed that Asians' participation could realistically be improved, because I noticed a good deal of fatigue and even cynicism in relation to this issue. As an older white woman once complained at one of the steering committee meetings: "we have been going down to Argyle, asking the businesses to put up CAPS flyers, and they just say 'No, I don't want anything to do with this.' Cultural difference. That's our barrier!" Expressing her frustration, she threw up her hands.

Another time, I spent an evening with Henry and William along Sheridan Road in the Argyle area for National Night Out, an annual positive loitering event organized by the National Association of Town Watch. Henry and William were committed safety activists: they were longtime block club members, CAPS participants, and positive loiterers. Early that evening, we observed a group of approximately fifty Asian seniors gathering in a local park for outdoor yoga under the leadership of a young white instructor. Henry told me that the Chinese Mutual Aid Association had organized this part of the event. As we watched the yoga exercises, I asked Henry and William whether they received good support from the Asian community for their efforts to reduce crime. William scoffed and said: "I see them once every year: here at National Night Out." Henry seemed slightly embarrassed by the tone of William's reply and, perhaps to add something more positive, said that he had two reliable contacts, Paul Wong and an influential local business owner. But overall, the safety activists seemed to feel that the Asians were free-riding—enjoying the fruits borne by safety initiatives without actively contributing to them.

Asian residents did appreciate the safety activists' efforts but also perceived a degree of condescension and paternalism. I first recognized this when I interviewed Julie, a Chinese American longtime business owner. She told me that she had been robbed twice in Uptown, first when she was only fifteen and helping out in her parents' restaurant. She felt that the neighborhood had certainly become safer since then and gave some of the credit to the safety activists. She said: "it helped that a lot of more affluent people moved into the neighborhood that cared about it." However, she added:

> They kind of expect, expected that we would do things their way because they're the new residents and because they can vote and they pay the taxes. . . . It took them a long time to finally let go of that kind of "We're in charge" grudge. But I don't think it will happen overnight. Maybe in thirty years, if another graduate student sits in front of me and asks me the same questions, I might be able to tell them that it's better.

In relation to gentrification and displacement, I observed no anxiety on the part of the Asian residents. The Asian character of the area was firmly established and, during the time of my fieldwork, was further reinforced by an urban beautification program that included developing the "Asia on Argyle" brand. While rents were rising, I heard no concerns about a lack of affordable housing for Asian residents. Mr. Wong, for example, said that the area continued to serve as a first place of settlement for many Asian immigrants because it was still inexpensive for them to live there. As for the growing wealth in the area, Asian business owners enthusiastically welcomed the increasing customer demand and spending power. In this regard, little had changed since Japonica Brown-Saracino (2009:236) studied the area between 2001 and 2005, reporting that Asian business owners "express an appreciation for gentrification that would surprise many [gentrification critics]."

Latinos and the Clark Street Community

Beginning in the 1960s, sizeable Latino communities developed in Rogers Park and Uptown. In Uptown, the Latino presence declined markedly after the onset of accelerated gentrification in the 1990s. In 2010, only about 13 percent of Uptown's residents still identified as Hispanic or Latino. Few visible vestiges of the neighborhood's Puerto Rican and Mexican communities remained. Rogers Park on the other hand maintained a large Latino population. In 2010, a quarter of Rogers Parkers identified as Latino. Many of the neighborhood's Latino residents lived in an enclave situated on and around Clark Street between Devon Avenue and Howard Street in the western part of Rogers Park. The enclave housed especially Mexican Americans but also Puerto Ricans, Peruvians, and other Latin Americans. Along with the inevitable corner stores and fast food joints, Clark Street was lined with shops selling quinceañera dresses, money transfer businesses, and Latin American restaurants. The annual Clark Street festival had a world music theme but specifically celebrated the area's Mexican identity with mariachi bands and the typical oompah tuba sounds.[11]

The Latin Kings claimed the Rogers Park section of Clark Street as their territory.[12] Interestingly, however, Rogers Parkers rarely ever talked or wrote about the Latin Kings. While the other gang crews in Rogers Park and Uptown were persistently at war with each other between 2011 and 2014, the Latin Kings did not participate in any of the local fighting. Hector, a Latino CeaseFire violence prevention worker, explained that the Latin Kings were content to be "just standing back" from the ongoing clashes so long as no one infringed on their territory or challenged the gang in some other way. Hector said:

These guys work. They're family men. They're good brothers, regular guys. They do whatever they do at their house, and then when it's time to come out, they have to come out.

For daily life in the neighborhood, this meant that the Latin Kings did not maintain a steady public presence along Clark Street, although Hector assured me that any incursion into their territory by other gangs would be noticed straight away. Hector pointed out that the Latin Kings regarded their gang affiliation as well as their territory not so much as an opportunity to make money but rather as a source of identity and honor. Other knowledgeable observers confirmed Hector's perspective. Robert was a preacher of Puerto Rican and Irish origins who had himself been in a gang as a young man. He was well connected in Rogers Park's underworld because he ran a ministry that specifically counseled gang members. He said: "the difference between a Latin gang and a black gang is: a black gang will fight for the position to make money from drugs, the drug market. A Latino gang, they just fight to fight." Since no other gang challenged the Latin Kings on Clark Street at the time, however, they remained largely invisible. Accordingly, the topic of the Latin Kings was almost never raised at CAPS or violence prevention meetings and none of the Rogers Parkers I spoke with identified the Latin Kings as a major issue of concern.

Even the police agreed. I interviewed a community organizer working for CAPS, Mayra Gomez, who was Mexican American. She served as a liaison between the police and residents, businesses, and community organizations. One of her projects was to establish and supervise CAPS meetings in Spanish for the Clark Street community in order to improve residents' communication and cooperation with the police. I asked her about the impact the Latin Kings had on the area. Given that they did not partake in drug dealing, I was wondering whether they might be running a protection or money laundering scheme or some other illicit activity that would remain largely hidden from public view. However, Mayra explained that the residents and businesses in the area did not face any particular threat from the Latin Kings. About the presence of the gang in the Clark Street community, she said: "it's a problem, but it's not an aggressive problem." Instead, she said that the main issue for Latino residents was the language barrier when communicating with the police, as well as a certain degree of concern about immigration enforcement—although she was quick to add that Chicago Police Department officers would never ask residents about their immigration status, Chicago being a "sanctuary city."

The Latin Kings themselves thus did not raise many concerns, but Latinos were obviously not living in isolation from the problems that troubled Rogers Park and Uptown. Certainly, Latino parents might have worried about seeing their children recruited into a gang, for example. For the Latin Kings, I was told that this was unlikely to happen, because gang membership was typically passed down within families. Robert, the gang ministry preacher, said: "you have generations of generations of young men who are in gangs. In a Latino organization, you're seeing a young man ten years old, his father twenty-two [sic] years old, his grandfather thirty-eight years old. And they are all Latin Kings." Hector from CeaseFire said that he had not heard of the Latin Kings pressuring students into joining them. He said: "you don't see that much of these guys trying to intimidate people. I'm thinking [people join] maybe more because of a sense of belonging that they want."

On the other hand Gangster Disciples crews in both Rogers Park and Uptown did pressure students to join, including Latinos. Reflecting this fact, some of the shooting victims I learned about were young Latino men.[13] Nevertheless, most Latino parents did not seem to be concerned about gang recruitment. I interviewed Doris Andrade, a staff member at Centro Romero, the largest Latino social service organization on the Far North Side, to ask her about gang recruitment and the corresponding concerns Latino parents might have. Centro Romero was located along Clark Street in Edgewater—between Rogers Park and Uptown—but served Latino residents from all over Chicago's Far North Side. Doris told me that she knew of only one Latino student who had been pressured to join a gang. She had referred him to Alternatives, a youth program in Uptown with particular expertise in the area of gang prevention, and believed that the young man was now doing fine. Centro Romero itself did not have specific programs for violence prevention or gang recruitment, and Doris did not consider such programs necessary, given that the Latino youth she encountered where very much focused on their academic success. Similarly, I interviewed Maria, a Mexican American college student who had grown up around Clark Street and still worked for the youth program at a local Catholic church. Maria said that neither the Latino teenagers in the church programs nor their parents had broached the topic of gang recruitment.

Regarding gentrification as the counterpart of the politics of crime, I again witnessed very little Latino concern or involvement. In this regard, my findings replicate Ellen Berrey's (2015:162) conclusion that "Latino residents were all but absent from development politics." Many of the Latino residents in the Clark Street enclave had bought houses, which reduced their vulnerability to displacement. Of course, many others were renters and might have well been affected by condo conversions and rising rents. One explanation for their absence from antigentrification activism might be that rampant gentrification had not quite reached Clark Street by 2014, when I concluded my fieldwork. On the other hand, as I've mentioned, gentrification had certainly affected the Latino community in Uptown—indeed so much so that only a fraction remained. Prior research on Uptown suggests that Latinos did participate in antigentrification activism in the 1980s and 1990s,[14] but this was no longer the case when I studied the neighborhood.

As a general rule, I only ever saw groups of Latinos at social justice events that brought out unusually large crowds, such as a peace march that ONE held in Rogers Park in the summer of 2012. That year, ONE drew on funds obtained through President Obama's Neighborhood Recovery Initiative and used them to establish a parent support network that included Latino residents. At the peace march, most of the Latinos I saw wore buttons that identified them as members of that parent network. But no durable Latino community mobilization emerged from this initiative. After funding for the program ran out, I again saw very few Latinos at social justice events, even the larger ones.

Conclusion

These brief snapshots show that crime and gentrification influenced ethnoracial communities differently. Latinos in Rogers Park's Clark Street enclave could afford to ignore political conflict because neither crime nor gentrification directly affected them very much. This tranquility could well have been disrupted if the Latin Kings had become embroiled in gang conflict or if a major influx of wealthy residents or real estate money had occurred. But neither of these things happened, and I cannot assess how the Clark Street community would have responded. By contrast, the Asian enclave in Uptown's Argyle area did have to grapple with street crime and violence on a regular basis. Asian residents certainly worried about this problem, much more than they seemed to worry about gentrification, which suggests that Asian residents and organizations would have been natural allies for Uptown's public safety camp. This is exactly what the safety activists thought, but to their frustration, very few Asians participated in safety initiatives or even called the police. As a result, there were feelings of resentment on both sides. Some safety activists resented the Asians' lack of support; some Asians found the safety activists to be overbearing.

Sub-Saharan African immigrants, finally, were affected by both crime and gentrification. Unlike Uptown's Asians and Rogers Park's Latinos, the Africans did not have an enclave that could at least partly shield them from the problems of the surrounding neighborhood. Instead, they frequently lived in the areas and even buildings that constituted the main battlegrounds in the fight over displacement and crime on the Far North Side. Due to their racial category, furthermore, they sometimes faced the same confrontations with the police and suspicious neighbors that African Americans so frequently experienced. In principle, African residents were thus structurally positioned between the safety and the antigentrification camps, but they generally appeared to accept the safety camp's focus on policing and social control.

Despite their sometimes inescapable entanglement in neighborhood conflicts, very little activism emerged from the three ethnoracial communities I've discussed here. But even these brief descriptions show that the racial confrontations in both neighborhoods did shape immigrants' social experiences. Frustration, distrust, and antagonism between activists, leaders, and organizations ran too deep to remain confined to non-Hispanic whites and African Americans. In addition, of course, many activist projects regarding housing and social control depended on basic support from immigrants. When the resulting encounters with immigrant residents did not go smoothly, such tensions were sometimes framed in ethnoracial terms—just like the tensions between safety and social justice activists. Thus, additional dividing lines occasionally became salient— African Americans resenting Africans for their perceived lack of solidarity; whites resenting Asians for their lack of involvement; and so forth. While very few Africans, Asians, or Latinos ever attended public safety or social justice events, it would thus be incorrect to suggest that they were disconnected from the politics of crime and gentrification. Instead, the larger conflicts in Rogers Park and Uptown were inflected by the specific ethnic, socioeconomic, and residential conditions that structured these residents' lives.

9

Conclusion

For the title of his 1997 assessment of race relations in America, sociologist Orlando Patterson chose *The Ordeal of Integration*. In the book, Patterson (1997:15) argued that "nothing short of astonishing" progress toward a more racially just society had been made since the civil rights movement and that this very success had increased racial tensions. Coming into increased contact in all spheres of society, black and white Americans were encountering a greater potential for strife. Patterson (52) believed that this was both necessary and transitory: "[things] appear to get worse, and are perceived as getting worse, because they are getting better. If the integration of two groups legally and socially separated for more than 350 years does not produce friction, it is the surest sign that no meaningful change has taken place." I am not sure whether the tensions I observed in Rogers Park and Uptown reflected progress in Patterson's sense. Certainly, many residents invoked the neighborhoods' residential integration as a sign of an increasingly open, tolerant society. When they temporarily put aside the contentious issues that divided them, residents of all backgrounds and persuasions indulged in the "happy talk" of racial diversity, expressing appreciation for the positive experiences and opportunities that residential integration enabled.[1] At the same time, Patterson's description of integration as an "ordeal" felt luminous during my fieldwork. The competing problems of crime and gentrification brought this ordeal out all too clearly. When I asked left-leaning residents about crime, their faces would sometimes drop in disappointment that this was what I had decided to study. Could I not see that white gentrifiers instrumentalized the suffering of criminalized black youth to push an agenda of racial displacement? On the other hand when safety activists heard me say that I was interested in learning how communities responded to crime, some chuckled and said: "well, you've come to the right place." Implicit in their laconic responses were the frustrations they had experienced in trying to make their neighborhoods safer. Why did some people make their hard work even harder by charging that it was racist to do so? In other words, all residents were wrestling

Us versus Them. Jan Doering, Oxford University Press (2020) © Oxford University Press.
DOI: 10.1093/oso/9780190066574.001.0001

with the complex tangle that race, crime, and gentrification formed. It was hanging over Rogers Park and Uptown like a dark cloud.

At the same time, the national context loomed forebodingly. In 2012, the shooting of Trayvon Martin in Sanford, Florida, ignited outrage and protest that later congealed into the Black Lives Matter movement, while police shootings of unarmed African Americans continued unabated. Meanwhile, it became apparent to Chicagoans that the steep declines in street crime and violence, which the city had experienced since the 1990s, had ended for the time being. Once again Chicagoans began to use the term "murder capital," as such divergent figures as Spike Lee and Donald Trump decried Chicago's gun violence.[2] Of course, Rogers Park and Uptown were never the locus of these problems. Crime there was a far cry from the dire situation in neighborhoods like Austin and Englewood, nor did a contentious case of police brutality occur on the Far North Side during the time of my fieldwork. But as residents of integrated neighborhoods, Rogers Parkers and Uptowners felt tied to these problems. Their neighborhoods bridged the divergent social worlds of privileged white neighborhoods and what some considered the high-crime "ghetto."[3]

Residents drew one of two political conclusions from all of this. Some concluded that they had to vigilantly protect their neighborhoods from rampant gentrification to make sure that at least a few thousand working-class black and Latino Chicagoans could live in a relatively safe and prosperous environment. Others concluded that in order for residential integration to work, they had to prevent crime from spiraling out of control and toward the dreaded conditions characterizing parts of the city's South Side and West Side. Some of those living in local gang hotspots claimed that their areas were already just as bad.

A neutral observer might interject that these positions were by no means incompatible. Why not fight for a safe and safely *integrated* neighborhood? While I occasionally heard appeals to this effect, they were almost always made by safety activists trying to neutralize racial challenges that framed their anticrime initiatives as racist. In practice, the neighborhoods' polarized political fields meant that reducing crime and protecting affordability and integration were largely seen as mutually exclusive goals. This division was deeper and more palpable in Uptown than in Rogers Park but nonetheless frequently materialized in both neighborhoods, pitting neighbors, activists, politicians, and community organizations against one another.

Race was at the moral and political core of these battles, although neither neighborhood was neatly divided along racial lines. Even in Uptown, where ongoing clashes in the political field further aggravated racial division, some residents collaborated across racial boundaries within the public safety and antigentrification camps. Nevertheless, the persistent tug of war over the racial implications of fighting crime left many people feeling alienated and aggrieved by their neighbors. These tensions not only unfolded as interracial conflict *between* whites and blacks but also inflected relationships *within* these groups. Moreover, community conflict sometimes drew in other ethnoracial groups, materializing across different axes, such as African versus African American or white versus Asian. From a bird's-eye perspective, therefore, the cases of Rogers Park and Uptown show how racial politics affect community patterns not just intensively but also extensively, reaching far and wide into many and perhaps *all* social relationships.

The Neighborhood Politics of Crime and Gentrification

Vital material outcomes depended on how individuals negotiated the politics of race and crime. When, if ever, was it acceptable or necessary to call the police? Was there a racially appropriate way for white residents to engage in civic safety initiatives, and if so, what was it? Under what circumstances, if any, were people justified in voting for a tough-on-crime politician? The ways residents answered these questions had substantial effects on racial inequality and urban change in Rogers Park and Uptown.

Urban scholars have long recognized the challenges crime poses for residential integration. Major scholarly works, including at least two classics of the urban ethnography tradition, have examined how whites and the community organizations they control adjust to the perceived risk of community decline and rapid racial turnover that they anticipate as a byproduct of integration.[4] But today, the direction of racial change tends to be reversed in the American city. As part of what Derek Hyra (2015) describes as the "back-to-the-city movement," educated, middle-class whites are seeking out inner-city neighborhoods, aspiring to secure attractive and reasonably priced housing that is situated close to professional opportunities and urban amenities. Gang violence, street crime, and notably also the ways they are perceived certainly constrain the residential options middle-class urbanites consider.[5] But some accept undesirable neighborhood conditions, hoping that they are temporary and will be eventually resolved. This was the case for many new as well as longtime residents in Rogers Park and Uptown.

Some residents took it upon themselves to actively address neighborhood problems by becoming involved in public safety initiatives. Those residents, I found, wielded a nontrivial degree of influence over the urban landscape. They strategically used the resources and direct access to the police, the state's attorney's office, and other agents of social control CAPS still provided, despite continued budget cuts. They also systematically called the police, using specific phrases and terms that would prioritize their requests to attain more patrols and police interventions. They went to court to advocate for tougher sentencing. They participated in positive loitering to reclaim street corners and other community spaces. Targeting units or buildings that seemed to shelter gang members or drug dealers, they demanded housing inspections and evictions, and sometimes triggered the transformation of entire buildings into boutique real estate. Their initiatives may have reduced crime—answering that question would require a different study design—but they certainly advanced gentrification, whether this was the safety activists' true goal or not.

Low-income residents, especially those who were black or Latino and thus more likely to be targeted by the police, found themselves in a difficult position. As Lance Freeman (2006) has argued, they could benefit from lower crime, greater neighborhood stability, and affluent neighbors. Gentrification could increase local job opportunities and improve schools, public transportation, and other city services. But minority residents also incurred costs. Most obviously, some found themselves displaced from the neighborhoods altogether as their buildings were refashioned into upscale housing. Burdensome for those who could stay, furthermore, were the frequent experiences of surveillance, suspicion, and harassment that stigmatized many blacks and Latinos. Many residents reported having undergone at least some such experiences—from being thrown onto the hood of a police car after walking home from playing basketball to simply being persistently watched and scrutinized. As an African American barber in his forties told me outside his shop: "sometimes, I am just standing here by the door, drinking a cup of coffee and smoking a cigarette, and I can see the police driving by slowly, eying over."

This book shows that these harmful forms of racial marginalization could not be attributed solely to zealous police officers or even the racial biases individual 911 callers might have had. The encompassing climate of social control in Rogers Park and Uptown resulted at least in part from safety activists' deliberate and coordinated efforts to draw in more police officers, housing inspectors, and other state agents. In addition, by demanding that the police act more preemptively and forcefully to suppress crime and violence, the safety activists encouraged an aggressive style of "warrior policing" that targeted black and Latino residents in particular.[6]

Accordingly, I argue that there is a demand side to interventions like police stops, evictions, CCTV surveillance, restrictions on the use of public spaces, and more. Police officers and other agents of social control implement these interventions not only as a simple result of independent state initiative— rather, their efforts are *also* influenced by the grievances and demands that vocal citizens and nonstate organizations articulate. This was true for invasive policing and housing interventions in Rogers Park and Uptown but is also true for other cases.[7] For instance, Forrest Stuart (2016) has argued that the mode of "therapeutic policing" in Los Angeles's Skid Row emerged when large service providers used the city's public safety consultations to reshape policing such that it would funnel low-income residents into their institutions and programs.

In principle, community policing and direct coordination with the police is democratic and therefore desirable, but it is not surprising that the most vocal citizens and well-resourced organizations will dominate and use this access to their advantage. They are in a much better position to exert influence through mechanisms of public consultation than low-income residents, whose immediate needs are often too pressing to consistently attend community meetings. Racially and socioeconomically biased modes of social control may then result.

Demand-side initiatives to marshal state interventions that contribute to neighborhood change materialize specifically in gentrifying and racially diverse neighborhoods. Media reports indicate this as much as scholarly work.[8] Analyzing 311 service requests from New York City, Joscha Legewie and Merlin Schaeffer (2016) found that people living in heterogeneous areas are particularly likely to complain about noise, public drinking, and other nuisances. Likewise, Matthew Desmond and Nicol Valdez (2013) have shown that "problem building" interventions, which result from recurrent 911 service requests and frequently yield evictions, cluster in Milwaukee's integrated neighborhoods. Just as in Rogers Park and Uptown, the denizens of heterogeneous New York and Milwaukee neighborhoods may be using their access to the police and other agents of social control to influence the direction of urban change.

Given the sizeable impact of public safety activism, it is no surprise that some decided to resist. This resistance took different forms. It could appear spontaneously in the form of racial challenges that residents voiced at community meetings or when they perceived safety activists to be harassing African Americans and Latinos. More encompassing resistance occurred when residents organized to protest gentrification, demand affordable housing, and elect supportive public officials. Nevertheless, their resistance ran up against gentrification's powerful momentum, which had already transformed all the other lakefront neighborhoods on Chicago's North Side, making them unaffordable to many. Under these circumstances, gentrification could hardly be stopped, let alone reversed. In addition to many small buildings, several large, low-income tenements were closed, converted, and upgraded during my fieldwork, despite repeated and sizable protests, while safety activists and the aldermen celebrated these transformations as decisive progress in the fight against crime. This happened at Lawrence House in Uptown, Hotel Chateau just south of Uptown's border with Lakeview, Astor House in Rogers Park, and other large buildings.[9] Perhaps the most justice activists could realistically hope to do was to decelerate gentrification and limit its impact. Indeed, they did accomplish occasional victories to this effect—helping their ally Helen Shiller win reelection one more time in 2007, securing at least some subsidized units for Lawrence House, reversing the displacement of black teenagers from Broncho Billy Park. Racial challenges played a major role in achieving all of these victories, and I will discuss their importance in more detail later.

In addition to these findings, two methodological and theoretical implications stand out. First, the fight against crime fostered racial displacement and marginalization but nonetheless did not always pit white against black residents. At least some African Americans sided with the public safety camp, whereas many whites, including some who were middle-class, fought gentrification. The neighborhoods' political dividing lines crisscrossed boundaries of class and race; accordingly, I observed not only interracial but also intraracial conflict.[10] In these confrontations, both African Americans and whites used racial challenges to attack their opponents. The *targets* of racial challenges were usually white, but even this was not always true. As I reported in chapter 7, Kay, a resident of Rogers Park's North of Howard area, had been derided by black neighbors for her public safety work and her middle-class habitus. In saying "you must think you're white," one neighbor even challenged Kay for betraying her race, for exhibiting behavior that one might expect from whites but certainly not from other African Americans.

Unusual political alignments and complex lines of alliance and conflict are not always fully acknowledged and reflected in sociological studies of race, but work on gentrification *has* actually done so. Lance Freeman (2006) revealed that many black and low-income Harlemites do not necessarily reject gentrification, although they certainly voice concerns and grievances. Japonica Brown-Saracino (2009) unpacked the catchall category of "the gentrifier," revealing heterogeneity, ambivalence, and sometimes even political activism in support of low-income residents. Recently, Derek Hyra (2017) has discussed the ways different neighborhood issues variably produce political coalitions that may foreground class, race, or sexuality, while deemphasizing other dividing lines. Overall, urban scholars are therefore increasingly following Rogers Brubaker's (2004) call to avoid methodological "groupness," the assumption that racial (or sexual, religious, etc.) identities inevitably congeal individuals into cohesive units. Instead, urban scholars assess carefully, from case to case, just how unified or divided people really are. This work should be carried on. For the sociology of race, it can yield a more complete picture of racial conflict. Applied to the cases of Rogers Park and Uptown, theories of racism and racial conflict would predict that whites would support any and all measures to crack down on crime in order to assert their privilege of living insulated from the symptoms of racialized poverty. And African Americans, of course, would be expected to resist.[11] When assessed against the findings I presented, these predictions were not wrong but they *were* incomplete, insofar as the actual battle lines were appreciably more complex.

A second implication that emerges from my fieldwork is the relevance of local political fields for interpreting community dynamics. Over recent decades, urban scholars have shown renewed interest in community organizations and their impact on urban space.[12] The findings I have cited underscore this impact. Going further, however, it must be recognized that organizations and their strategies are shaped by their shifting relationships with other actors in the local political field. Urban scholars should therefore pay close attention to political fields and the changes within them. Regarding such changes, electoral campaigns in particular turned out to be important junctures in the shifting relationships between influential local actors. Not only could elections change the access organizations had to political support; they could also alter local lines of conflict by pitting organizations against one another. Sustained conflict in the political field, which I observed in Uptown, in turn filtered down and produced tangible distrust and hostility even among relatively uninvolved residents. On the other hand a savvy incumbent like Rogers Park's Joe Moore could reduce community conflict by pacifying the local political field.

Urban ethnographers have often neglected this complex interdependence between residents, organizations, and politics.[13] Two notable exceptions are Nicole Marwell's (2007) study of competition between Jewish and Latino community organizations in Brooklyn and Robert Vargas's (2016) study of violence prevention in Chicago's Little Village. Vargas argues that political "turf wars" between reform-minded and more conservative aldermen over Little Village left parts of that neighborhood so divided that its ability to combat crime declined precipitously. The specific configuration of conflict in Little Village differed from Rogers Park and Uptown, but Vargas's point that political battles produce divided and thus inefficacious communities resonates with the results I presented. Urban ethnographers must account for the ways the phenomena they study are embedded in both local and non-local processes and relationships.

Racial Challenges, Neutralizations, and Neighborhood Change

The fight against crime increased racial discrimination and inequality in Rogers Park and Uptown. But whether it was discussed as a racial matter or not depended on racial claims-making and, more specifically, on the interplay of racial challenges and neutralizations. These rhetorical practices moved specific urban interventions—from positive loitering to sweeping transformations of the housing stock—into or out of the domain of racial politics. They were crucial tools for the politics of crime and gentrification, because they could bestow or withdraw the moral legitimacy many interventions ultimately required.[14] Depending on their success, an act like shutting down Lawrence House could constitute either a laudable contribution to the security of all Uptowners or a tangible instance of white homeowners forcing minority tenants out of the neighborhood under the guise of fighting crime. This, then, raises the question of actual outcomes—under what circumstances did racial challenges succeed over neutralizations? To conclude, I will aggregate findings from various settings so as to return, once more, to racial challenges and neutralizations as strategic practices. I will examine the contexts in which these practices occurred, the forms they took, and the outcomes they produced.

First of all, for racial challenges to succeed, racial challenges had to be made. That may sound obvious, but it is necessary to distinguish *opportunities* for challenges from the situations in which individuals or organizations *act on* those opportunities. Given enduring racial inequality in all areas of life in America, a motivated individual could make racial challenges about virtually anything at virtually any time. But most people do not talk about race all the time, nor did even the most fervent social justice activists in Rogers Park and Uptown.

One factor that shaped the prevalence of racial challenges on Chicago's Far North Side was the presence or absence of organized campaigns that entailed attacking opponents in the local political field. Outside organized campaigns, individual residents certainly made racial challenges on the basis of their personal experience. They decried encounters with police harassment or confronted positive loiterers over aggressive practices, for example. But such challenges were intermittent because they were spontaneous. Community organizations on the other hand could raise the level of racial contestation by *systematically* challenging opponents and their plans. After James Cappleman was elected alderman in 2011, this occurred in Uptown. Social justice organizations there sought to disrupt the emerging political program of the newly elected alderman and his allies in the public safety camp. The justice activists wanted to prove to the entire neighborhood that Cappleman really was the coldhearted exponent of racial displacement they believed him to be. Launching protests, holding public meetings, distributing flyers, and mobilizing sympathetic journalists, they disseminated information about gentrification and left few opportunities for making racial challenges unused. In Rogers Park, things were different. Social justice organizations in that neighborhood lobbied for affordable housing and social service funding but did not attack Alderman Moore or the safety initiatives, and thus racial challenges remained sporadic.

When they saw themselves confronted with racial challenges, individuals could respond in various ways. In principle, they could also *not* respond, but this happened only rarely. In some situations, the Lakesiders, a group of positive loiterers who were particularly dismissive of racial justice concerns, ignored racial challenges by literally walking away. But typically they did respond, as did most members of the public safety camp. In fact, safety activists preventively deployed racial neutralizations even in the absence of racial challenges. Since they wanted to portray the battle against crime in a favorable way and mobilize a broader set of residents to join (or vote for) them, they often appealed to the value of unity and to residents' shared interest in safety. From CAPS beat facilitators to tough-on-crime aldermanic candidates, the members of the public safety camp neutralized the fight against crime by distributing race-neutral counter-narratives.

In addition to spreading positive counter-narratives, individuals facing racial challenges could engage in defensive or corrective impression management that might discourage continued conflict.[15] For example, safety activists frequently encouraged their critics to attend public safety events, which made those events seem inclusive rather than divisive. Another tactic was to implement minor changes when particular interventions became overly contentious. An Uptown CAPS group stopped projecting mug shots of black offenders at their meetings in order to reduce discontent, although the group continued to share these images in private. Similarly, Alderman Cappleman and FLATS, a housing developer, designated a small number of units in Lawrence House as subsidized housing in an effort to appease critics of the tenement's conversion. Alderman Cappleman had initially refused to do this but changed his strategy after sizable protests occurred in the neighborhood and both the *Chicago Tribune* and the *Chicago Sun-Times* published articles that had highlighted the threat of racial displacement.[16] Keeping some units affordable made the building's conversion appear less offensive.

Alternatively, individuals could refute the racial challenges they faced. During the heated 2007 aldermanic campaign in Rogers Park, the candidate Don Gordon saw himself forced not only to defend his campaign's focus on street crime but also his canvassing strategy of handing out bananas to commuters, which some residents framed as a "racist joke."[17] Gordon neutralized the bananas by responding that they "taste delicious and they're good for you. . . . So I'm sticking with this."[18] Dropping the bananas from his campaign could have looked like an admission of guilt that might have given a boost to his opponent, so it makes sense from a strategic perspective that Gordon's campaign continued on with the practice.

Beyond refuting racial challenges, individuals could also turn the tables and attack their attackers for aggravating racial division. In their classic study of neutralizations, Gresham Sykes and David Matza (1957:668) write that ostracized individuals can fend off identity threats by claiming that their "condemners [are] hypocrites, deviants in disguise, or impelled by personal spite." Along these lines, Don Gordon charged that those who were expressing outrage about his bananas were not ordinary community members but campaign activists for Joe Moore, who was seeking to win a close election by grasping at (racial) straws. Accordingly, Gordon criticized Moore for his "polarizing rhetoric when what we need most in our community is the dialogue of unity." In this way, Gordon tried to use the initial racial challenge against Joe Moore, hoping to undermine his racial legitimacy and portray him as needlessly divisive.

Finally, individuals could try to suppress racial challenges. This was Alderman Cappleman's tactic during the uproar over the removal of basketball hoops from Broncho Billy Park, which displaced black teenagers from that location. When journalists from the *Chicago Reader* wanted to interview Cappleman about his decision to remove the hoops, he warned them to not focus their story on race, threatening to never speak with them again if they did. This strategy backfired, because the journalists and many readers interpreted the warning as evidence that the social justice activists' portrayal of the park's transformation as a case of racist criminalization had been accurate. Under such circumstances, even allies may run for cover. Thus, when protesters from Uptown appeared at a Chicago Park District board meeting, the board quickly agreed to reinstall the basketball hoops even against the express will of the alderman.

These findings point to the significant role of the public sphere in adjudicating racial challenges and neutralizations. When racial challenges spill over—or threaten to spill over—into the wider public sphere by drawing in journalists, pundits, and their unpredictable audiences, those challenges can exert substantial pressure. As the philosopher and sociologist Jürgen Habermas (1996) has noted, a healthy public sphere serves as a system of normative control that pushes organizations and individuals to justify or change problematic behavior.[19] Politicians, whose power is typically rooted in legitimacy in democratic societies, are especially susceptible to public pressure. As the gatekeepers of this pressure, journalists and the media were valuable allies in battles over urban change in Rogers Park and Uptown.

The legitimacy of urban interventions hinged on how residents and outside observers did or did not connect these interventions to race—hence the continual tug of war over the racial implications of fighting crime. Accordingly, the scenarios I have invoked here and throughout this book underscore the strategic nature of racial challenges and racial neutralizations. In analyzing these practices as strategic, I am not suggesting that they were necessarily insincere, however. Strong emotions and deeply held beliefs underpinned many confrontations, as I've shown particularly in chapter 7. But in the context of these confrontations, residents, activists, and politicians used their options for making racial challenges and neutralizations to their advantage as best they could—precisely *because* they were so attached to their neighborhoods and the visions of urban change they were pursuing.[20] As Arlie Hochschild (1985) has long argued, emotions and strategic action do not contradict but rather inform one another.

Rogers Park and Uptown were good field sites for studying racial challenges and neutralizations, because their increasingly threatened racial diversity elicited these practices in abundance. But battles over racial meanings and identities unfold across the United States, shaping and reshaping the national political landscape. Race scholars widely acknowledge the importance of racial neutralizations in the form of color-blind rhetoric,[21] which enable white Americans to reject affirmative action, criminal justice reform, the construction of subsidized housing, higher taxes, and other policies that might benefit racial minorities while reducing white privilege. But race scholars have devoted relatively little attention to the contested interplay of challenges and neutralizations,[22] which represents a huge part of America's racial discourse. Are voter ID laws common-sense protections against election fraud or are they deliberate efforts to disenfranchise African American voters? Do considerations of racial diversity in college admissions discriminate against Asian Americans? Should Confederate monuments remain in place or should they be removed? For these and other debates, race scholars should examine the ways racial challenges and neutralizations ultimately influence decision-making and policy. Much work remains to be done to understand their relative success or failure in different social contexts. Without incorporating the deployment and effects of challenges and neutralizations, the study of color-blindness remains incomplete.

Racial challenges and neutralizations shape major social debates, but they do more than that. When individuals and organizations clash about the racial entanglements involved in local or national issues, they also contest existing understandings and delineate new understandings of what race and racism actually are. Mustafa Emirbayer and Matthew Desmond (2015:166) write that debates about the racial nature of specific issues "never are concerned exclusively with the particular" but always also with "securing the authority to describe the very nature of racial domination itself." Similarly, Ashley Doane (2006:256) notes that racial "discourse is not merely communication or 'debate,' it is an attempt to influence both the rules of the game and others' perceptions of social reality." In other words, as they fought about stereotyping, police harassment, and displacement in Rogers Park and Uptown, residents also negotiated the proper definition of racism, appropriate and inappropriate forms of blackness and whiteness, and the ways racial claims-making could and should occur. It stands to reason that such discourses affect the social organization of race not only in racially diverse neighborhoods but throughout America.

About the Fieldwork

I launched this project with an interest in urban politics and in the ways individuals make sense of, and strategically navigate, categories of social stratification, especially race and ethnicity. After reading Elijah Anderson's (1990) *Streetwise*, I decided that racially diverse neighborhoods would represent good sites for pursuing an empirical research project that could incorporate both of these interests. Residents of different backgrounds would have local interests and needs that would regularly bring them into mutual contact, which I could then observe and analyze. In 2010, as I conducted online research to identify potential field sites, I learned about the practice of positive loitering in Uptown. Positive loitering appeared to be a particularly promising setting in which to study how residents negotiated race and urban change. I thus began exploratory research in the fall of 2010.

The approximately fifteen positive loiterers I joined during my first fieldwork excursion were an all-white group of mostly middle-class neighborhood residents who lived in an impressive condo building with floor-to-ceiling windows that looked out over the street where the positive loitering event took place. I was told that the positive loiterers were trying to "reclaim," as several participants put it, the street after an outbreak of brawls, shootings, and occasional drug dealing that had begun that summer. No one discussed race, and I did not observe any focused interaction across racial boundaries,[1] but I nonetheless concluded that civic initiatives of this kind must be rich subjects for studying race.

First, the positive loitering group represented a clear exception in the urban street scene. All the other groups I saw in the neighborhood that night—on the way to the event, during the event, after the event—were either multiracial or comprised only black residents. Many looked like they were probably low-income, drinking from bagged bottles and wearing slightly ragged clothing.[2] In this context, how could positive loitering not bring out racial meaning-making and also conflict? Second, I learned that the positive loiterers were extremely unhappy with their current city council representative (Alderwoman Shiller), whom they charged with failing to support efforts to reduce crime and disorder in the neighborhood. One of the positive loiterers I met that night was Frank, one of the leaders of Uptown's public safety camp. I would see Frank again and again at CAPS, court advocacy, and block club meetings, and many other crime-related events. Frank was carrying a clipboard, collecting petition signatures for James Cappleman's 2011 aldermanic campaign. Signing his name, one positive loiterer approvingly said that Cappleman was going to "clean up" the neighborhood after Helen Shiller had allowed it to decline for years. Against this background of neighborhood conflict about crime and disorder, I felt all the more assured that Uptown's racial politics were a rich object of study.

The outing left me with a taste for more, and so I began to plan my research project in more detail. To prepare, I conducted further exploratory research on the Far North Side in the winter and spring of 2011. I asked residents and social workers about pertinent local issues. I read blogs and gathered statistical data on neighborhood change and crime. I sifted through newspaper articles at the Chicago History Museum as well as a set of organizational documents and newspaper clippings from and about Uptown that Professor

Richard Taub of the University of Chicago had gathered in the 1980s and 1990s. I also conducted fieldwork during the aldermanic elections in the winter of 2011.

On the basis of these initial findings, I decided to study Uptown in combination with Rogers Park. The neighborhoods resembled each other in terms of their composition and crime rates but exhibited different degrees of political contestation—I realized this very early, because Uptowners clearly had very strong and incompatible perspectives on the 2011 election while hardly anyone in Rogers Park seemed to be discussing the aldermanic election there. Comparing two "strategically matched" neighborhoods, I could then try to explain divergent observations within them by drawing on their different histories and political fields.[3] Except for helping me understand the neighborhoods' political trajectories, which yielded different degrees of organizational polarization over crime and gentrification, this comparative design ultimately proved less central to the study than I had initially expected, because most of the community dynamics I observed in the two neighborhoods turned out to be relatively similar after all. However, in addition to interpretive and explanatory leverage, studying two neighborhoods also gave me the opportunity to observe more community organizations and expanded the pool of activists I could interview.

I moved into an apartment in Edgewater—the area between the two neighborhoods—so as to live close to the field sites, and I began intensive fieldwork in the summer of 2011. While I also conducted field research in Edgewater, which is largely white but has some racially integrated areas, I found much less to observe, so I do not include findings from there in this book. In both Rogers Park and Uptown, I identified and approached all the community groups and organizations that were engaging issues of crime and violence as well as gentrification and racial justice. I gradually built ties by attending as many events as possible, getting to know community activists on both sides, and learning about other possibly relevant organizations and events.

Participant Observation and Access in a Field of Competing Organizations

Access is a fundamental requisite of ethnography. Trying to gain access, an ethnographer must frequently struggle until finding a sympathetic gatekeeper who essentially makes the study possible. Ethnographers receive important information and guidance from gatekeepers, but most important, they receive an advance of trust they can use when talking with other members of the gatekeeper's network. To take some examples from urban ethnography, Doc in *Street Corner Society*, Tally in *Tally's Corner*, and Hakim in *Sidewalk* enabled Whyte (1993 [1943]), Liebow (1967), and Duneier (1999) to enter distinct and bounded social worlds and provided them with foundational knowledge they needed to understand them. Finding a sympathetic gatekeeper and convincing that person to help with one's project requires hard work and good fortune, but once it has happened things appear to get easier.

I conducted the fieldwork for this book without one central gatekeeper who could be compared to Doc, Tally, or Hakim. Since I studied a number of groups and organizations, as well as individuals' experiences outside collective settings, no single person could have provided me with comprehensive access. Instead, I had to continually negotiate my access with block club presidents, social workers, aldermanic staffers, community organizers, and so forth. Beyond the challenges this posed, repeatedly negotiating access provided useful data, because I could compare the ways a variety of people made sense of my social identities and my presence as a researcher.

When introducing myself to the groups and organizations I wanted to observe, I said that I wanted to learn what residents and community organizations were doing in relation to crime and neighborhood change. I was ultimately allowed at least some access to all the groups and organizations I approached, although I had to overcome some barriers—I'll discuss those later. As an observer, I maintained a quiet presence, occasionally asking questions to better understand what people were talking about or what they were doing. Importantly, I did not ask about race unless participants brought up race themselves. I wanted to learn how residents dealt with race in situ and so I needed to avoid producing the very engagements I hoped to examine. In Gary Fine's (1993:276) terms, I thus operated under a "shallow cover," which means that "the ethnographer announces the research intent but is vague about the goals." Of course, this is not to say that my presence did not influence the ways people behaved, but I do think it helped that they could not know for sure that I mainly studied race. I should add, however, that this approach had the considerable downside of having to spend many hours observing and interviewing residents without learning anything at all about racial politics, marginalization, and inequality.

After I concluded my fieldwork, Matthew Desmond (2014) published a useful article on relational ethnography, and I believe that my fieldwork illustrates some of the promises and problems a relational approach entails. Examining community processes through the interplay of organizations and individual actors proved insightful but also complicated the fieldwork because many of the organizations and groups I studied regarded each other with skepticism or even overt hostility. I thought about this problem a lot. Building close connections to one group, I feared, might preclude access to others. In order to study all the major actors who made up the field of neighborhood politics, I had to maintain the continued support of key organizations and leaders. I hoped that taking a self-avowedly neutral position would ensure this, so I cautiously managed my involvement to avoid sending signals that I had joined either the safety or the justice camp.

Sometimes, the natural flow of fieldwork endangered my neutrality. In January 2013, ONE held a protest outside the home of a developer who was methodically buying run-down rental buildings across the Far North Side and turning them into fashionable rentals for young professionals. I observed the event and rode along on the buses that transported the protesters there. The logic of the protest swept me right into it. When I got off the bus, someone handed me a lit candle and chaperoned me into the picket line with the other protesters.[4] It was a fun night because it temporarily relieved me from the awkward feeling of marginal membership that ethnographers typically have to endure. But over the following days, I anxiously searched the Internet for reports about the event, because I suddenly realized that pictures and videos might show me protesting gentrification, which could have endangered my rapport with the safety camp. It did not happen, but more than ever I wished that I was conducting an ethnography not of a political field but of a single group in which I could simply build relationships and participate in collective activities without having to worry about such things.

For the most part, navigating rivalries simply meant that I had to frequently reiterate that I wanted to gather the widest possible range of opinions about crime, violence, and neighborhood change. My contacts generally seemed to accept this goal. They sometimes commented on having seen me with adversaries, but these conversations were often humorous. Gayle, a safety activist, once mentioned that she had seen me as I was interviewing Ben, a leftist community organizer. She said: "when he sees me, he makes faces at me. Like a child. He acts like child. So when I saw you with him, I thought, 'Poor Jan!'" Rather than being angry that I was talking to Ben, Gayle expressed mock compassion for me having to suffer through a conversation with him. I never encountered a situation in which I was denied access as a result of my fieldwork with other groups and individuals. This could mean that my worries were unfounded—maybe my contacts did not care very much about who I spoke with after all. Nonetheless, embracing a relational and thus more distanced approach might have had subtle consequences, influencing what study participants said and did when I was present.

I wrote up detailed field notes on returning home from my field sites, and I repeatedly read these notes to develop analytic ideas and interrogate my emerging interpretations and explanations.[5] In this context, I should note how I logged conversations and talk in field settings. Unlike Mitchell Duneier (1999) or Matthew Desmond (2016), I audio recorded only a few of my field observations. Aside from in-depth interviews, I recorded larger public events, such as town hall meetings. One problem that ethnographers encounter in the absence of audio recordings is dealing with talk, because it is essentially impossible to remember exact phrases after hours of fieldwork. (Nonetheless, many ethnographies contain sentences upon sentences of speech in direct quotes without indicating how such a naturalistic account was made possible.) In my field notes, I logged conversation in two different ways. When I realized in the field that particular statements might prove important, I did my best to preserve them verbatim. I often jotted them down when it was neither disruptive nor suspicious to do so, using Erving Goffman's (1989:130) technique of "off-phase note taking," that is, I wrote notes in such a way that it was difficult for others to know which situation I was logging. When jotting down notes was not possible, I tried to memorize crucial statements word for word. This meant that I could never remember more than a few sentences or sentence fragments per event. Nevertheless, those key sentences I logged as direct speech in my field notes, and this is also how they appear throughout the book. If I was not quite sure about the wording, which was often the case, I logged talk as indirect speech, summarizing a conversation's content and development. I acknowledge that this strategy of reproducing speech may nonetheless distort what people said, despite my best efforts.

I continued fieldwork through the spring of 2014, observing hundreds of gatherings and events of any kind. I developed amicable relationships with almost all of the people I regularly encountered in field settings. Like most ethnographers, I experienced some of the advantages and even pleasures of good rapport: I was invited to parties, dinners, art shows, and music recitals; I was called up to help install shelves or accompany acquaintances to court; people would take me aside and share gossip; regulars reported talking about whether I was sick when I missed an event; and so on. However, I encountered one noteworthy exception. Studying Uptown's public safety camp, it appeared that several leaders became increasingly suspicious the longer I stayed in the field. This decline in rapport struck me as interesting, because it differs from the general experience of ethnographers, who usually gain trust as the fieldwork progresses. At first, Uptown's safety activists unanimously welcomed my presence. The leading activists, those who were involved in several safety initiatives, would joke about my commitment, saying things like "You're everywhere, Jan!" As time went on, I noticed that this appreciation cooled. It was replaced by a wary alertness.

A good example is Henry, an older white man, who organized a positive loitering group, worked with CAPS and the court advocacy program, and served on a public safety advisory board for the alderman. When in September 2012 he introduced me at a meeting of the Uptown Chicago Commission, an umbrella organization of block clubs, he commented that I had been showing up to a lot of community events for my research. He paused and said: "I guess that means he is trying to do a good job." If this statement does not yet convey suspicion, more overt expressions of apprehension followed. At a subsequent meeting of the Commission in January 2013, he remained silent and made no eye contact when I greeted the participants as I took a seat next to him. During that meeting, one agenda item was the paperwork that had to be submitted to renew the Commission's nonprofit status. Henry explained that this status allowed the Commission to avoid having to pay taxes and then added: "and it tells everyone that we're good people." While he said that, he turned his head slightly toward me and looked at me out of the corner of his eyes. In doing this, I think he wanted to tell me that he knew what I was "really" doing—to assess (and presumably question) whether the safety activists were good people.

This pattern of declining rapport, I would argue, reflects two things. First, it corresponds to the general climate of disunity and distrust in Uptown. The ongoing conflict with the social justice camp heightened safety activists' concerns about facing racial challenges. In this context, any kind of outside observer would have been undesirable, but especially a graduate student who presumably sympathized with the justice camp even if he did not admit it. Second, the safety activists may have assumed that the only reason I could have for continuing fieldwork for multiple years—certainly a timeline that surprises many outside academia—was that I would not give up until I had found the "dirty laundry." The declining rapport did not make the fieldwork impossible, although it did make it somewhat uncomfortable. But data about rapport are important and valuable in their own right. In this case, they bolster my findings about the intense polarization of Uptown's political field, which increased safety activists' sensitivity about being observed and possibly charged with racism.

Researcher Effects

As a participant observer, I necessarily inhabited a number of social identities that people used as cues to evaluate whether I could be trusted and what my motives might be. Obviously, people wanted to know whether I would portray them favorably or at least fairly. Under the "mask" of scholarly neutrality, what were my actual allegiances? As I came to learn in the course of the research, my identities took on conflicting meanings for different people and produced a number of situations I had not expected. Interestingly, my whiteness came up quite rarely—which is not to say that it did not matter. But residents repeatedly drew explicitly on two aspects of my identity to make inferences about my political views: being a sociologist and being from the University of Chicago.

The University of Chicago, founded with support from industrial magnate John D. Rockefeller, is a private research institution that boasts one of the largest university endowments in the nation. While it has a tradition of progressive scholarship that reaches back to Jane Addams and John Dewey, the university is better known for the gospel of unfettered markets: libertarian economists from Milton Friedman to Gary Becker have called the university their home. Well-off whites in Rogers Park and Uptown seemed to find my affiliation with the University of Chicago reassuring and I think it may have opened some initial doors into the public safety camp.

Others found my university affiliation off-putting. After spending several months with RYCH, I was hanging out with Wes on a cold and rainy Saturday morning. Over the past months, RYCH had organized protests, fielded a petition, and much more. The group was clearly in decline at this point—fewer and fewer people were coming to the meetings and events. This time it was just five people, including Wes and myself. Wes was tired and frustrated that more people had not shown up. As I was getting ready to leave, Wes said that he appreciated that he could rely on me to do the things I had signed up to do.[6] Then he added: "you know, I'm color-blind. As long as you love people, I love you. But when I heard that, Jan, you're from the University of Chicago . . . and you are going to take notes . . . because that's an elite-run institution. Wasn't that started by some super rich guy?" Wes here suggested that my whiteness was not so much of a problem for him as my affiliation with an elite institution. Although his comment suggests that I had by then overcome his concerns, it is possible that Wes and the others had previously withheld some of their views and plans.

Interestingly, others thought the exact opposite: since I studied sociology at the University of Chicago, I presumably inhabited a leftist parallel universe. I am not entirely sure if the following utterance was linked to my fieldwork, but it is revealing either way. The blog *Uptown Update* was an important prodevelopment forum for discussions of crime and disorder. Heated debates about racism and gentrification would often unfold in the blog's comments sections when the occasional left-leaning reader would confront the bloggers and commenters about their views on crime. In late 2013, one of the bloggers replied to a commenter who had lectured the blog's readers about the "the many matrices of oppression" in Uptown that nurtured the gangs. As a reflection on public perceptions of sociology, the reply is worth quoting at length.

> Oh, good lord. You sound like someone who is either a current or former University of Chicago student—recent, at that—who absorbs all the reading assignments in sociology classes and becomes quite proficient at spouting all the lovely terminology that you had to regurgitate for your exams. Unfortunately, the real world doesn't always conform to those tidy case studies that the sociology professors like to expound upon. AND . . . most of us were once 20-somethings like you appear to be and believed that we could put our shiny university idealism to use and change the world (or at least one corner of it). A good number of us have tried over the years to be helpful and constructive about solving problems that other people bring upon themselves, and many of us have had it thrown back in our faces, despite our social idealism. . . . Give it a whirl, but make sure that you're walking a mile in the shoes of those you feel you have to berate, too.[7]

This writer may not have thought that I had personally posted the initial comment, but it is more than possible that the reference to sociology at the University of Chicago was a stab at me, intended to communicate that the writer knew that I was planning to "berate" white Uptowners with my "shiny university idealism." In support of this interpretation, I would invoke the process of declining rapport I've outlined, and this comment was indeed posted toward the end of my fieldwork. Even if it had nothing to do with me personally, it still sheds light on what some residents thought about sociology—and, by extension, sociologists.[8] It is difficult to imagine that individuals holding such views would speak freely, without reservations, to a sociological observer or interviewer.

Another time, the evidence was more straightforward. I was standing on Howard Street with Gayle and two other safety activists, talking about crime and disorder in the area. Prefacing her causal analysis, which revolved around the adverse effects of welfare without accountability, Gayle said: "I know you are a sociologist, Jan, but you have to understand that . . ." Gayle thought that sociology was a discipline of leftists whose ideas had no bearing on the real world. For her, it appears, this meant simply that she had to be patient with me and educate me more slowly. For other, less self-confident people than Gayle, it may have meant that it was probably best to avoid me altogether or at least exercise caution when interacting with me.

Most of the members of the social justice camp shared the interpretation of sociology as leftist scholarship and therefore assumed that I was going to eventually take their side. This produced sporadic tensions. For example, I faced some hostility from Jack, a white community activist for a Rogers Park organization named Hope for Youth; Jessica, who I introduced in chapter 7, was also a member of that organization. Hope for Youth maintained an in-depth mentoring program for black and Latino teenagers who had come in contact with the criminal justice system. I observed a book club that was held as a part of this program. We discussed Michelle Alexander's (2010) *The New Jim Crow* and William Rhoden's (2006) *Forty Million Dollar Slaves*—critical accounts of racism in the criminal justice system and in professional sports, respectively—as well as the race-conscious art of Kara Walker. During the last session devoted to *The New Jim Crow*, three black teenagers talked about their experiences with police harassment, and I was asked for my opinion. Rather than offering an opinion, I said that at a recent CAPS meeting, the police commander had described his strategy of "proactive policing" to curtail violence, which involved searching pedestrians and cars for guns before those guns could be used. The officers' aggressive behavior, which the teenagers had just described, could have something to do with this, I suggested. Later, as we concluded the session by going around the room and summarizing what we had learned, Jack said: "Jan mentioned that he is writing a dissertation. He is looking at these issues from both sides, from the people who sit down with the police to us here. And from what he said it seems like he's made up his mind. So, I'd like to give him props for that. Fuck those CAPS meetings!"

I did not correct Jack's interpretation, although I did not agree. Strategically, I believe that by interpreting what I had said in this way, Jack was trying to make it true—endowing me with a political self by ascribing it to me.[9] Jack saw value in activist scholarship like *The New Jim Crow* but not in more purely academic pursuits. When a white participant suggested that we next read Sudhir Venkatesh's (2008) *Gang Leader for a Day*, Jack said: "let's not. I learned nothing from that book. Stop being so fucking amazed at everything all the time! If this is the level on which we are going to stay, we can't make any progress." Given his distaste for the scholarly gaze—exemplified by Venkatesh's book and luminously described as "being so fucking amazed at everything all the time"—I think Jack wanted to convert me into a proper activist scholar.

In sum, these situations show that people thought of me differently depending on whether they foregrounded my discipline (sociology) or my institutional affiliation (University of Chicago). Both could serve as political proxies. The former was interpreted as an indicator of leftist politics. The latter could be interpreted as a proxy of my class and social aspirations, which in turn suggested a conservative outlook. Thus, some safety activists seemed mollified by my institutional affiliation, while those who emphasized my disciplinary background responded with suspicion. Leftist residents were torn between considering me a potential ally because I studied sociology and considering me elitist because of my institutional affiliation. Even Jack would have probably been more comfortable with me if I had been a student at a different university—he made derogatory comments specifically about the University of Chicago several times.

I had expected that my other social identities would lead to more discussion. What about being white? And male? And a foreigner (I am a German citizen)? Residents rarely brought up these identities. White racism and whiteness were frequently discussed in social justice environments, including RYCH and Hope for Youth's book club. But I was never singled out in these discussions, and only rarely was I the only white person. The situation I've described in which Wes discounted my racial identity and instead stressed my affiliation with the University of Chicago was one of the very few times anyone commented on my racial category. Of course, this is not to say that my race—or, for that matter, my gender and foreign background—did not influence the fieldwork. To state a simple counterfactual, it is inconceivable that Andy (see chapter 7) would have shared his racist sentiments if I had been black. On the other hand a black fieldworker would undoubtedly have learned things that remained hidden to me.[10]

Independent of the study participants' response, being a white, male foreigner facilitated certain aspects of the fieldwork. Being a foreigner enabled me to ask questions that might appear painfully naïve to some people, such as "What would it take to fix the gang problem?"[11] And being male and white allowed me to feel comfortable in environments that might have felt threatening to nonwhites and women. After positive loitering events, for example, I would freely walk and bike through the neighborhood without having to worry about being accosted by strangers or the police.

Interviews and Other Supplementary Data Sources

In addition to countless conversations in the field, I conducted interviews with seventy-eight activists, residents, and experts on specific topics, such as neighborhood history or the local Chinese community. A few interviews with particularly busy experts were as short as thirty minutes; others lasted over four hours. The average length of the interviews was eighty minutes. The interviews were intended to complement and extend findings from my participant observations in three ways.

First, I interviewed forty-eight safety and social justice activists. In most cases, I already knew quite a bit about these interviewees and had observed them in various field settings before I interviewed them. That way, I could ask them for details about their views and also about how they had experienced interesting situations I had witnessed. For instance, when I interviewed positive loiterers, I would, among other things, ask them about situations in which I had seen others voice racial challenges to them about their public safety efforts. This allowed me to understand their perspective without having to challenge their work myself. Consequently, interviewing the activists largely served the purpose of enriching and specifying observational data.

I also conducted twenty-six interviews with various kinds of experts to gather more information about the neighborhoods and the social context in which the fieldwork dynamics I observed unfolded. The experts' perspective was typically filtered through their professions. For example, I interviewed journalists and a campaign strategy consultant to learn about the neighborhoods' political histories. I also interviewed police officers, social workers, and clergy with ties to gang members so as to better understand the extent and quality of gang activity and street crime. Some of these interviewees did not live in Rogers Park or Uptown; many of them did.

Finally, I interviewed nineteen residents from various ethnoracial backgrounds who were largely uninvolved in their neighborhoods or who participated primarily in community activities that did not, in any immediate sense, deal with crime or gentrification. It is important to note that the vast majority of Rogers Parkers and Uptowners fell under this rubric. Most residents hardly ever attended any neighborhood-specific events and had limited knowledge of local politics. What did they think about crime, policing, and displacement? In addition to speaking with uninvolved blacks and whites, I made a particular effort to speak with immigrant residents. After having conducted fieldwork for about a year, I realized that without also interviewing largely uninvolved residents, I would gain very little insight into the perspectives of Latinos, Africans, and Asians, because almost none of them participated in public safety or social justice groups in the two neighborhoods.

Each interview was different, and I rarely asked two interviewees the exact same set of questions. Nevertheless, in addition to each interview's unique components I generally covered certain themes. I asked when and why the interviewees had moved into the neighborhood; what they liked or disliked about it; how they saw the neighborhood changing; what they thought about neighborhood change; what they knew and thought about specific community organizations and initiatives; how much of a problem crime was; whether crime had any implications for their personal activities; and what needed to be done to deal with crime. Overall, I interviewed twenty-three African Americans, one African, four Asians, six Latinos, and forty-four whites. The high proportion of whites resulted from the fact that most of the experts I interviewed—journalists, police officers, aldermanic staffers, and so forth—were white.

In addition to field notes and interview transcripts, I also gathered a broad set of archival and secondary data. I read several Chicago-based publications—the *Chicago Tribune*, the *Chicago Sun-Times*, the *Chicago Reader*, and the *Chicago Reporter*—as well as local news and opinion blogs, such as *Uptown Update* and *DNAinfo*. I also monitored the Internet presences of community organizations so as to examine the ways people discussed race and crime online. Researching neighborhood history, I scavenged through electronic databases and the archives of the Chicago History Museum and the Chicago Public Library. I also read existing scholarship about the two neighborhoods. Furthermore, I collected and archived documents I came across during the fieldwork. They include, for example, meeting agendas and minutes, all kinds of flyers, and brochures that advertised community organizations. To study electoral politics, I made a particular effort to find canvassing material from aldermanic campaigns. With the help of several helpful informants, I was able to assemble a set of 103 such documents from the 2007, 2011, and 2015 elections in both neighborhoods. Finally, I used secondary datasets to learn about neighborhood change: crime data from the Chicago Police Department as well as sociodemographic data from the decennial census and the American Community Survey. When analyzed in combination, I believe these data sources provide a thick portrait of race, crime, and gentrification in Rogers Park and Uptown.

Notes

Chapter 1

1. "Gentrification" is a multifaceted and complex concept. Using it in an analytically precise fashion has become harder in part as a result of its diffusion throughout public discourse, which means that it exists simultaneously as a scholarly and as a folk concept—both of which take on a plethora of meanings (Brown-Saracino 2011, 2017). Insofar as I invoke it as an analytic tool, I follow Neil Smith's (1996:32) simple definition of gentrification as "the process by which poor and working-class neighborhoods in the inner city are refurbished via an influx of private capital and middle-class homebuyers and renters." I provide figures that describe the status of gentrification in Rogers Park and Uptown in chapter 2.

2. The blog *Uptown Update* and its affiliated Facebook site were the main online platforms for debating neighborhood issues in Uptown. The blog's rule against making charges of racism stated that "any post that tells anyone else to STFU [shut the fuck up] will be deleted. Ditto for calling someone racist." However, especially after shootings occurred, the bloggers and commenters frequently expressed stark opinions about the shootings' perceived roots in subsidized housing, deficient parenting, and lax social control. They also occasionally used derogatory terms like "thugs," "scum," and "human waste" to describe alleged gang members. Unsurprisingly, some residents found these statements unacceptably aggressive, stereotypical, and—ultimately—racist. Elsa, for example, an African American single mother living in affordable housing, told me: "People on *Uptown Update*, they talk about us in the low-income housing and we're all labeled as—it's like we're the leaders of the gangs, the single mothers. That's pretty much what we're labeled as. . . . And you're saying to me that I can't go on there [*Uptown Update*] and call someone a racist. I find that so insulting for you to even be able to put that on there." In Rogers Park, residents mostly relied on Everyblock, a location-based social network platform, to discuss neighborhood matters on the Internet. This platform is now defunct.

3. On the postwar process of metropolitan segregation, see Hirsch (1983); Massey and Denton (1993); Sugrue (2005); Taub, Taylor, and Dunham (1984). On the decline of urban manufacturing and its effects, see Wilson (1987, 1978). On the durability of urban poverty, see Sampson (2011).

4. Bursik and Grasmick (1993); Harding (2010); Harding, Morenoff, and Herbert (2013); Massey and Denton (1993); Sampson (2011); Venkatesh (2000); Wilson (1987).

5. This literature is now so large that only a smattering can be cited here. For broad overviews of the punitive turn in criminal justice policy and the concomitant rise in the mass incarceration especially of African Americans, see Alexander (2010);

Garland (2001); Wacquant (2002a); Western (2006). On the harmful effects of surveillance and intensive policing, see Goffman (2014); Legewie and Fagan (2019);
Rios (2011); Stuart (2016). On the negative consequences of focusing on punishment
rather than rehabilitation, see Gonzales Van Cleve (2016); Manza and Uggen (2006);
Pager (2009); Soyer (2016). Harding, Morenoff, and Herbert (2013), Sharkey (2013,
2018), and Wacquant (2002) discuss the racially disparate neighborhood impacts of
punitive criminal justice policy.

6. The potential impact of desegregation and poverty deconcentration is contested.
Policy interventions that pursue these goals, such as the Gautreaux Assisted Housing
and the Moving to Opportunity programs, have yielded some positive outcomes but
certainly not the sweeping improvements policy advocates had hoped and expected
to find (de Souza Briggs, Popkin, and Goering 2010). For some evidence of positive
impacts, see Chetty, Hendren, and Katz (2016). Considering the resistance integration policies face as well as the limited evidence for their efficacy, Goetz (2018) has
argued that racial justice interests might actually be better served by building affordable housing in low-income neighborhoods, where such construction is welcomed,
rather than devoting scarce resources to costly battles for desegregation.

7. Goetz (2018); Massey et al. (2013).

8. Logan and Stults (2011). On white perceptions of black criminality and how they
affect residential choices and responses to integration measures, see Gould (2000);
Hwang and Sampson (2014); Quillian and Pager (2001).

9. For studies that engage the link between crime and neighborhood racial change in
detail, see Gould (2000); Hwang and Sampson (2014); Nyden, Maly, and Lukehart
(1997); Quillian and Pager (2001); Taub et al. (1984). From the more general theoretical perspectives of Lawrence Bobo (1999) and Eduardo Bonilla-Silva (1997),
whites would be expected to respond to experiences of gang-related street crime
with aggressive efforts at defending their racial privilege. It may be worthwhile to
deduce this conclusion from their work. Restating and elaborating a short but influential article by Herbert Blumer (1958), Lawrence Bobo (1999:450) positions at
the center of his theory of race the "sense of group position," an "understanding
on where the dominant group should stand relative to the subordinate group."
This sense becomes salient and consequential especially when "dominant group
members believe that subordinate group members are encroaching on their rightful
prerogatives" (1999:450). The right to be insulated from gang-related street crime
certainly constitutes a widely held white prerogative, and therefore one would predict that crime would activate white resistance against integration.

Eduardo Bonilla-Silva (1997:470), in his structural theory of racism, argues that
racial conflict is ultimately driven by the "objective interests" of racial groups. He
acknowledges that some whites may temporarily act in less racially oppressive ways
than other whites "because they have greater control over the form and the outcome
of their racial interactions" (1997:476). Accordingly, whites in segregated, low-crime
neighborhoods may feel that they can afford to take a relatively progressive stance
on policing. Nevertheless, Bonilla-Silva (1997:476) portrays this progressivism as
fragile, easily evaporating as soon as white privilege is threatened: "[in] the case of

revolts, general threats to Whites, Blacks moving into 'their' neighborhood[,] they behave much like other members of the dominant race." As is the case for Lawrence Bobo's theory, therefore, Bonilla-Silva's work leads to the prediction that the presence of black street gangs will unite and mobilize the white against the black population.

10. Anderson (1990).

11. For a summary of several such incidents, see Victor (2018).

12. Broken windows theory has galvanized social scientists as few other scholarly contributions have. Many social scientists now hold that the theory's fundamental argument—that unpunished minor infractions set in motion a spiral of escalating crime—is wrong (Harcourt 2001; Sampson 2011; Sampson and Raudenbush 1999; but see Skogan 2015). Even if it is wrong, however, it could still be the case that a shared interest in safety and order unites residents across racial lines. Theoretically, the view that collaboration produces trust and relationships is rooted in Gordon Allports's (1954) contact hypothesis. For a more recent statement, see Pettigrew (1998). In relation to urban neighborhoods, many scholars have expressed concern that residents in integrated areas live more or less parallel lives and exhibit weak neighborhood attachment as well as low levels of neighborly trust (Guest, Kubrin, and Cover 2008; Putnam 2007; Stolle, Soroka, and Johnston 2008). Accordingly, a shared task (fighting crime) could provide a social focus (Feld 1981) that allows residents to collaborate and create relationships. Especially Fung (2004) has provided empirical support for this perspective (see also Skogan 1988).

13. Given the fact that African Americans tend to suffer from street crime more than whites (Peterson and Krivo 2010), it is, in principle, not surprising that at least some of them became active in anticrime initiatives. This activism is consistent with a longstanding commitment to tough-on-crime policies among a sizable segment of the black community. For an insightful study of the roots of this political tradition, see Forman Jr. (2017).

14. Logan and Stults (2011).

15. Regarding the diagnosis of "racial integration," it is necessary to consider questions of scale. Demographic studies typically use the census tract unit in order to approximate neighborhoods (e.g., Gould 2000; Logan and Zhang 2010). By contrast, Rogers Park and Uptown are two of seventy-seven Chicago "community areas" that are quite large and consist of several census tracts each. Due to the continued use of the community area names and boundaries for almost a century now, they are very engrained in Chicagoans' "cognitive maps" (Lynch 1960) of the city. Residents know and widely use more specific names for particular territories within their community areas, but these areas remain important units in residents' perspectives on their urban environment. Since Rogers Park and Uptown are quite large, they exhibit substantial internal variation, and some parts of them are much more racially diverse than others. Overall, however, residents frequently encountered members of other ethnoracial groups in their day-to-day local activities. Whether waiting for the train to downtown or attending a community meeting, residents expected to encounter racial diversity.

16. One of the most systematic studies in this regard remains Molotch's (1972) book about South Shore, Chicago. See also Anderson (1990); Mayorga-Gallo (2014); Perry (2017).

17. During the 2013–2014 school year, Uptown's Uplift Community high school had a mere 10 non-Hispanic white students among 327 African Americans and Latinos. During the same year, Rogers Park's Sullivan High School's student body was about 80 percent African American and Hispanic but less than 5 percent non-Hispanic white. For Chicago Public Schools racial composition data, see https://cps.edu/ SchoolData/Pages/SchoolData.aspx, accessed March 4, 2019.

18. See George and Bennett (2005). On this method in the study of urban places, see Molotch, Freudenburg, and Paulsen (2000); Paulsen (2004).

19. See Bennett (1997); Berrey (2005; 2015); Brown-Saracino (2009); Burke (2012); Gitlin and Hollander (1970); Maly (2005); Marciniak (1981); Rai (2016); Schloss 1957; Sonnie and Tracy (2011); Welter (1982). On the method of using past ethnographies as additional data points for new analyses, see Burawoy (2009). For the case of Uptown, I draw especially on Bennett's (1997) detailed account.

20. These figures are taken from the Chicago Data Portal: https://data.cityofchicago.org/ Public-Safety/Crimes-2001-to-present/ijzp-q8t2, accessed April 17, 2019.

21. Emmanuel (2014).

22. Sobol (2014).

23. Between 2000 and 2010, the median family income in both neighborhoods grew by about 50 percent, while it grew at only half that pace throughout Chicago. These figures, as well as the ones in the main text, are based on my analysis of the 2000 and 2010 Census and the American Community Survey's five-year estimates for 2008–2012.

24. For some classics of the community studies tradition, see Drake and Cayton (1993); Du Bois (1899); Gans (1962); Lynd and Lynd (1929); Suttles (1968).

25. For general literature on social fields, see Bourdieu (1993, 2000); Martin (2003, 2011). For an application of field theory to the study of race, see Emirbayer and Desmond (2015). Urban scholars increasingly draw on field theory in the study of neighborhoods (see Marwell 2007; Stuart 2016; Vargas 2016).

26. For historical accounts of the relations between community organizations in Rogers Park and Uptown, see Bennett (1997); Berrey (2015); Rai (2016); Sonnie and Tracy (2011); Welter (1982).

27. These calls have been made by scholars with very different (and sometimes conflicting) perspectives on urban research. All of them suggest expanding the scope of urban ethnography, however. For instance, McQuarrie and Marwell (2009) as well as Small (2004) have highlighted the role of organizations in shaping the neighborhood dynamics urban ethnographers can observe. Burawoy (1991), Wacquant (2002b), and Walton (1993) call on ethnographers to situate their cases in the (urban) political economy. Katz (2010) and McRoberts (2003) emphasize careful contextualization and historicization as an imperative for understanding neighborhoods and their community structure. Duneier's (1999) notion of the "extended place method" requires that ethnographers observe not only a specific group but also other social

actors that may influence the group's situation. Of course, I cannot claim to satisfy all of these demands, but I have made substantial efforts to comprehensively incorporate at least the neighborhood-level forces that were shaping the politics of crime and race in Rogers Park and Uptown.

28. See Fields (2016).

29. Racial challenges thus engender self-referential moments for "doing" race in the ethnomethodological sense. For the theoretical foundation of that approach, see Garfinkel (1967). The ethnomethodological tradition is vibrant in gender studies (Schilt 2010; West and Fenstermaker 1995; West and Zimmerman 1987, 2009) and has also been used in work on race (Rawls and David 2005).

30. On face work, see Goffman (1967). As readers familiar with the criminological tradition may have noticed, I take the term "neutralization" from Gresham Sykes and David Matza's (1957) work on delinquency. For more general discussions of techniques of neutralization and the related concept of accounts, see Scott and Lyman (1968); Hewitt and Stokes (1975); Stokes and Hewitt (1976).

31. Mendelberg (2001).

32. Scott and Lyman (1968).

33. Blum and McHugh (1971) provide an insightful ethnomethodological discussion of how discourse confers social identities.

34. My definition of "racial challenge" resembles Emirbayer and Desmond's (2015:166) concept of "racialization" as well as Brubaker et al.'s (2006) parallel concept of "ethnicization." However, I avoid these terms, for two reasons. First, "racialization" and "ethnicization" in Emirbayer, Desmond, and Brubaker's sense would include any affixing of ethnoracial meanings—whether positive, negative, or neutral—to a person, event, or object. My goals in this book are too specific for this terminology, because I aim to examine only the moral negotiation of racial identities. Second, there are currently too many competing definitions of "racialization" to rule out misunderstandings when using this term. British and Canadian scholars, for example, frequently speak of racialization as an alternative to the quotation marks often seen around the word "race." By referring to "racialized" rather than "racial" groups, these scholars indicate that they do not regard these as biologically real categories whereas society treats these groups as if they did exist in a biological sense (for overviews, see Barot and Bird 2001; Murji and Solomos 2005).

35. A great deal of scholarship has since followed in that tradition. For one recent example, see Gonzales Van Cleve (2016).

36. See also Bobo, Kluegel, and Smith (1997); Bonilla-Silva (2003).

37. After leaving his position at the White House, Trump's former advisor Steve Bannon went so far as to state that the Right should treat charges of racism as a "badge of honor" (quoted in Reid 2018).

38. On the general shift toward racial resentment among a segment of the white population, see Valentino, Neuner, and Vandenbroek (2018). For some recent examples of apologies, firings, or resignations in the aftermath of racial challenges, see Koblin (2018); Stevens (2018); Silverstein (2016); Wenzel and Zieller (2018).

39. Bosman and Smith (2017).

40. The quotes from Trump appear in Glanton (2016), Stafford (2016), and Cherone (2017).

41. Alvarez was trying to prevent the release of dashboard video footage that depicted the shooting. Allegedly, she suppressed the footage to support the reelection of Mayor Rahm Emanuel in 2015. After a court ordered the police department to release the footage, protesters insisted that Emanuel step down. Emanuel refused but eventually fired Police Superintendent Garry McCarthy in an effort to appease his critics (Husain 2017).

42. Corley (2019); US Department of Justice (2017).

43. For a selection of work on black-white integrated neighborhoods that has been published since Anderson (1990), see Berrey (2015); Brown-Saracino (2009); Freeman (2006); Gould (2000); Hyra (2017); Mayorga-Gallo (2014); Nyden, Maly, and Lukehart (1997); Perry (2017); Quillian and Pager (2001).

44. Bailey and Nixon (2010); Skogan and Hartnett (1997).

45. Hyra (2017). Recently, Richard Florida (2017), whom many urban scholars regard as gentrification's main apologist, has revisited his prior arguments and acknowledged a growing crisis of affordability in American cities that have undergone substantial gentrification.

46. E.g., Brown-Saracino (2009); Freeman (2006); Jackson (2001).

47. E.g., Levine (2016); Marwell (2007); Smock (2004); Warren (2001).

48. See also Legewie and Fagan (2019).

49. These monikers have been awarded to whites who have called the police on African Americans engaging in nondeviant, everyday activities. For an overview, see Victor (2018).

50. It is important to note that gangs can be important political actors, especially when they have a deep foothold in their neighborhoods. For studies of neighborhoods with politically connected gangs, see Pattillo (2013); Sánchez-Jankowski (1991); Vargas (2016); Venkatesh (2008).

Chapter 2

1. Main (2012).

2. While Rogers Park and Uptown have fewer than 100,000 inhabitants each, this is the standard denominator for crime rates. I computed the community area average by dividing the city's average homicide count between 2008 and 2017 by seventy-seven. The population tally of community areas varies, but the figure may serve as a reasonable point of comparison.

3. For maps of gang boundaries and general information about the gangs and their alliances—although somewhat outdated—see Chicago Crime Commission (2012). Intergang alliances and even membership within the same gang have lost most of their meaning in Chicago over recent years (Hagedorn et al. 2019).

4. Papachristos, Hureau, and Braga (2013) have shown that turf adjacency and a history of conflict predict gang violence. The frequent outbursts of violence between factions of the same gang may also be related to organizational atrophy, produced by arresting leaders (Papachristos 2001; Vargas 2016; Venkatesh 2006).

5. The complete list comprises homicide, sexual assault, aggravated assault, aggravated battery, burglary, theft, motor vehicle theft, and arson.

6. Sampson (2011).

7. For the Chicago Police Department's annual reports, see https:// home.chicagopolice. org/inside-the-cpd/statistical-reports/annual-reports/ accessed September 10, 2019. For unknown reasons, annual reports were no longer published after 2010. I thus solicited index crime data through a Freedom of Information Act request for the years 2011, 2012, and 2013. Since the city eventually made all crime data since 2001 available online, data for subsequent years could be drawn from the Chicago Data Portal: https://data.cityofchicago.org/Public-Safety/Crimes-2001-to-present/ijzp-q8t2 accessed September 10, 2019.

8. Warr (2000).

9. Sampson and Bartusch (1998).

10. Occasionally, there were shootings in a racially diverse part of Edgewater, the neighborhood wedged between Uptown and Rogers Park. Residents of Edgewater usually agreed with Uptowners and Rogers Parkers, however, that Edgewater's problems were less severe.

11. By necessity, this overview focuses only on select historical processes and events. For other accounts of history, social life, and politics in Rogers Park and Uptown, see Archer and Santoro (2007); Bennett (1997); Berrey (2005); Burke (2012); Gitlin and Hollander (1970); Henderson (2007); Malooley (2011); Maly (2005); Marciniak (1981); Rai (2016); Savage (2009); Sonnie and Tracy (2011); Welter (1982).

12. In his work on the extended case method, Michael Burawoy (2009) argues that, in studying the local, ethnographers can disentangle macro processes from their cases' idiosyncratic features. An extended case method approach to neighborhood change might try to assess how forces like globalization or the transformation of the labor market shape neighborhoods in order to refine theories of urban change. This is not my primary goal in this book. In a nutshell, however, I can report that the dynamics of change I found in Rogers Park and Uptown were inconsistent with Robert Park and Ernest Burgess's (1925) ecological model of the city, which posits that neighborhood change occurs through an uncoordinated cycle of population invasion and succession. The timing and patterns of both integration and gentrification in Rogers Park and Uptown clearly reflected intentional political efforts. A systematic analysis of the roots of urban change in Rogers Park and Uptown would thus produce results much more consistent with the political economic approach to urban sociology (see Harvey 1989; Logan and Molotch 2007; Smith 1996; Walton 1993; Zukin 1980).

13. Pacyga (2009).

14. Van den Berghe (1967).

15. Hauser and Kitagawa (1953:18).

16. See Massey and Denton (1993) for a detailed discussion of racial segregation. For a study of the Black Belt, its emergence, and social life within it, see Drake and Cayton's (1993) seminal *Black Metropolis*.

17. In many ways, the response of established residents to the southern whites mirrored how residents would later respond to black settlement. A study conducted for the Uptown Chicago Commission—a community organization founded in 1955 to curtail neighborhood decline—portrayed the Appalachians as a dangerously unadjusted group, citing lawlessness, a deficient work ethic, and even incest (see Schloss 1957).

18. The federal state's Indian Relocation Act had brought many Native Americans to the neighborhood. The National Museum of the American Indian in Washington, D.C., still showcases exhibits that represent Native American life in Uptown.

19. The state of Illinois fueled this process by channeling large numbers of deinstitutionalized mental health patients to Uptown.

20. Oppenheim (1974).

21. At first, African Americans could access only the most dilapidated housing in Uptown. In the 1960s, the black population grew in only one census tract along the "L" tracks, where the initial black enclave was already located. The 1960 Census estimated that 60 percent of the units in this tract were in substandard condition—an astronomical figure.

22. Myler (1983); Oppenheim (1974).

23. Specifically in Uptown, developers drew on a federal loan insurance program to build low-income rental towers (Bennett 1997). Nonprofit housing providers in both neighborhoods also used subsidies to create project-based Section 8 housing (Myler 1983). In addition, the Chicago Housing Authority built a small contingent of scattered site public housing in Rogers Park and Uptown as part of the *Hill v. Gautreaux* Supreme Court decision. On the Gautreaux desegregation program, see de Souza Briggs, Popkin, and Goering (2010).

24. Quoted in Bennett (1997:177).

25. Quoted in Ansley (1981).

26. This redevelopment was part of an ambitious growth coalition program to enhance Chicago's economic vitality (Ferman 1996; for theoretical statements of growth machine theory, see Logan and Molotch 2007; Stone 1989). Under the leadership of Mayor Richard J. Daley, the growth coalition refashioned downtown into a center for business services and corporate headquarters and shielded the area from black and Latino neighborhoods to the south and west. On the Near South Side, borders between downtown and the black Bronzeville neighborhood were erected with the construction of the Eisenhower Expressway and McCormick Center, a trade show facility. To the west, the Kennedy and Dan Ryan Expressways buffered downtown, as well as the strategic placement of the University of Illinois on the Near West Side through an urban renewal program (Suttles 1968). At the same time, the growth coalition invested in North Side neighborhoods to attract and retain middle-class whites. Over the following decades, gentrification thus slowly moved north along the lakefront—first into the Near North Side, then Lincoln Park, and then Lakeview (Taub, Taylor, and Dunham 1984). The new residents bought and renovated houses, formed neighborhood associations, and lobbied for code enforcement and better city services. They were aided by urban renewal projects that demolished low-income housing. The proportion of middle-class residents increased, and income levels and housing values swelled close to downtown.

27. "The Uptown Gamble" (1988); Bennett (1997). The negative impact of Uptown's reputation can be gleaned, for example, from the successful campaign of community organizations in Edgewater, an area south of Rogers Park that was officially a part of Uptown, to convince the city to recognize Edgewater as a distinct community area in order to symbolically distance itself from Uptown (Marciniak 1981).

28. Uptown's housing market is and has been driven less by individual landlords, tenants, and buyers and more by large developers and institutional interventions, such as historic district designations, tax increment financing, and state-funded loan insurance programs. One important case in point is the construction of Truman College through the federal Model Cities program in the 1970s (Bennett 1997), but other examples abound. In the mid-1980s, developers persuaded the National Register of Historic Places to establish two historic districts in Uptown ("It Costs Money to Make Money" 1988; McCarron 1988). This designation made tax credits available for building renovations that then became profitable in spite of Uptown's blemished reputation. More recently, developers have been able to purchase and upgrade low-income residential hotels with the help of the alderman, building inspectors, and housing courts (e.g., Emmanuel and Woodard 2013; Tekippe 2013). I discuss an example of the latter in chapter 3.

29. Feldman (1995); Palmer (2001).

30. The following figures are based on my analysis of census and American Community Survey data. Other studies that explore this process or related issues on Chicago's Far North Side include Bennett (1997); Berrey (2005; 2015); Brown-Saracino (2009); Burke (2012); Maly (2005); Rai (2016).

31. The actual share of African Americans must be somewhat smaller than 20 percent, because Uptown has a sizeable population of African immigrants.

32. Rogers Park and Uptown had, respectively, 20,849 and 23,279 renter-occupied units in 2000 and 17,155 and 20,191 in 2010. The number of owner-occupied units increased from 4,688 and 7,354 to 7,137 and 9,528 over the same period.

33. In designated areas, TIFs redirect a certain percentage of property tax revenues to fund designated development programs. This may include infrastructure investments, beautification, and the construction of new residential and commercial buildings.

34. Quoted in Ruklick (2003:2).

35. Quoted in Ruklick (2003:2).

36. For select journalistic accounts, see "Noise and Fury in Uptown" (2004); Bowean (2013); Chandler (2001); Eight Forty-Eight (2011); Meyer (2004); Mowatt (2000); Roeder (2006); Palmer (2001); Woodard (2013).

37. See Papachristos et al. (2011) for an overview. A direct causal link between gentrification and crime is widely implied in public discourse, however. Recently, the *Onion* published a satirical article, "Neighborhood Starting to Get Too Safe for Family to Afford" (2015), about Humboldt Park, another gentrifying Chicago neighborhood.

38. Community policing was implemented in many large police departments in the 1990s. The quick spread of community policing can be explained in part by the exploding rates of drug crime and violence American cities experienced at that time. Mayors and police superintendents had to demonstrate that they were trying new ways to control escalating crime rates. Nonetheless, it has often been difficult for police departments to adopt community policing. Police officers across the ranks tend to be skeptical of community policing because it takes time away from core duties and requires officers to commit to some degree of external priority-setting, which can entail having to work on tedious "quality-of-life" issues—graffiti, loitering, littering, and so forth (Skogan and Hartnett 1997).

39. Kelling and Coles (1996); Skogan and Hartnett (1997).

40. Neither the police department nor Mayor Richard M. Daley initially favored police reform, but during his second term (1991–1995), Daley, who was under pressure to respond to rising crime rates, embraced community policing (Martin 1995). Community organizations from around Chicago had lobbied the city for several years to adopt community policing, arguing that it would make policing more effective and progressive (see Friedman 1991, 1996; Friedman and Matteo 1988; Recktenwald 1991). It would be more effective because it would target crime as a community-rooted syndrome, not as a set of quasi-isolated incidents, as the strategy of rapid response had necessarily done. And it would be progressive, because it sought to improve the relationships between civilians—particularly those of color—and the police force, which was widely perceived as aloof and unresponsive to citizen concerns.

   Some social justice activists in Rogers Park and Uptown at first welcomed community policing, because they hoped that it would provide an opportunity to increase police accountability and to push for greater efforts to target the systemic roots of criminal behavior. But they became frustrated with CAPS very quickly. Elliot, one social justice activist, commented laconically: "we didn't get community policing, we got CAPS." He explained: "the grassroots folks that were calling for community policing were very clear that it was both a safety and a police accountability kind of issue. That it was about having policing that was rooted in a community that was not just enforcement-based." But Elliot and his fellow activists in Rogers Park and Uptown quickly concluded that increasing police accountability through CAPS was going to be out of the question. After all, CAPS was not an independent institution but was implemented by the police department itself.

41. In addition to Skogan's (2006) favorable evaluation, Fung (2004) has celebrated CAPS beat meetings as a model of deliberative urban democracy.

42. See Taub, Taylor, and Dunham (1984); Skogan and Maxfield (1981). Molotch's (1972) study of the racial integration of Chicago's South Shore neighborhood also includes an excellent discussion of civic efforts to control crime.

43. Stuart (2016) describes a similarly synergetic relationship between large social service providers and community policing in Los Angeles's skid row neighborhood.

44. For discussions and more examples, see Fung (2004); Skogan and Hartnett (1997).

45. Allport (1954); Pettigrew (1998).

46. Fligstein and McAdam (2012).

47. I should add that safety activists did not oppose all affordable housing and social services—nor did they support all private development. Regarding the latter, for example, they fought projects they considered overly dense (tall buildings) and those that appeared to clash with the area's architectural heritage.

48. Several organizations promoted gentrification more than safety. Among these were the chambers of commerce and developers' associations. These organizations quietly worked to encourage development and improve the vitality of businesses and commerce in Rogers Park and Uptown. In describing their work as "quiet," I mean that they did not, for instance, endorse candidates for public office or mobilize residents for protests. Nor did they make any notable efforts to shape public discourse about

development or street crime. That is not to say that these organizations did not matter—in fact, they may have well mattered more precisely *because* they operated quietly. Along these lines, some urban scholars argue that one aspect of power is the ability to implement policy without overt conflict even when opposing interests exist. For fundamental statements of this tradition, see Hunter (1953) and Bachrach and Baratz (1962), as well as the competing tradition of pluralism (Dahl 1961; Polsby 1959). For two influential studies that examine the indirect exercise of power, see Crenson (1971) and Gaventa (1980). For the purpose of this book, which focuses specifically on manifest conflict and its racial features, the chambers of commerce and developers' associations turned out to be of little importance, however. For a study of Rogers Park that was conducted at an earlier point in time and that includes development organizations, see Berrey (2015). Berrey reports that in the early 2000s, these organizations behaved differently, working explicitly to convince the alderman and residents that gentrification was good and necessary.

49. In mid-2013, ONE merged with a similar organization, the Lakeview Action Coalition, and rebranded itself as ONE Northside. To avoid confusion, I refer to the organization only by its old name.

50. CeaseFire was renamed "CureViolence" in 2012, but no one I knew used that name.

51. The boundaries of the 49th Ward matched Rogers Park relatively well, but the overlap between the 46th Ward and Uptown was less perfect. The 46th Ward included most of Uptown but also parts of Lakeview. Uptown's westernmost section, the area west of Clark Street, was located in the 47th Ward, and a part of northern Uptown, including a piece of the Argyle area, belonged to the 48th Ward. Regarding the politics of crime, this made very little difference, as all three of Uptown's gang hotspots were located in the 46th Ward. Although street crime and gang activity sometimes spilled over into the 48th Ward, conflict over the politics of crime played out mostly in the 46th Ward.

52. See Fremon (1988). Some Chicago aldermen have been accused of using their influence over the police to protect gangs within their wards. This is also the case for Uptown's former Alderwoman Helen Shiller (see Bernstein and Isackson 2011). I cannot assess these accusations, but it is clear that aldermen could shape local police priorities and the tactics police officers adopted in dealing with street crime.

Chapter 3

1. For an analysis of such interactions, see Duneier and Molotch (1999).

2. See City of Chicago Building Department record 9828959 for the inspection that occurred on December 29, 2011: https://www.chicago.gov/city/en/depts/bldgs/provdrs/inspect/svcs/building_violationsonline.html; accessed November 5, 2017. For a recent study of building inspectors and their decisions to "go after" or "go easy" on certain landlords, see Bartram (2019). Quite consistently with the case of Lawrence House, Bartram found that inspectors tend to strictly pursue professional landlords, "who inspectors believe can afford to maintain buildings but fail to." The inspectors thereby aim to punish bad landlords, but Bartram suggests that strict inspection practices can also lead to rent hikes and evictions.

3. Bowean (2012). At a block club meeting the week after that article was published, Henry, a white retiree, complained that the *Chicago Tribune* article ignored the fact that tenants felt "terrorized" by the crime in the building. He dismissed the article, arguing that its slant was predictable, given that the reporter had recruited her informants through ONE. He called on the members of the block club to submit letters to the editor in order to correct the article's perceived biases.

4. Emmanuel and Woodard (2013).

5. Emmanuel (2014).

6. See Bartram (2019).

7. For some examples, see Cottrell (2012, 2013).

8. Between 1992 and 1995, Chicago had an ordinance that allowed police officers to arrest individuals for loitering "in any one place with no apparent purpose" (Greenhouse 1999). The ordinance has since been found unconstitutional—first by the Illinois Supreme Court in 1997 and again by the U.S. Supreme Court in 1999—despite the fact that thirty-one states and the Clinton administration filed briefs supporting it.

9. Since cases of police brutality and general disaffection with the police can lead residents in poor black and Latino neighborhoods to underreport crime (Desmond, Papachristos, and Kirk 2016; Sampson and Bartusch 1998), service requests as a criterion for reassigning officers are likely to lead to a skewed distribution of police service throughout the city. Whether one thinks that is a good or a bad thing depends on whether one believes that more policing overall benefits or harms low-income minority neighborhoods. For some contrasting perspectives on this question, see Alexander (2010); Desmond and Valdez (2013); Leovy (2015); Rios (2011); Sharkey (2018).

10. While one could construe this as a deliberate misuse of 911, police officers were well aware of this practice and did nothing to discourage it. One argument that officers made in favor of the practice was that the police could obtain a clearer picture of the incident if more residents called because callers might have observed different things. In addition, police district leadership had incentives to keep the number of service requests high because they had to log enough to keep their district well-resourced.

11. It is by no means obvious that whites would not be adversely affected by increased policing, particularly in the North of Howard area. Since it was perceived as a black neighborhood, patrol officers could have suspected whites of coming there to buy drugs (see also Goffman 2009). Nevertheless, I never heard complaints from whites about being stopped and questioned—here or elsewhere in Rogers Park or Uptown. One possible explanation might be that most whites did not have to circle the block in search of parking because they owned or rented private parking spots.

12. While court advocates did not testify, state's attorneys made sure to use the court advocates to the prosecution's advantage. In some cases, state's attorneys asked the court advocates to stand up during court hearings so the judge could see them. Some judges did not allow this practice, but even in these cases the state's attorneys found ways to signal the presence of the court advocates. During breaks, for example, they would demonstratively walk over to the court advocates and chat with them. These practices were intended to convince judges to impose harsher sentences when defendants were found guilty.

13. Safety activists also pressed the city to provide better maintenance services, such as more quickly replacing burned-out light bulbs, removing graffiti, cutting overgrown bushes and trees that could shield potential offenders from public view, or mending

torn fences. Just as 911 calls mobilized limited police services, 311 calls mobilized the city's limited capacities to provide maintenance and landscaping. Safety activists could also ask the city to install CCTV cameras in crime hotspots, but many residents had mixed feelings about cameras because they might make the neighborhood look "ghetto." Unlike other forms of safety work, maintaining or altering public spaces and amenities did not usually engender contestation, perhaps because activities like picking up trash could not be interpreted as racially aggressive. There were exceptions, however. In chapter 5, I discuss how removing basketball hoops from a local park in Uptown initiated a bitter conflict between social justice and public safety activists.

14. Having African American participants was considered much more important than, for instance, incorporating East Asians. Mustafa Emirbayer and Matthew Desmond's (2015) theory of the racial order as a hierarchical field of racial domination helps to explain this. In this field, whites and blacks occupy opposite poles. Some groups are situated more closely to the dominated pole (working-class Puerto Ricans, say), while others gravitate toward the pole of domination (Chinese professionals, for example). For public safety activists, nonwhites became more valuable as collaborators the more closely their social location approached the dominated pole.

15. Cappleman (2011:5).

16. Cappleman (2011:6).

17. On vocabularies of motive and similar narrative devices, see Mills (1940); Scott and Lyman (1968).

18. See Bowean (2012). The safety camp also received occasional support from journalists. For example, the *Chicago Sun-Times* published an article about a repeat offender from Uptown with 396 arrests and expressed sympathy for the public safety activists, charging the criminal justice system with failing "to save [the offender] from herself or to help the communities she menaces" (Esposito 2013). The woman in question was infamous in Uptown. She had been convicted of robbing a seventy-five-year-old at knifepoint. Another noteworthy incident occurred when this woman was arrested in 2012 for allegedly assaulting Alderman Cappleman. There was also a stock story among residents about an incident she had allegedly caused at Magnolia Café, which was celebrated as the neighborhood's first genuine fine dining option when it opened in 2001. The story goes that on the day of the restaurant's opening, the woman asked to use the restroom and then covered the bathroom walls in feces, which forced the restaurant to delay its opening. (Obviously, the story resonated in part because it had rich symbolic implications for thinking about gentrification in Uptown.) Reporting some of these stories, the *Sun-Times* article vindicated safety activists by suggesting that their efforts were both necessary and laudable.

Chapter 4

1. On Saul Alinsky's program of working-class empowerment through radical community organizing, see Alinsky (1989); Gitlin and Hollander (1970); Halpern (1995). For more information about Shiller's political background and career, see Bennett (1997).

2. The quote is from former aldermanic candidate Sandra Reed, cited in Bernstein and Isackson (2011).

3. For reports on these events, see Dumke (2011); Esposito (2011).

4. Malooley (2010). For a study of the Robert Taylor Homes, see Venkatesh (2000).

5. Hyra (2017); Vargas (2016).

6. See Beckett (1997); Gilens (1999); Kinder and Sanders (1996); Mendelberg (2001). These studies demonstrate that political initiative has a crucial impact on perceptions of crime and race. Campaigning on crime, politicians can mobilize racial resentment and fears among white voters without overtly appealing to white racial superiority (Mendelberg 2001). The most famous example is the Willie Horton advertisement for George H. W. Bush's 1988 presidential campaign in which threatening images of a black criminal were used to depict Bush's opponent, Michael Dukakis, as soft on crime. At the same time, campaigning on crime further escalates fear of crime—and attendant racial stereotypes—and thus keeps crime on the political agenda (Beckett 1997). For an analysis specifically of urban politics that focuses on the mobilization of nonwhite rather than white voters, see Doering (2019).

7. Mendelberg (2001); Metz and Tate (1995).

8. Brubaker et al. (2006).

9. I focus on the direct effects electoral politics had on conflict (or its absence) between community organizations. Going further, one could also argue that campaigning influences community dynamics by molding place-based culture. The concept of place-based culture accounts for the fact that neighborhoods are not only material but also cultural entities that take on distinct meanings through collective actions and narratives. On the emergence and reproduction of place-based culture, see Brown-Saracino (2015); Goodman (2014); Molotch, Freudenburg, and Paulsen (2000); Suttles (1984). For a study of place-based culture that explicitly incorporates electoral campaigning as a factor, see Kaufman and Kaliner (2011).

10. Bennett (1997).

11. Kleine (1999); Joravsky (2007). On "rubber stamp" aldermen and the politics of Chicago's city council, see Simpson (2001). Shiller's opponents were Michael Quigley in 1991 and Robert Kuzas in 1995. Voters in Uptown did not recognize these candidates for their local civic engagement. Quigley did not even live in Uptown but moved there shortly before the deadline that requires aldermanic candidates to demonstrate their residence in the ward where they want to run for office. Because Quigley and Kuzas received substantial campaign support from the mayor and his allies, both elections were nonetheless contested—Shiller won with 55 percent in 1991 and 57 percent in 1995.

12. Struzzi (1999:4).

13. Garza (1999:1).

14. Kleine (1999).

15. Quoted in Kleine (1999). Regarding the insinuation of racism, Reed had distributed flyers in the neighborhood that depicted black children in a playground as well as a group of white adults. The latter had been pasted into the flyer to add visual "diversity," but, according to Kleine, the whites "looked like they were waiting for a limo to drive them to opening night at the Chicago Symphony." The flyer's title was "Quality of Life." Shiller's campaign interpreted the flyer as a sign of who Reed perceived to be

her constituency. They reprinted Reed's flyer, simply adding the following commentary: "Look closely and see if you 'fit' Sandra's picture for 'quality people in the ward'" Kleine (1999).

16. Pick (1999).

17. Reed claimed that the incumbent had failed to make Uptowners feel safe. At a press conference, Reed said: "people are scared to walk the streets. One businessman told me, 'My business is suffering because of the loitering. Customers don't want to go in. There's drug dealing'" (quoted in Kleine 2003). As in 1999, Reed's campaign conjured and legitimized fear. Crime purportedly deterred locals from frequenting parks and businesses and hence fed a spiral of neighborhood decline. Reed called for a heavier police presence and other security measures that would allow law-abiding residents to reclaim Uptown.

18. Brown (2003).

19. Roeder (2006a).

20. Meyer (2004).

21. Eight Forty-Eight (2011).

22. "Noise and Fury in Uptown" (2004). Safety activists were distraught by how they were being portrayed. In letters to the editor printed in the *Chicago Sun-Times* (see Roeder 2006b), several writers complained about incendiary rhetoric. One writer criticized the alderwoman for "insisting that it was a racist and gentrification-oriented attitude that was fueling the thought [of artist housing]."

23. Dumke (2011).

24. Dumke (2007b).

25. I was not able to obtain a complete copy of this flyer. For one partial image, see "Wow, Alderman Shiller, Really?," *Uptown Update*, August 30, 2009, http://www.uptownupdate.com/2009/08/wow-alderman-shiller-really.html; accessed January 27, 2015.

26. http://buenaparkneighbors.yuku.com/reply/2231/Woman-Shot-At-Clarendon-Park-Field-House-CBS2#reply-2231; accessed November 19, 2015.

27. Esposito (2011).

28. Quoted in Washington (2015).

29. Quoted in Riley (2015).

30. For portraits of the candidates and their campaigns in 2019, see Dukmasova (2019a); Hopkins (2019); Pratt (2019). The run-off took place between Cappleman and Marianne Lalonde, a white woman who was a relatively recent newcomer to the neighborhood and largely unknown before the election. Nevertheless, the race became so close that its outcome could be announced only weeks after Election Day, since late-arriving mail ballots could have made a decisive difference.

31. Hardy (1991); Welter (1982).

32. Quotes in this paragraph are taken from Joravsky (1991).

33. Moore said: "trim a tree and suddenly it's not dark and shadowy on the block and someone is grateful because they're not so scared to walk home at night. It's those simple things that have the most meaning" (quoted in Joravsky 1991).

34. "Final City Council Endorsements" (1995).

35. Quoted in Ihejirika (1995).
36. Joravsky (2009).
37. Becker and Mihalopoulos (2007).
38. Quoted in Dumke (2007a).
39. Quoted in Dumke (2007a).
40. In contrast to other Rogers Park campaign material I reference from 2007, I have not been able to retrieve a copy of this mailer. However, several informants independently described it to me and their descriptions matched each other.
41. For example, Moore instituted a participatory budgeting program that allows residents to democratically allocate infrastructure funds for the 49th Ward. Moore received accolades from the National League of Cities for his leadership in promoting participatory budgeting (see Hoene, Kingsley, and Leighninger 2013).
42. The NRI aimed to reduce violence and its root causes in twenty-three neighborhoods and municipalities that had been hit by the recent recession. The NRI funds benefited Moore's political standing, but the NRI also had strategic value on a higher political level. When he announced the initiative in late 2010, Illinois's Democratic governor, Pat Quinn, was embroiled in a tough fight for reelection. Republicans and political commentators widely interpreted the NRI as a tactic to increase electoral turnout among African American voters (Groden 2014; Long 2015). Quinn narrowly won reelection, but after substantial public pressure, Illinois's auditor general released a report finding that as much as 40 percent of the initiative's expenses were of questionable validity (Holland 2014). The report also noted that no documentation existed for how NRI target communities had been selected and pointed out that some high-violence communities in Chicago had gone without NRI support while several NRI areas (including Rogers Park) exhibited rather lower crime rates. It appears that well-connected political representatives like Alderman Moore were able to secure funds while less connected ones could not. After the audit, the federal state launched a criminal investigation against key administrators involved in the NRI program (Long and Garcia 2014), which was still ongoing at the time of this writing.
43. As Nicole Marwell (2007) has shown in a study of Brooklyn, community organizations are engines of political mobilization. Community organizations are usually registered as nonprofits, which means that they cannot explicitly support political candidates, but they nonetheless have powerful tools to influence electoral outcomes. Community organizers working for ONE and its affiliated social service agencies, who were obviously well connected among residents, could freely discuss politics outside their professional role. Perhaps most important, ONE usually hosted aldermanic debates but, tellingly, did not do so in 2011, a year after Moore had secured the NRI funds for ONE. This made it difficult for Brian White to reach ONE's potentially receptive constituents. In contrast to the registered nonprofit organizations in the social justice camp, grassroots organizations like NA4J did not receive any funds, so their loyalty to Moore continued to erode. Realizing that the odds did not favor Brian White, however, they too stayed away from his campaign. As Elliot, a member of NA4J, tersely explained, "I could see the slaughter coming."

44. In 2015, Gordon ran against Moore once more. As in 2007, Gordon claimed that Moore did not pay sufficient attention to street crime, but Gordon discussed crime less aggressively and less prominently, instead concentrating on Moore's reliance on campaign donations from big developers. To distinguish himself, Gordon vowed to accept no donations at all and ran his entire campaign on $2,500 of his own money (Woodard 2015). Given these financial constraints, it is not surprising that Gordon's campaign failed to reach voters who might have appreciated his stance on crime. Shortly before the 2015 election, I reconnected with Melissa, a white woman in her thirties who had moved to Chicago from the rural Midwest. She had always expressed great alarm about street crime in Rogers Park and wanted to see more of a crackdown. But during our conversation I learned that she had not heard anything about Gordon's electoral campaign—she thus said that she would vote for Moore. Accordingly, Moore easily won the 2015 election with two-thirds of the vote. The result of the 2019 election, in which Maria Hadden roundly defeated Moore, appeared to reflect citywide politics more than local issues. Voters specifically expressed discontent about Moore's support for the contested 2011–2019 administration of Mayor Rahm Emanuel (Dukmasova 2019b; Pratt 2019). Even former 49th Ward alderman David Orr criticized Joe Moore, his longtime political protégé, for his close ties to the Emanuel administration. Hadden benefited from this discontent. In terms of neighborhood issues, she highlighted affordability and gentrification as Rogers Park's main problems. Neither Moore nor Hadden emphasized street crime as a challenge.

45. For election results since 2003, see Chicago Board of Election Commissioners: https://chicagoelections.gov/en/election-results.html accessed September 11, 2019. Results for earlier years were taken from the *Chicago Tribune*. See "Aldermanic Results" (1991); "Aldermanic Results" (1995); "Chicago Aldermanic Races" (1999). Homicide figures for all years after 2010 were taken from the Chicago Data Portal: https://data.cityofchicago.org/Public-Safety/Crimes-2001-to-present/ijzp-q8t2 accessed September 10, 2019. Earlier homicide figures were taken from the Chicago Police Department's annual reports: https://home.chicagopolice.org/inside-the-cpd/ statistical-reports/annual-reports/ accessed September 10, 2019.

46. See also Beckett (1997). The fact that contenders so readily chose crime as a campaign issue does not imply that campaigning on crime always worked; no matter what campaign platforms they selected, most candidates failed in challenging incumbents. In local, nonpartisan elections, incumbency provides a powerful bonus that challengers rarely overcome (Trounstine 2013). Nevertheless, in selecting their central campaign issue, electoral challengers frequently settled on crime.

47. On crime remaining a salient issue in Uptown, see Riley (2015). Since gang violence was the main political grievance in both neighborhoods, it is worth mentioning that homicides were actually more frequent in Rogers Park than in Uptown. Between 1998 and 2018, Rogers Park experienced 125 homicides and Uptown 96, a non-trivial difference given that both neighborhoods have approximately the same population.

48. For example, one case of building turnover I observed in Rogers Park was the fight over Astor House, a low-income tenement building that resembled Uptown's Lawrence House. At local block club meetings, public safety activists discussed how

Astor House contributed to crime and disorder in the area. They agreed to systematically call 911 in relation to the building in order to bring in housing inspectors, whose reports would give the residents and the alderman leverage for pressuring the landlord to evict troublesome tenants. The building inspectors visited the building in 2012. The owner, however, decided to sell the building to a developer, BJB Properties, rather than make long-overdue renovations and police his tenants (Woodard 2013b). Together with activists from NA4J, the tenants resisted their eviction. They demanded help from Alderman Moore and called on the city to protect the building's residents from being displaced (Brown 2013; Kunichoff 2013a, 2013b; Woodard 2013a). Eventually, however, most of the tenants were evicted (Woodard 2014).

49. For other analyses of how politicians shape the salience of race and ethnicity in social life, see Brubaker et al. (2006); Jenkins (1994); Rothschild (1981).

Chapter 5

1. Tocqueville (2000 [1835]).
2. Park and Burgess (1925:106). Community organizations were regarded as so critical to the vitality of the city that the influential tradition of criminology that emanated out of the Chicago School used the absence of organization—social disorganization—as both its name and its primary explanatory variable of interest (Shaw and McKay 1942). Strictly speaking, Shaw and McKay used the concept of social disorganization in contradistinction to "social organization," which designates the smooth interweaving of joint action in Mead's (1934) and Cooley's (1902) social theory. But given Shaw and McKay's roots in the works of Park and Burgess (1925), the concept of disorganization is also clearly linked to the absence of effective community organizations, an important source of social organization, although not necessarily the only one.
3. Robert Sampson and colleagues (2005) found that the presence of nonprofit organizations in a neighborhood invigorates political and civic life. The more organizations a neighborhood has, the more civic events take place. Those events do not have to be conflictual—but of course they *can* be.
4. As mentioned in chapter 4, Alderman Moore's efforts to support both justice and safety organizations helped to facilitate a modicum of peace between local organizations. Not everyone was happy, but community leaders on both sides suggested that Moore was trying to accommodate both sides. Elizabeth, a senior community organizer working in the North of Howard area, said the following about how she felt Moore addressed concerns about crime in Rogers Park: "from my perception, I think he [Moore] is trying his best. You know, people have biases within the community, so I think he [Moore] takes the flak for that sometimes when he's really trying to be evenhanded and not hysterical."
5. "Ald. Shiller Will Not Run For Re-Election," *Uptown Update*, August 2, 2010, http://www.uptownupdate.com/2010/08/ald-shiller-will-not-run-for-re.html, accessed May 9, 2016.

6. On banishment as a strategy of urban change, see Beckett and Herbert (2009).

7. Dumke and Warwick (2011:17).

8. Quoted in Dumke and Warwick (2011:18).

9. Dumke and Warwick (2011:18).

10. I did not observe these barbeques because they happened before I began my field-work, but I learned about them from Leticia, one of RYCH's African American core members, who had taken the lead in organizing them. She was a friendly and assertive single parent. She lived in a subsidized building and worked for a nonprofit agency. As she recounted, the young men and their parents pointed to a lack of youth programs in the neighborhood but also talked about a history of conflict between the gangs that went back as far as twenty years and still produced violent altercations today.

11. That day, I joined a newly formed positive loitering group from the Sheridan Park area, where Broncho Billy Park was located. Having learned from one participant that the hoops had been reinstalled, the dumbfounded safety activists walked over to the park and watched in silence as a group of young black men joyfully played basket-ball as if nothing had happened. I could see the energy draining from the positive loiterers. Five minutes later, the group decided to disband for the day, but they actu-ally disbanded for good. The frustration had apparently been too much.

12. My discussion of this case builds on Demby and Marisol Meraji (2019) as well as Lang (2019).

13. Quoted in Demby and Marisol Meraji (2019).

14. See, for example, Sampson (1999, 2011); Sampson, Raudenbush, and Earls (1997).

Chapter 6

1. On group culture, see Eliasoph and Lichterman (2003); Fine (2012).

2. See also Hartmann, Gerteis, and Croll (2009); McIntosh (1988); McKinney (2005). For theoretical explorations of whiteness, see Frankenberg (1993); Lewis (2004); Roediger (1999).

3. Some participants carried pepper spray, but I never witnessed or heard of any physical altercations that occurred in the context of positive loitering. Carrying a gun in public was illegal in Illinois during the time of my fieldwork. A court overturned Illinois's concealed carry ban in December 2012 (Long, Sweeney, and Garcia 2012), but the state did not issue its first concealed carry licenses until February 2014 (Glanton 2014).

4. Brubaker and his colleagues (2006) studied ethnicity and ethnic politics in Cluj, a Romanian town with a sizeable Hungarian population. The researchers found that despite political leaders' and ethnic organizations' aggressive agitation, ethnic tension rarely materialized in the individual interactions between Romanians and Hungarians.

5. In order to prevent group members from being identified, I have to withhold some information about dates, specific areas, and the people the groups encountered.

6. Trayvon Martin's killer, George Zimmerman, has Hispanic origins through his mother, but the incident is largely remembered as a case of white-on-black violence.

7. Frankenberg (1993); Hartmann, Gerteis, and Croll (2009); Rich (1979).

Chapter 7

1. While all of them offer powerful insights, these theories in their current form do not account for political variation and tensions among the members of racial groups, a fact Eduardo Bonilla-Silva (2015) has recently acknowledged and highlighted as a limitation that will have to be overcome in order to advance work on racism and racial conflict.

2. See also Forman, Jr. (2017).

3. I do not know precisely how this situation developed and what occurred. Chloe was very shaken up as she talked about this time in her life, and I decided not to ask her to elaborate.

4. Social isolation in cities can be a response to adverse neighborhood conditions, although it can also simply be a symptom of urban anonymity (Klinenberg 2002; Wirth 1938). Alice Goffman (2014:165–96) describes the way a group of black men strategically minimized their exposure to the police and to criminalized residents by socializing indoors.

5. See Emirbayer and Desmond (2015) as well as Monk's (2016) review; Hall (2017); Jackson (2001, 2005). For more examples of how certain attitudes and characteristics can lead black observers to attribute negative identities to African Americans, see Doering (2014).

6. Together with Kay, Gayle wrote grant applications to obtain funding for additional youth programs at the Howard Street field house. She also helped to organize a fundraiser for the field house. One time, Gayle and Margaret (and I) hosted a public picnic and game night for children in a park on Howard Street. This combination of tough-on-crime views and personal efforts to support low-income residents was not atypical of white safety volunteers.

7. After this particular passage in the interview, Andy seemed intent to soften the combative nature of his previous statements by comparing his black neighbors with the staff at an African American theater, where, he said, he had volunteered as an usher. He described the theater company in this way: "They're so good. You should see their productions. Absolutely mind-bogglingly wonderful. And you see civilized, human, black people. Like you, like me. Respectful, human, dignified." Talking about this theater, Andy probably tried to demonstrate that he still differentiated among black people, reserving his hostility and racial slurs for his low-income neighbors.

8. For example, see Bobo (1999); Bonilla-Silva (1997); Feagin (2006).

9. More axes would have to be added if individuals from other racial backgrounds had participated more substantially in local politics. Since I rarely had the opportunity to observe such individuals in the context of community activism, I do not include them in this summary.

10. In addition to gender and class, I explored whites' proximity to shooting incidents as a potential explanation for their divergent political views on crime and gentrification. Spatial proximity could have been an indicator of racial threat: whites living a "safe distance" away from gang hotspots could have entertained sympathies for

low-income residents, while those living closer would respond more aggressively. Nevertheless, respondents like Jessica and others showed that this hypothesis did not determine whites' political views.

11. For important contributions to the scholarly debate on this issue, see Bonilla-Silva (1997, 1999); Brubaker (2004); Loveman (1999); Wimmer (2015); Winant (2015).

Chapter 8

1. In addition to ethnic communities, one might also mention the strong LGBTQ presence that was especially pronounced in Uptown. My findings in this regard suggest that LGBTQ residents were just as divided over the politics of crime and gentrification as the neighborhoods were overall. Some of the most prominent members of the public safety camp—first and foremost Alderman Cappleman, of course—identified as gay or lesbian, but so did a number of leftist activists and community organizers. Historically, Uptown's LGBTQ community had sided more with the social justice camp overall and with prior Alderwoman Helen Shiller, who was widely recognized for her LGBTQ advocacy on the city council (Kleine 1999). The gentrification-critical organization Queer to the Left, now long-defunct, was an important political force in Uptown in the 1990s and early 2000s (Brown-Saracino 2009; Rai 2016). Nevertheless, there had always been dissenters. In a piece published during the 1999 electoral campaign, the *Chicago Reader* quoted two gay residents who were going to vote for Shiller's opponent Sandra Reed as saying that "the city's gay [and pro-Shiller] leadership doesn't have to live with the litter and crime" in Uptown (quoted in Kleine 1999).

2. See Avila (2003); Olivo (2013).

3. Befekadu Retta, an Ethiopian immigrant, and Andy Lam, a Chinese-American, received 4.37 percent and 1.34 percent of the vote, respectively. Emily Stewart, who had Japanese origins, did better and received 14.61 percent, placing her behind only James Cappleman and Molly Phelan. In terms of her social identities, however, Stewart's sexual identification as a lesbian woman shaped her campaign much more than her ethnic background did. In other words, even if elected, one would not have necessarily considered her a representative of Uptown's immigrant communities.

4. Importantly, in asking a question like "How do Uptown's Africans feel about gentrification?," there is always the risk of reifying ethnicity by suggesting that there is one perspective that all (or most) individuals within that category share. Of course, the category "African" encompasses a huge range of cultural and political backgrounds. But, more important, many immigrants may not really be "members" of any ethnic community at all insofar as they are uninvolved in ethnic networks and associations. The portraits in this chapter cannot do justice to these complexities but instead are intended to provide general insights into common—rather than representative—experiences of crime and gentrification.

5. Black Caribbeans experienced problems similar to the ones I describe in this section. Many of them resided in Rogers Park's North of Howard area, which was regularly

affected by gang violence. But I have much less information about Rogers Park's Caribbean community and thus focus on Africans instead.

6. In the broader sociological terms provided by segmented assimilation theory, one might say that African immigrants faced the risk of downward assimilation and concomitant criminalization. See Portes and Zhou (1993); Haller, Portes, and Lynch (2011); Alba, Kasinitz, and Waters (2011).

7. By highlighting a distinct ethnic identity, Waters (1999:286) argued, black Caribbeans could try "to remove themselves from the negative stereotypes of blacks in the United Sates, and, perhaps, to maintain some sense of superiority over American blacks." But by embracing African American culture, the Caribbeans could make sense of their encounters with discrimination and racism, which haunted especially the second generation. Waters reports that middle-class subjects tended to select an "ethnic response" of immigrant identity maintenance while poorer black Caribbeans living in segregated neighborhoods more frequently assimilated by adopting a race-based identity.

8. I have withheld more specific information about places, people, and organizations in this passage in order to avoid revealing the identities of study participants who requested confidentiality.

9. For sources on the Argyle area's early Asian settlement period, see Congbalay (1986); Phillips (1976).

10. The most recent ward remapping, which took effect with the 2015 elections, united the Argyle enclave politically. It is now completely situated in Edgewater's 48th Ward.

11. On the enshrinement of urban identities through cultural practices (such as parades and festivals), see Suttles (1984).

12. Years ago, the southern stretch of Clark Street in Uptown was also considered Latin Kings territory, but I never witnessed or heard of a gang presence on Clark Street in Uptown. CeaseFire staff as well as police officers told me that the presence of the Latin Kings in Uptown had ended.

13. A violent death in the family sometimes mobilized African American parents to become involved in community activism. At shooting vigils and other peace initiatives that the neighborhoods' social justice organizations launched, I met several African American mothers who had each lost a son to gun violence. I never met a Latino parent with a similar background, however.

14. Bennett (1997:244).

Chapter 9

1. On racial "happy talk," see Bell and Hartmann (2007). See also Berrey (2015); Perry (2017). As an innocuous type of social discourse that leaves racial inequality and structural imbalances unchallenged, "happy talk" about residential integration fit particularly well with the Obama presidency. It would be interesting to consider how, if at all, the Trump presidency changed this type of discourse in Rogers Park and Uptown, but my fieldwork concluded too early to shed light on this matter.

2. See Spike Lee's 2015 film *Chi-Raq*. For some of Donald Trump's comments on gun violence in Chicago, see Glanton (2016), Stafford (2016), and Cherone (2017).

3. Peterson and Krivo (2010).

4. Anderson (1990); Molotch (1972); Skogan and Maxfield (1981); Taub et al. (1984).

5. A recent boom in scholarship illuminates the connection between race and the search for housing. See, for example, Desmond (2016); Korver-Glenn (2018); Krysan and Crowder (2017).

6. Rahr and Rice (2015); Sharkey (2018).

7. James Forman Jr. (2017) has also demonstrated civic influence on criminal justice policy. He argues that the punitive turn in the American criminal justice system resulted not only from the politics of the Republican Party's Southern Strategy of recruiting white voters but also from demand for tough-on-crime measures that African American civic groups expressed.

8. Many tensions about policing and social control in racially diverse spaces have recently been reported in the media. For example, see Fayyad (2017); Holson (2018); Mervosh (2018a, 2018b); Zraick (2018).

9. For information about the fight over Hotel Chateau, see Cottrell (2012); Dai (2013); Emmanuel (2013). On the case of Astor House, see Brown (2013a); Kunichoff (2013a, 2013b); Woodard (2013a, 2013b, 2014).

10. As the flip side of cross-cutting conflict, interracial coalitions formed within social justice as well as public safety organizations. This is an interesting finding insofar as many scholars have found interracial community to be an elusive outcome. See, for example, Anderson (1990); Chaskin and Joseph (2010); Emerson (2006); Flippen (2001); Guest, Kubrin, and Cover (2008); Lichterman (2005); Nyden, Maly, and Lukehart (1997); Oliver (2010); de Souza Briggs (1998); and Suttles (1968).

11. Bobo (1999); Bonilla-Silva (1997). Emirbayer and Desmond's (2015) theory of the racial order and Omi and Winant's (2014) racial formation theory are more flexible in this regard. In Omi and Winant's theory, the central concept of competing racial projects does not require political homogeneity among groups or even a correspondence between the advocates of a given project and racial boundaries. Racial projects may have advocates from different racial groups, and conversely, racial groups may struggle over the projects that best serve their interests (Doering 2014).

12. Levine (2016); Marwell (2007); Marwell and McQuarrie (2009); Small (2004, 2009); Vargas (2016).

13. Urban ethnography's focus on face-to-face community at the expense of politics is rooted in the discipline's Chicago School origins, wherein scholars depicted the city as an ecological system of groups and individuals rather than an outcome of political decisions (Park and Burgess 1925; see also Walton 1993). But even scholars working with a political economy approach have expressed skepticism about the significance of urban politics because of its limited ability to mold processes of urban change (Logan and Molotch 2007; see also Peterson 1981). This skepticism may be justified, but politics matters at least insofar as it affects perceptions, discourse, and conflict. In this context, it helps to recall that neighborhoods today play a limited role in the lives of most city dwellers (Chaskin 1997; Janowitz 1952; Putnam 2000, 2007; Wellman and Leighton 1979). Residents pay attention to their neighborhoods chiefly when organizations and politicians can convince them that serious local changes are afoot

that will directly impact their lives. Electoral campaigns in particular provide opportunities to do so. In the lead-up to elections, even those who are usually uninvolved in local affairs may attend meetings, read local news outlets, and discuss community issues with neighbors. Consequently, urban sociologists should carefully examine these and other fleeting moments when urban change actually becomes a salient feature in the minds of residents.

14. Austin (1975); Bakhtin (1986); Mills (1940).

15. On defensive and reparative impression management, see Goffman (1959, 1967); Scott and Lyman (1968); Stokes and Hewitt (1976).

16. See Bowean (2012); Brown (2013b).

17. Quoted in Joravsky (2007). The racial challenge here apparently built on racist depictions of African Americans as monkeys, which extends to bananas as a food associated with monkeys.

18. Quoted in Joravsky (2007).

19. An important consideration I cannot address here in full is the ongoing process of disintegration that is tearing the American public sphere into disjointed factions with fundamentally incompatible views about many issues, including race. Habermas (1996) notes that public spheres are never fully integrated, but in contemporary America the process of disintegration appears to be reaching worrisome levels. For racial politics, this could mean that the moral authority of racial claims-making is bifurcating. Racial justice claims would then resonate only among some while leaving others more or less unmoved. In support of this hypothesis, survey researchers have shown that many white Americans have become less responsive to racial claims-making. As the political scientist Nicholas Valentino and his colleagues (2018:768) write, "many whites now view themselves as an embattled and even disadvantaged group, and this has led to both strong in-group identity and a greater tolerance for expressions of hostility toward out-groups." These changes predate the election of Donald Trump, which they probably facilitated. Presumably, Trump has also further undercut commitment to the value of racial equality among his supporters through his nonchalant flirtations with racist groups and white nationalism.

20. It may seem that this argument applies to activists and community organizations more than to ordinary residents, but here, too, emotional involvement and strategic action typically went hand in hand. For instance, in chapter 3 I discussed how an African American couple decried incessant police harassment at a large public meeting in the North of Howard area. The couple's anger and distress were plain for everyone to see. But they also acted strategically insofar as they did not simply write a complaint, which would have then been filed away among the countless others the city's Independent Police Review Authority (now defunct) had failed to address (US Department of Justice 2017). Rather, the couple used this public forum to voice their grievance in front of an audience that included the police commander, the alderman, journalists, and hundreds of neighbors. In this context, they could at least expect that their complaint would not be ignored.

21. All of the recent theoretical investigations of racism and racial politics assign some role to the rhetoric of color-blindness. See Bobo et al. (1997); Bonilla-Silva (2003);

Emerson and Yancey (2011); Emirbayer and Desmond (2015); Feagin (2006); Golash-Boza (2016); Omi and Winant (2014).

22. Sociologists may have studied racial challenges less than neutralizations because they prefer to reserve their critical analysis skills for political strategies they find distasteful. Thus, antiracist scholars like Bonilla-Silva (2003) study color-blind rhetoric, while right-wing pundits, such as Dinesh D'Souza (1995), delight in dissecting—and then dismissing—racial justice claims-making.

Appendix

1. On focused and unfocused interaction, see Goffman (1963).

2. As I became more familiar with Uptown, I realized that most of the groups I had seen that night must have been tenants of a nearby rooming house.

3. George and Bennett (2005); Paulsen (2004).

4. The event was framed as a prayer vigil for compassion and led by a reverend. While riding the bus, organizers instructed us that this was a precaution to avoid a police intervention. In addition, we were told to stay on the sidewalk, not engage potential hecklers, and keep walking at all times. On the connection between religious involvement in protest activities and police responses, see Beyerlein, Soule, and Martin (2015).

5. See Tavory and Timmermans (2014).

6. I sometimes took on small tasks for the groups I observed. For RYCH, I wrote up meeting minutes and recorded and transcribed the second youth speak-out event the group organized. Wes and Kareem were almost inordinately thankful when I gave them the transcript.

7. "Chateau Gets Scaffolding, Neighborhood Changes Apparent," *Uptown Update*, November 5, 2013, http://www.uptownupdate.com/2013/11/chateau-gets-scaffolding-neighborhood.html, accessed February 5, 2016.

8. Of course, this is what a lot of people think about sociology, as well as the social sciences in general, and this interpretation is not entirely unfair (Duarte et al. 2015).

9. Cooley (1902); Mead (1934).

10. In terms of assessing ethnography, this means that replicability cannot be a quality criterion. Different fieldworkers will see and hear different things in part because people will respond to their presence in systematically different ways. In relation to the perennial question of whether researchers should only study "their own" groups or, conversely, study only outgroups so as to avoid "me-search," I therefore submit that everyone should study everything.

11. I once asked an aldermanic staffer whether she knew why Rogers Park had seen a spike in shootings in 2011. Impatiently, she replied: "no, nor does anyone else." Her terse answer startled me and I paused. When she realized this, she looked at me, chuckled, and added facetiously: "you were hoping for the answer. 'She has the answer!' I don't have the answer." Obviously, she thought it had been a stupid question to ask.

References

Alba, Richard, Philip Kasinitz, and Mary C. Waters. 2011. "Commentary: The Kids Are (Mostly) Alright: Second-Generation Assimilation: Comments on Haller, Portes and Lynch." *Social Forces* 89(3): 763–73.

"Aldermanic Results." 1991. *Chicago Tribune*, February 28, 4.

"Aldermanic Results." 1995. *Chicago Tribune*, March 2, 7.

Alexander, Michelle. 2010. *The New Jim Crow: Mass Incarceration in the Age of Colorblindness*. New York: New Press.

Alinsky, Saul D. 1989. *Reveille for Radicals*. New York: Random House.

Allport, Gordon W. 1954. *The Nature of Prejudice*. Cambridge, MA: Addison-Wesley.

Anderson, Elijah. 1990. *Streetwise: Race, Class, and Change in an Urban Community*. Chicago: University of Chicago Press.

Anderson, Elijah. 1999. *Code of the Street: Decency, Violence, and the Moral Life of the Inner City*. New York: Norton.

Anderson, Elijah. 2011. *The Cosmopolitan Canopy: Race and Civility in Everyday Life*. New York: Norton.

Ansley, Mary Holm. 1981. "Rogers Park Offers Diversity in Housing." *Chicago Tribune*, February 1, B2.

Archer, Jacque Day, and Jamie Wirsbinski Santoro. 2007. *Rogers Park*. Charleston, SC: Arcadia.

Austin, J. L. 1975. *How to Do Things with Words*. 2nd ed. Cambridge, MA: Harvard University Press.

Avila, Oscar. 2003. "Organizations Try to Unite African Immigrants." *Chicago Tribune*, July 31, 1.

Bachrach, Peter, and Morton S. Baratz. 1962. "Two Faces of Power." *American Political Science Review* 56(4): 947–52.

Bakhtin, M. M. 1986. *Speech Genres and Other Late Essays*. Austin: University of Texas Press.

Barot, Rohit, and John Bird. 2001. "Racialization: The Genealogy and Critique of a Concept." *Ethnic and Racial Studies* 24(4): 601–18.

Bartram, Robin. 2019. "Going Easy and Going After: Building Inspections and the Selective Allocation of Code Violations." *City & Community* 18(2): 594–617.

Bayley, David H., and Christine Nixon. 2010. *The Changing Environment for Policing, 1985–2008*. Washington, DC: National Institute of Justice.

Becker, Robert, and Dan Mihalopoulos. 2007. "Nothing Left up to Chance." *Chicago Tribune*, April 6, 2.

Beckett, Katherine. 1997. *Making Crime Pay: Law and Order in Contemporary American Politics*. New York: Oxford University Press.

Beckett, Katherine, and Steve Herbert. 2009. *Banished: The New Social Control in Urban America*. New York: Oxford University Press.

Bell, Joyce M., and Douglas Hartmann. 2007. "Diversity in Everyday Discourse: The Cultural Ambiguities and Consequences of 'Happy Talk.'" *American Sociological Review* 72(6): 895–914.

Bennett, Larry. 1997. *Neighborhood Politics: Chicago and Sheffield*. New York: Garland.

Bernstein, David, and Noah Isackson. 2011. "Gangs and Politicians in Chicago: An Unholy Alliance." *Chicago Magazine*. Accessed December 15, 2011 (http://www.chicagomag.com/Chicago-Magazine/January-2012/Gangs-and-Politicians-An-Unholy-Alliance/).

Berrey, Ellen. 2005. "Divided over Diversity: Political Discourse in a Chicago Neighborhood." *City and Community* 4(2):143–70.

Berrey, Ellen. 2015. *The Enigma of Diversity: The Language of Race and the Limits of Racial Justice*. Chicago: University of Chicago Press.

Beyerlein, Kraig, Sarah A. Soule, and Nancy Martin. 2015. "Prayers, Protest, and Police: How Religion Influences Police Presence at Collective Action Events in the United States, 1960 to 1995." *American Sociological Review* 80(6): 1250–71.

Blum, Alan F., and Peter McHugh. 1971. "The Social Ascription of Motives." *American Sociological Review* 36(1): 98–109.

Blumer, Herbert. 1958. "Race Prejudice as a Sense of Group Position." *Pacific Sociological Review* 1(1): 3–7.

Bobo, Lawrence D. 1999. "Prejudice as Group Position: Microfoundations of a Sociological Approach to Racism and Race Relations." *Journal of Social Issues* 55(3): 445–72.

Bobo, Lawrence D., James R. Kluegel, and Ryan A. Smith. 1997. "Laissez Faire Racism: The Crystallization of a 'Kinder, Gentler' Anti-Black Ideology." Pp. 15–44 in *Racial Attitudes in the 1990s: Continuity and Change*, edited by S. A. Tuch and J. Martin. Greenwood, CT: Praeger.

Bonilla-Silva, Eduardo. 1997. "Rethinking Racism: Toward a Structural Interpretation." *American Sociological Review* 62(3): 465–80.

Bonilla-Silva, Eduardo. 1999. "The Essential Social Fact of Race." *American Sociological Review* 64(6): 899–906.

Bonilla-Silva, Eduardo. 2003. *Racism without Racists: Color-Blind Racism and the Persistence of Racial Inequality in the United States*. Lanham, MD: Rowman and Littlefield.

Bonilla-Silva, Eduardo. 2015. "More Than Prejudice: Restatement, Reflections, and New Directions in Critical Race Theory." *Sociology of Race and Ethnicity* 1(1): 73–87.

Bosman, Julie, and Mitch Smith. 2017. "Chicago Police Routinely Trampled on Civil Rights, Justice Dept. Says." *New York Times*. Accessed January 17, 2017 (https://www.nytimes.com/2017/01/13/us/chicago-police-justice-department-report.html).

Bourdieu, Pierre. 1993. *The Field of Cultural Production: Essays on Art and Literature*. Boston, MA: Polity Press.

Bourdieu, Pierre. 2000. *Pascalian Meditations*. Stanford, CA: Stanford University Press.

Bowean, Lolly. 2012. "At Uptown Building, Anxiety among Vulnerable Residents." *Chicago Tribune*. Accessed June 8, 2012 (http://www.chicagotribune.com/news/local/ct-met-lawrence-house-20120608,0,3409109.story).

Bowean, Lolly. 2013. "Cubicle Hotel in a Tight Spot." *Chicago Tribune*, March 31, 1.4.

Brown, Mark. 2003. "Daley Greases Council's Last Squeaky Wheel." *Chicago Sun-Times*, January 20, 2.

Brown, Mark. 2013a. "Brown: Low-Income Residents Rattled by Take Over of North Side Apartment Building." *Chicago Sun-Times*. Accessed July 11, 2013 (http://www.

suntimes.com/news/brown/21160108-452/brown-low-income-residents-rattled-by-take-over-of-north-side-apartment-building.html).

Brown, Mark. 2013b. "'Where Is He Going to Put These People?'" *Chicago Sun-Times.* Accessed March 4, 2013. (http://www.suntimes.com/news/brown/18522480-452/aldermans-reason-for-shuttering-cubicle-hotel-cock-and-bull.html).

Brown-Saracino, Japonica. 2009. *A Neighborhood That Never Changes: Gentrification, Social Preservation, and the Search for Authenticity.* Chicago: University of Chicago Press.

Brown-Saracino, Japonica. 2011. "Diverse Imageries of Gentrification: Evidence from Newspaper Coverage in Seven US Cities." *Journal of Urban Affairs* 33(3): 289–315.

Brown-Saracino, Japonica. 2015. "How Places Shape Identity: The Origins of Distinctive LBQ Identities in Four Small U.S. Cities." *American Journal of Sociology* 121(1): 1–63.

Brown-Saracino, Japonica. 2017. "Explicating Divided Approaches to Gentrification and Growing Income Inequality." *Annual Review of Sociology* 43(1): 515–39.

Brubaker, Rogers. 2004. *Ethnicity without Groups.* Cambridge, MA: Harvard University Press.

Brubaker, Rogers, Margit Feischmidt, Jon Fox, and Liana Grancea. 2006. *Nationalist Politics and Everyday Ethnicity in a Transylvanian Town.* Princeton, NJ: Princeton University Press.

Burawoy, Michael. 2009. *The Extended Case Method: Four Countries, Four Decades, Four Great Transformations, and One Theoretical Tradition.* Berkeley, CA: University of California Press.

Burawoy, Michael, Alice Burton, Ann A. Ferguson, Kathryn J. Fox, Joshua Gamson, Nadine Gartrell, Leslie Hurst, Charles Kurzman, Leslie Salzinger, Josepha Schiffman, and Shiori Ui. 1991. *Ethnography Unbound: Power and Resistance in the Modern Metropolis.* Berkeley: University of California Press.

Burke, Meghan A. 2012. *Racial Ambivalence in Diverse Communities: Whiteness and the Power of Color-Blind Ideologies.* Lanham, MD: Lexington Books.

Bursik, Robert, and Harold G. Grasmick. 1993. *Neighborhoods and Crime: The Dimensions of Effective Community Control.* New York: Lexington.

Cappleman, James. 2011. "46th Ward Master Plan: Public Safety Section." Accessed April 18, 2013 (http://www.james46.org/46th-ward/ward-master-plan/).

Carr, Patrick J. 2005. *Clean Streets: Controlling Crime, Maintaining Order, and Building Community Activism.* New York: New York University Press.

Chandler, Susan. 2001. "Megamall's Merchants Face a Shaky Future." *Chicago Tribune,* February 6.

Chaskin, Robert J. 1997. "Perspectives on Neighborhood and Community: A Review of the Literature." *Social Service Review* 71(4): 521–47.

Chaskin, Robert J., and Mark L. Joseph. 2010. "Building 'Community' in Mixed-Income Developments." *Urban Affairs Review* 45(3): 299–335.

Cherone, Heather. 2017. "Trump on Chicago Violence: 'What the Hell Is Going On?'" *DNAinfo Chicago.* Accessed January 27, 2017 (https://www.dnainfo.com/chicago/20170126/fuller-park/trump-on-chicago-violence-what-hell-is-going-on).

Chetty, Raj, Nathaniel Hendren, and Lawrence F. Katz. 2016. "The Effects of Exposure to Better Neighborhoods on Children: New Evidence from the Moving to Opportunity Experiment." *American Economic Review* 106(4): 855–902.

"Chicago Aldermanic Races." 1999. *Chicago Tribune,* April 15, 6.

Chicago Crime Commission. 2012. *The Chicago Crime Commission Gang Book: A Detailed Overview of Street Gangs in the Chicago Metropolitan Area*. Chicago: Chicago Crime Commission.

Chicago Fact Book Consortium. 1984. *Local Community Fact Book: Chicago Metropolitan Area, Based on the 1970 and 1980 Censuses*. Chicago: Chicago Review Press.

Chicago Fact Book Consortium. 1995. *Local Community Fact Book: Chicago Metropolitan Area, 1990*. Chicago: University of Illinois at Chicago.

Congbalay, Dean. 1986. "Argyle Street Shopping Strip Weaves Pattern of Prosperity." *Chicago Tribune*, March 31, A3.

Cooley, Charles Horton. 1902. *Human Nature and the Social Order*. New York: Scribner's.

Corley, Cheryl. 2019. "'The Consent Decree Will Make Us Better,' Federal Oversight of Chicago Police Begins." *NPR*. Accessed March 26, 2019 (https://www.npr.org/2019/03/01/699439896/the-consent-decree-will-make-us-better-federal-oversight-of-chicago-police-begin).

Cottrell, Megan. 2012. "Dwindling SROs: Hotel Chateau Residents Fear They'll Soon Be Homeless." *Chicago Muckrakers*. Accessed February 1, 2013 (http://www.chicagonow.com/chicago-muckrakers/2013/01/for-chateau-residents-a-new-home-may-be-hard-to-come-by/).

Cottrell, Megan. 2013. "SROs, the 'Housing of Last Resort,' Face Extinction as Chateau Hotel Closes." *DNAinfo*. Accessed June 20, 2013 (http://www.dnainfo.com/chicago/20130620/lakeview/sros-housing-of-last-resort-face-extinction-as-chateau-hotel-closes).

Crenshaw, Kimberlé. 1989. "Demarginalizing the Intersection of Race and Sex: A Black Feminist Critique of Antidiscrimination Doctrine, Feminist Theory and Antiracist Politics." *University of Chicago Legal Forum* (1): 139–67.

Crenson, Matthew A. 1971. *The Un-politics of Air Pollution: A Study of Non-decision-making in the Cities*. Baltimore: Johns Hopkins University Press.

Dahl, Robert A. 1961. *Who Governs? Democracy and Power in an American City*. New Haven: Yale University Press.

Dai, Serena. 2013. "Chateau Hotel Tenants Served Evictions: 'We're All Looking for Places.'" *DNAinfo*. Accessed March 29, 2013 (http://www.dnainfo.com/chicago/20130329/lakeview/chateau-hotel-tenants-served-evictions-were-all-looking-for-places).

Dawson, Michael C. 1994. *Behind the Mule: Race and Class in African-American Politics*. Princeton, NJ: Princeton University Press.

Demby, Gene, and Shereen Marisol Meraji. 2019. "Can the Go-Go Go On?" *NPR Code Switch*. Accessed April 22, 2019. (https://www.npr.org/templates/transcript/transcript.php?storyId=713866839).

Desmond, Matthew. 2014. "Relational Ethnography." *Theory and Society* 43: 547–79.

Desmond, Matthew. 2016. *Evicted: Poverty and Profit in the American City*. New York: Crown.

Desmond, Matthew, Andrew V. Papachristos, and David S. Kirk. 2016. "Police Violence and Citizen Crime Reporting in the Black Community." *American Sociological Review* 81(5): 857–76.

Desmond, Matthew, and Nicol Valdez. 2013. "Unpolicing the Urban Poor: Consequences of Third-Party Policing for Inner-City Women." *American Sociological Review* 78(1): 117–41.

Doane, Ashley. 2006. "What Is Racism? Racial Discourse and Racial Politics." *Critical Sociology* 32(2–3): 255–74.

Doering, Jan. 2014. "A Battleground of Identity: Racial Formation and the African American Discourse on Interracial Marriage." *Social Problems* 61(4): 559–75.

Doering, Jan. 2019. "Ethno-Racial Appeals and the Production of Political Capital: Evidence from Chicago and Toronto." *Urban Affairs Review*. Prepublished March 6. DOI: 10.1177/0003122419826020.

Drake, St. Clair, and Horace R. Cayton. 1993. *Black Metropolis: A Study of Negro Life in a Northern City*. Rev. and enl. ed. Chicago: University of Chicago Press.

D'Souza, Dinesh. 1995. *The End of Racism: Principles for a Multiracial Society*. New York: Free Press.

Du Bois, W. E. B. 1899. *The Philadelphia Negro: A Social Study*. Philadelphia: University of Pennsylvania Press.

Duarte, Jose L., Jarret T. Crawford, Charlotta Stern, Jonathan Haidt, Lee Jussim, and Philip E. Tetlock. 2015. "Political Diversity Will Improve Social Psychological Science." *Behavioral and Brain Sciences* 38: 1–58.

Dukmasova, Maya. 2019a. "Five Challengers Take on 46th Ward Alderman Cappleman from the Left." *Chicago Reader*. Accessed April 17, 2019 (https://www.chicagoreader.com/chicago/46th-ward-james-cappleman-uptown-helen-shiller/Content?oid=67989938).

Dukmasova, Maya. 2019b. "No More Joe Moore? The 49th Ward Prepares to Vote . . . or Not." *Chicago Reader*. Accessed April 16, 2019 (https://www.chicagoreader.com/chicago/49th-ward-aldermanic-election-joe-moore-maria-hadden-bill-morton/Content?oid=66662180).

Dumke, Mick. 2007a. "Aldermania: The Final Round." *Chicago Reader*. Accessed November 4, 2013 (http://www.chicagoreader.com/chicago/aldermania-the-final-round/Content?oid=924723).

Dumke, Mick. 2007b. "Elections/Aldermania!" *Chicago Reader*. Accessed April 25, 2013 (http://www.chicagoreader.com/chicago/electionsaldermania/Content?oid=924280).

Dumke, Mick. 2011. "Crime Dominates Talk in 46th Ward Campaign." *New York Times*. Accessed January 30, 2011 (http://www.nytimes.com/2011/01/30/us/30cncward.html?_r=2).

Dumke, Mick, and Kevin Warwick. 2011. "Criminal Courts?" *Chicago Reader*, September 22, 17–19.

Duneier, Mitchell. 1999. *Sidewalk*. New York: Farrar, Straus and Giroux.

Duneier, Mitchell, and Harvey Molotch. 1999. "Talking City Trouble: Interactional Vandalism, Social Inequality, and the 'Urban Interaction Problem.'" *American Journal of Sociology* 104(5): 1263–95.

Eight Forty-Eight. 2011. "Mayor Monday: Race Relations and What the Next Mayor Can Expect." *WBEZ*. Accessed September 24, 2013 (http://www.wbez.org/episode-segments/2011-02-07/mayor-monday-race-relations-and-what-next-mayor-can-expect-81897).

Eliasoph, Nina, and Paul Lichterman. 2003. "Culture in Interaction." *American Journal of Sociology* 108(4): 735–94.

Emerson, Michael O. 2006. *People of the Dream: Multiracial Congregations in the United States*. Princeton, NJ: Princeton University Press.

Emerson, Michael O., and George A. Yancey. 2011. *Transcending Racial Barriers: Toward a Mutual Obligations Approach*. New York: Oxford University Press.

Emirbayer, Mustafa, and Matthew Desmond. 2015. *The Racial Order*. Chicago: University of Chicago Press.

Emmanuel, Adeshina. 2013. "Chateau Hotel Residents Disappointed after Meeting with Cappleman." *DNAinfo*. Accessed February 9, 2013 (http://www.dnainfo.com/chicago/20130209/uptown/chateau-hotel-residents-disappointed-after-meeting-with-cappleman).

Emmanuel, Adeshina. 2014a. "Landlord Criticized for Displacing Poor Tenants to Offer Affordable Housing." *DNAinfo Chicago*. Accessed September 3, 2015 (http://www.dnainfo.com/chicago/20140722/uptown/landlord-criticized-for-displacing-poor-tenants-offer-affordable-housing).

Emmanuel, Adeshina. 2014b. "Uptown Shooting Spurs Retaliation Fears, More Concerns about Strip Mall." *DNAinfo*. Accessed May 29, 2014 (http://www.dnainfo.com/chicago/20140529/uptown/uptown-shooting-spurs-retaliation-fears-more-concerns-about-strip-mall).

Emmanuel, Adeshina, and Benjamin Woodard. 2013. "Flats Chicago Adds Lawrence House to Its Uptown Holdings, Plans $14M Rehab." *DNAinfo*. Accessed August 21, 2013 (http://www.dnainfo.com/chicago/20130806/uptown/flats-chicago-adds-lawrence-house-its-uptown-holdings-plans-14m-rehab).

Esposito, Stefano. 2011. "Crime Takes 46th Ward Focus." *Chicago Sun-Times*. Accessed January 31, 2011 (http://www.suntimes.com/news/elections/3538301-505/ward-uptown-crime-phelan-cappleman.html).

Esposito, Stefano. 2013. "Arrested 396 Times, Woman Knows How to Work the System." *Chicago Sun-Times*. Accessed April 26, 2013 (http://www.suntimes.com/photos/galleries/19542640-417/arrested-396-times-woman-knows-how-to-work-the-system.html).

Fayyad, Abdallah. 2017. "The Criminalization of Gentrifying Neighborhoods." *Atlantic*. Accessed December 31, 2017 (https://www.theatlantic.com/politics/archive/2017/12/the-criminalization-of-gentrifying-neighborhoods/548837/).

Feagin, Joe R. 2006. *Systemic Racism: A Theory of Oppression*. New York: Routledge.

Feld, Scott L. 1981. "The Focused Organization of Social Ties." *American Journal of Sociology* 86(5): 1015–35.

Feldman, Amy. 1995. "Lure of the Lake Lifts Rogers Park Condos." *Chicago Tribune*, November 26, 1.

Ferman, Barbara. 1996. *Challenging the Growth Machine: Neighborhood Politics in Chicago and Pittsburgh*. Lawrence: University Press of Kansas.

Fields, Corey D. 2016. *Black Elephants in the Room: The Unexpected Politics of African American Republicans*. Berkeley: University of California Press.

"Final City Council Endorsements." 1995. Editorial. *Chicago Tribune*, February 17, 22.

Fine, Gary A. 1993. "Ten Lies of Ethnography: Moral Dilemmas of Field Research." *Journal of Contemporary Ethnography* 22(3): 267–94.

Fine, Gary A. 2003. "Towards a Peopled Ethnography." *Ethnography* 4(1): 41–60.

Fine, Gary A. 2012. *Tiny Publics: A Theory of Group Action and Culture*. New York: Russell Sage Foundation.

Fligstein, Neil, and Doug McAdam. 2012. *A Theory of Fields*. New York: Oxford University Press.

Flippen, Chenoa. 2001. "Neighborhood Transition and Social Organization: The White to Hispanic Case." *Social Problems* 48(3): 299–321.

Florida, Richard. 2017. *The New Urban Crisis*. New York: Basic Books.

Forman, James, Jr. 2017. *Locking Up Our Own: Crime and Punishment in Black America*. New York: Farrar, Straus and Giroux.

Frankenberg, Ruth. 1993. *White Women, Race Matters: The Social Construction of Whiteness*. Minneapolis: University of Minnesota Press.

Freeman, Lance. 2006. *There Goes the 'Hood: Views of Gentrification from the Ground Up*. Philadelphia: Temple University Press.

Fremon, David K. 1988. *Chicago Politics, Ward by Ward*. Bloomington: Indiana University Press.

Friedman, Warren. 1991. "The Promise of Community Policing." *Chicago Tribune*, September 13, 19.

Friedman, Warren. 1996. "Grassroots and Persistent: The Chicago Alliance for Neighborhood Safety." *National Institute of Justice Journal* (231): 8–12.

Friedman, Warren, and Karen Matteo. 1988. *Police Service in Chicago: 911, Dispatch Policy and Neighborhood-Oriented Alternatives*. Chicago: Chicago Alliance for Neighborhood Safety.

Fung, Archon. 2004. *Empowered Participation: Reinventing Urban Democracy*. Princeton, NJ: Princeton University Press.

Gans, Herbert J. 1962. *The Urban Villagers. Group and Class in the Life of Italian-Americans*. New York: Free Press of Glencoe.

Garfinkel, Harold. 1967. *Studies in Ethnomethodology*. Englewood Cliffs, NJ: Prentice-Hall.

Garland, David. 2001. *The Culture of Control: Crime and Social Order in Contemporary Society*. Chicago: University of Chicago Press.

Garza, Melita M. 1999. "Residents Clash over Future of Uptown; Shiller Critics Say She's Stuck in Past." *Chicago Tribune*, April 11, 1.

Gaventa, John. 1980. *Power and Powerlessness: Quiescence and Rebellion in an Appalachian Valley*. Champaign: University of Illinois Press.

George, Alexander L., and Andrew Bennett. 2005. *Case Studies and Theory Development in the Social Sciences*. Cambridge, MA: MIT Press.

Gilens, Martin. 1999. *Why Americans Hate Welfare: Race, Media, and the Politics of Antipoverty Policy*. Chicago: University of Chicago Press.

Gitlin, Todd, and Nanci Hollander. 1970. *Uptown; Poor Whites in Chicago*. New York: Harper and Row.

Glaeser, Edward, and Jacob Vigdor. 2012. *The End of the Segregated Century: Racial Separation in America's Neighborhoods, 1890–2010*. New York: Manhattan Institute for Policy Research.

Glanton, Dahleen. 2014. "Illinois' First Concealed Carry Licenses in the Mail—5,000 of Them." *Chicago Tribune*. Accessed September 7, 2015 (http://articles.chicagotribune.com/2014-02-28/news/chi-illinois-first-concealed-carry-licenses-in-the-mail-5000-of-them-20140228_1_law-enforcement-licenses-paper-application-process).

Glanton, Dahleen. 2016. "Trump Considers Chicago America's Dumping Ground." *Chicago Tribune*. Accessed January 17, 2017 (http://www.chicagotribune.com/news/columnists/glanton/ct-trump-blacks-crime-glanton-20161024-column.html).

Goetz, Edward G. 2018. *The One-Way Street of Integration: Fair Housing and the Pursuit of Racial Justice in American Cities*. Ithaca, NY: Cornell University Press.

Goffman, Alice. 2009. "On the Run: Wanted Men in a Philadelphia Ghetto." *American Sociological Review* 74(3): 339–57.

Goffman, Alice. 2014. *On the Run: Fugitive Life in an American City*. Chicago: University of Chicago Press.

Goffman, Erving. 1959. *The Presentation of Self in Everyday Life*. Garden City, NY: Doubleday.

Goffman, Erving. 1963a. *Behavior in Public Places: Notes on the Social Organization of Gatherings*. New York: Free Press.

Goffman, Erving. 1963b. *Stigma: Notes on the Management of Spoiled Identity*. Englewood Cliffs, NJ: Prentice-Hall.

Goffman, Erving. 1967. *Interaction Ritual. Essays in Face-to-Face Behavior*. Chicago: Aldine.

Goffman, Erving. 1989. "On Fieldwork." *Journal of Contemporary Ethnography* 18(2): 123–32.

Golash-Boza, Tanya. 2016. "A Critical and Comprehensive Sociological Theory of Race and Racism." *Sociology of Race and Ethnicity* 2(2): 129–41.

Gonzales Van Cleve, Nicole. 2016. *Crook County: Racism and Injustice in America's Largest Criminal Court*. Stanford, CA: Stanford University Press.

Goodman, Philip. 2014. "Race in California's Prison Fire Camps for Men: Prison Politics, Space, and the Racialization of Everyday Life." *American Journal of Sociology* 120(2): 352–94.

Gould, Ingrid Ellen. 2000. *Sharing America's Neighborhoods: The Prospects for Stable Racial Integration*. Cambridge, MA: Harvard University Press.

Greenhouse, Linda. 1999. "Loitering Law Aimed at Gangs Is Struck Down by High Court." *New York Times*, June 11.

Groden, Claire. 2014. "An 'Antiviolence' Boondoggle in Murder-Plagued Chicago." *Wall Street Journal*. Accessed May 18, 2016 (http://www.wsj.com/articles/claire-groden-an-antiviolence-boondoggle-in-murder-plagued-chicago-1407537166).

Guest, Avery M., Charis E. Kubrin, and Jane K. Cover. 2008. "Heterogeneity and Harmony: Neighbouring Relationships among Whites in Ethnically Diverse Neighbourhoods in Seattle." *Urban Studies* 45(3): 501–26.

Habermas, Jürgen. 1996. *Between Facts and Norms: Contributions to a Discourse Theory of Law and Democracy*. Cambridge, MA: MIT Press.

Hagedorn, John, Roberto Aspholm, Teresa Córdova, Andrew Papachristos, and Lance Williams. 2019. *The Fracturing of Gangs and Violence in Chicago: A Research-Based Reorientation of Violence Prevention and Intervention Policy*. Chicago: Great Cities Institute, University of Illinois at Chicago.

Hall, Stuart. 2017. *The Fateful Triangle: Race, Ethnicity, Nation*. Cambridge, MA: Harvard University Press.

Haller, William, Alejandro Portes, and Scott M. Lynch. 2011. "Dreams Fulfilled, Dreams Shattered: Determinants of Segmented Assimilation in the Second Generation." *Social Forces* 89(3): 733–62.

Halpern, Robert. 1995. *Rebuilding the Inner City: A History of Neighborhood Initiatives to Address Poverty in the United States*. New York: Columbia University Press.

Harcourt, Bernard E. 2001. *Illusion of Order: The False Promise of Broken Windows Policing*. Cambridge, MA: Harvard University Press.

Harding, David J. 2010. *Living the Drama: Community, Conflict, and Culture among Inner-City Boys*. Chicago: University of Chicago Press.

Harding, David J., Jeffrey D. Morenoff, and Claire W. Herbert. 2013. "Home Is Hard to Find: Neighborhoods, Institutions, and the Residential Trajectories of Returning Prisoners." *Annals of the American Academy of Political and Social Science* 647(1): 214–36.

Hardy, Thomas. 1991. "49th Ward Race May Be Daley vs. Orr Preview." *Chicago Tribune*, February 17, 3.

Hartigan, John. 1999. *Racial Situations: Class Predicaments of Whiteness in Detroit*. Princeton, NJ: Princeton University Press.

Hartmann, Douglas, Joseph Gerteis, and Paul R. Croll. 2009. "An Empirical Assessment of Whiteness Theory: Hidden from How Many?" *Social Problems* 56(3): 403–24.

Harvey, David. 1989. *The Urban Experience*. Baltimore: Johns Hopkins University Press.

Hauser, Philip M., and Evelyn Mae Kitagawa, eds. 1953. *Local Community Fact Book for Chicago, 1950*. Chicago: University of Chicago Press.

Henderson, Harold. 2007. "The High Ground." *Chicago Reader*. Accessed September 19, 2013 (http://www.chicagoreader.com/chicago/the-high-ground/Content?oid=924637).

Hewitt, John P., and Randall Stokes. 1975. "Disclaimers." *American Sociological Review* 40(1): 1–11.

Hill Collins, Patricia. 2000. *Black Feminist Thought: Knowledge, Consciousness, and the Politics of Empowerment*. New York: Routledge.

Hirsch, Arnold R. 1983. *Making the Second Ghetto: Race and Housing in Chicago, 1940–1960*. New York: Cambridge University Press.

Hochschild, Arlie Russell. 1985. *The Managed Heart: Commercialization of Human Feeling*. Berkeley: University of California Press.

Hochschild, Arlie Russell. 2016. *Strangers in Their Own Land: Anger and Mourning on the American Right*. New York: New Press.

Hoene, Christopher, Christopher Kingsley, and Matthew Leighninger. 2013. *Bright Spots in Community Engagement*. Washington, DC: National League of Cities.

Holland, William G. 2014. *State Moneys Provided to the Illinois Violence Prevention Authority for the Neighborhood Recovery Initiative. Performance Audit*. Springfield, IL: Office of the Auditor General.

Holson, Laura M. 2018. "Hundreds in Oakland Turn Out to BBQ While Black." *New York Times*. Accessed August 23, 2018 (https://www.nytimes.com/2018/05/21/us/oakland-bbq-while-black.html).

Hopkins, Madison. 2019. "Candidates in 46th Ward Make Gentrification Key Issue in Challenging Uptown's Alderman." *Block Club Chicago*. Accessed April 17, 2019 (https://blockclubchicago.org/2019/01/31/candidates-in-46th-ward-make-gentrification-key-issue-in-challenging-uptowns-alderman/).

Hunter, Floyd. 1953. *Community Power Structure: A Study of Decision Makers*. Chapel Hill: University of North Carolina Press.

Husain, Nausheen. 2017. "Laquan McDonald Timeline: The Shooting, the Video and the Fallout." *Chicago Tribune*. Accessed January 17, 2017 (http://www.chicagotribune.com/news/laquanmcdonald/ct-graphics-laquan-mcdonald-officers-fired-timeline-htmlstory.html).

Hwang, Jackelyn, and Robert J. Sampson. 2014. "Divergent Pathways of Gentrification: Racial Inequality and the Social Order of Renewal in Chicago Neighborhoods." *American Sociological Review* 79(4): 726–51.

Hyra, Derek. 2015. "The Back-to-the-City Movement: Neighbourhood Redevelopment and Processes of Political and Cultural Displacement." *Urban Studies* 52(10): 1753–73.

Hyra, Derek S. 2017. *Race, Class, and Politics in the Cappuccino City*. Chicago: University of Chicago Press.

Ihejirika, Maudlyne. 1995. "Time for Another Change, 49th Ward Challengers Say." *Chicago Sun-Times*, February 23, 12.

"It Costs Money to Make Money in Uptown's Historic Districts." 1988. *Chicago Reporter* 17(11): 5, 11.

Jackson, John L. 2001. *Harlemworld: Doing Race and Class in Contemporary Black America*. Chicago: University of Chicago Press.

Jackson, John L. 2005. *Real Black: Adventures in Racial Sincerity*. Chicago: University of Chicago Press.

Jacobs, Jane. 1961. *The Death and Life of Great American Cities*. New York: Random House.

Janowitz, Morris. 1952. *The Community Press in an Urban Setting*. Glencoe, IL: Free Press.

Jenkins, Richard. 1994. "Rethinking Ethnicity: Identity, Categorization and Power." *Ethnic and Racial Studies* 17(2): 197–223.

Joravsky, Ben. 1991. "Politics by Proxy: It's Clarke vs. Moore (Daley vs. Orr) in the 49th Ward." *Chicago Reader*. Accessed September 13, 2013 (http://www.chicagoreader. com/chicago/politics-by-proxy-its-clrake-vs-moore-daley-vs-orr-in-the-49th-ward/ Content?oid=877294).

Joravsky, Ben. 2007a. "Bananas for Gordon." *Chicago Reader*. Accessed April 23, 2013 (http://www.chicagoreader.com/Bleader/archives/2007/04/02/bananas-for-gordon).

Joravsky, Ben. 2007b. "Helen's Voters." *Chicago Reader*. Accessed April 28, 2012 (http:// www1.chicagoreader.com/features/stories/uptown/politics/).

Joravsky, Ben. 2009. "MVP or Mope?" *Chicago Reader*. Accessed December 6, 2015 (http://www.chicagoreader.com/chicago/mvp-or-mope/Content?oid=1103207).

Katz, Jack. 2010. "Time for New Urban Ethnographies." *Ethnography* 11(1): 25–44.

Kaufman, Jason, and Matthew E. Kaliner. 2011. "The Re-accomplishment of Place in Twentieth Century Vermont and New Hampshire: History Repeats Itself, until It Doesn't." *Theory and Society* 40(2): 119–54.

Kelling, George L., and Catherine M. Coles. 1996. *Fixing Broken Windows: Restoring Order and Reducing Crime in Our Communities*. New York: Martin Kessler.

Kinder, Donald R., and Lynn M. Sanders. 1996. *Divided by Color: Racial Politics and Democratic Ideals*. Chicago: University of Chicago Press.

Kleine, Ted. 1999. "Radical Chick." *Chicago Reader*. Accessed November 11, 2015 (http:// www.chicagoreader.com/chicago/radical-chick/Content?oid=898847).

Kleine, Ted. 2003. "Aldermania!" *Chicago Reader*. Accessed April 25, 2013 (http://www. chicagoreader.com/chicago/aldermania/Content?oid=911162).

Klinenberg, Eric. 2002. *Heat Wave: A Social Autopsy of Disaster in Chicago*. Chicago: University of Chicago Press.

Koblin, John. 2018. "After Racist Tweet, Roseanne Barr's Show Is Canceled by ABC." *New York Times*. Accessed June 19, 2018 (https://www.nytimes.com/2018/05/29/business/ media/roseanne-barr-offensive-tweets.html).

Korver-Glenn, Elizabeth. 2018. "Compounding Inequalities: How Racial Stereotypes and Discrimination Accumulate across the Stages of Housing Exchange." *American Sociological Review* 83(4): 627–56.

Krysan, Maria, and Kyle Crowder. 2017. *Cycle of Segregation: Social Processes and Residential Stratification*. New York: Russell Sage.

Kunichoff, Yana. 2013a. "Astor House Court Date Brings Another Delay for Residents Eagerly Awaiting Resolution." *Chicago Muckrakers*. Accessed July 31, 2013 (http:// www.chicagonow.com/chicago-muckrakers/2013/07/astor-house-court-date-brings- another-delay-for-residents-eagerly-awaiting-resolution/).

Kunichoff, Yana. 2013b. "Rogers Park Building Could Be Last Truly Affordable Housing Option on Chicago's North Side." *Chicago Muckrakers*. Accessed July 31, 2013 (http://www.chicagonow.com/chicago-muckrakers/2013/07/rogers-park-building-could-be-last-truly-affordable-housing-option-on-chicagos-north-side/).

Lamont, Michèle, Graziella Moraes Silva, Jessica S. Welburn, Joshua Guetzkow, Nissim Mizrachi, and Elisa Reis. 2016. *Getting Respect: Responding to Stigma and Discrimination in the United States, Brazil, and Israel*. Princeton, NJ: Princeton University Press.

Lang, Marissa J. 2019. "'The Music Will Go On': Go-Go Returns Days after a Complaint Silenced a D.C. Store." *Washington Post*. Accessed April 22, 2019 (https://www.washingtonpost.com/local/the-music-will-go-on-t-mobile-ceo-says-go-go-music-will-return-after-complaint-silenced-a-dc-store/2019/04/10/ceab190a-5ba8-11e9-9625-01d48d50ef75_story.html).

Legewie, Joscha, and Jeffrey Fagan. 2019. "Aggressive Policing and the Educational Performance of Minority Youth." *American Sociological Review* 84(2): 220–47.

Legewie, Joscha, and Merlin Schaeffer. 2016. "Contested Boundaries: Explaining Where Ethnoracial Diversity Provokes Neighborhood Conflict." *American Journal of Sociology* 122(1): 125–61.

Leovy, Jill. 2015. *Ghettoside: A True Story of Murder in America*. New York: Spiegel and Grau.

Levine, Jeremy R. 2016. "The Privatization of Political Representation: Community-Based Organizations as Nonelected Neighborhood Representatives." *American Sociological Review* 81(6): 1251–75.

Lewis, Amanda E. 2004. "'What Group?' Studying Whites and Whiteness in the Era of 'Color-Blindness.'" *Sociological Theory* 22(4): 623–46.

Lichterman, Paul. 2005. *Elusive Togetherness: Church Groups Trying to Bridge America's Divisions*. Princeton, NJ: Princeton University Press.

Liebow, Elliot. 1967. *Tally's Corner: A Study of Negro Streetcorner Men*. Boston: Little, Brown.

Logan, John R., and Harvey Molotch. 2007. *Urban Fortunes: The Political Economy of Place*. Berkeley: University of California Press.

Logan, John R., and Brian J. Stults. 2011. "The Persistence of Segregation in the Metropolis: New Findings from the 2010 Census." *Census Brief prepared for Project US2010*. Accessed September 26, 2019 (https://s4.ad.brown.edu/Projects/Diversity/Data/Report/report2.pdf).

Logan, John R., and Charles Zhang. 2010. "Global Neighborhoods: New Pathways to Diversity and Separation." *American Journal of Sociology* 115(4): 1069–109.

Long, Ray. 2015. "Lawmaker Wants Ban on Grant Announcements before Elections." *Chicago Tribune*. Accessed May 18, 2016 (http://www.chicagotribune.com/news/local/politics/ct-nri-grant-oversight-met-0422-20150421-story.html).

Long, Ray, and Monique Garcia. 2014. "Feds Subpoena Emails in Quinn Anti-violence Fund Inquiry." *Chicago Tribune*. Accessed May 18, 2016 (http://articles.chicagotribune.com/2014-07-04/news/ct-quinn-program-federal-subpoena-0704-20140704_1_neighborhood-recovery-initiative-quinn-spokesman-grant-klinzman-anti-violence-program).

Long, Ray, Annie Sweeney, and Monique Garcia. 2012. "Concealed Carry: Court Strikes Down Illinois' Ban." *Chicago Tribune*. Accessed September 7, 2015 (http://www.chicagotribune.com/news/local/breaking/chi-us-appeals-court-strikes-down-states-concealedcarry-ban-20121211-story.html).

Loveman, Mara. 1999. "Is 'Race' Essential?" *American Sociological Review* 64(6): 891–98.

Lynch, Kevin. 1960. *The Image of the City*. Cambridge, MA: MIT Press.

Lynd, Robert Staughton, and Helen Merrell Lynd. 1929. *Middletown: A Study in American Culture*. New York: Harcourt.

Main, Frank. 2012. "Gangs Are under 'Audit' in Rogers Park Neighborhood." *Chicago Sun-Times*. Accessed April 16, 2012 (http://www.suntimes.com/11885191-417/gangs-are-under-audit-in-rogers-park-neighborhood.html).

Malooley, Jake. 2010. "Fixed Wilson Yard." *Time Out Chicago*. Accessed September 26, 2013 (http://www.timeoutchicago.com/arts-culture/museums/85653/fixed-wilson-yard).

Malooley, Jake. 2011. "The 'Hood That Helen Shiller Built." *Time Out Chicago*, February, 12–16.

Maly, Michael T. 2005. *Beyond Segregation: Multiracial and Multiethnic Neighborhoods in the United States*. Philadelphia: Temple University Press.

Manza, Jeff, and Christopher Uggen. 2006. *Locked Out: Felon Disenfranchisement and American Democracy*. New York: Oxford University Press.

Marciniak, Ed. 1981. *Reversing Urban Decline: The Winthrop-Kenmore Corridor in the Edgewater and Uptown Communities of Chicago*. Washington, DC: National Center for Urban Ethnic Affairs.

Martin, Andrew. 1995. "Daley, Foes Alike on Crime up to a Point." *Chicago Tribune*, February 5, 1.

Martin, John Levi. 2003. "What Is Field Theory?" *American Journal of Sociology* 109(1): 1–49.

Martin, John Levi. 2011. *The Explanation of Social Action*. New York: Oxford University Press.

Marwell, Nicole P. 2007. *Bargaining for Brooklyn: Community Organizations in the Entrepreneurial City*. Chicago: University of Chicago Press.

Massey, Douglas S., Len Albright, Rebecca Casciano, Elizabeth S. Derickson, and David N. Kinsey. 2013. *Climbing Mount Laurel: The Struggle for Affordable Housing and Social Mobility in an American Suburb*. Princeton, NJ: Princeton University Press.

Massey, Douglas S., and Nancy A. Denton. 1993. *American Apartheid: Segregation and the Making of the Underclass*. Cambridge, MA: Harvard University Press.

Mayorga-Gallo, Sarah. 2014. *Behind the White Picket Fence: Power and Privilege in a Multiethnic Neighborhood*. Chapel Hill: University of North Carolina Press.

McCarron, John. 1988. "Shiller Guards against Uptown Progress." *Chicago Tribune*, September 1, 1.

McDermott, Monica. 2006. *Working-Class White: The Making and Unmaking of Race Relations*. Berkeley: University of California Press.

McIntosh, Peggy. 1988. *Unpacking the Knapsack of White Privilege*. Working Paper 189. Wellesley, MA: Wellesley College Center for Research on Women.

McKinney, Karyn D. 2005. *Being White: Stories of Race and Racism*. New York: Routledge.

McQuarrie, Michael, and Nicole P. Marwell. 2009. "The Missing Organizational Dimension in Urban Sociology." *City and Community* 8(3): 247–68.

McRoberts, Omar M. 2003. *Streets of Glory: Church and Community in a Black Urban Neighborhood*. Chicago: University of Chicago Press.

Mead, George Herbert. 1934. *Mind, Self, and Society from the Standpoint of a Social Behaviorist*. Chicago: University of Chicago Press.

Mendelberg, Tali. 2001. *The Race Card: Campaign Strategy, Implicit Messages, and the Norm of Equality*. Princeton, NJ: Princeton University Press.

Mervosh, Sarah. 2018a. "A Black Man Wore Socks in the Pool. After Calling the Police on Him, a Manager Got Fired." *New York Times*. Accessed July 11, 2018 (https://www.nytimes.com/2018/07/09/us/memphis-pool-manager-fired-socks.html).

Mervosh, Sarah. 2018b. "Woman Assaulted Black Boy after Telling Him He 'Did Not Belong' at Pool, Officials Say." *New York Times*. Accessed July 13, 2018 (https://www.nytimes.com/2018/07/01/us/pool-patrol-paula.html).

Metz, David Haywood, and Katherine Tate. 1995. "The Color of Urban Campaigns." Pp. 262–77 in *Classifying by Race*, edited by P. E. Peterson. Princeton, NJ: Princeton University Press.

Meyer, H. Gregory. 2004. "Uptown Factions at Odds. As Neighborhood Changes, Housing for Poor Debated." *Chicago Tribune*, August 23, 1.

Mills, C. Wright. 1940. "Situated Actions and Vocabularies of Motive." *American Sociological Review* 5(6): 904–13.

Molotch, Harvey. 1972. *Managed Integration: Dilemmas of Doing Good in the City*. Berkeley: University of California Press.

Molotch, Harvey, William Freudenburg, and Krista E. Paulsen. 2000. "History Repeats Itself, But How? City Character, Urban Tradition, and the Accomplishment of Place." *American Sociological Review* 65(6): 791–823.

Monk, Ellis P. 2016. "The Racial Order by Mustafa Emirbayer and Matthew Desmond." *American Journal of Sociology* 122(2): 620–22.

Moskos, Peter. 2008. *Cop in the Hood: My Year Policing Baltimore's Eastern District*. Princeton, NJ: Princeton University Press.

Mowatt, Raoul V. 2000. "Rogers Park Rally Protests Loss of Affordable Housing." *Chicago Tribune*, May 14, 4C3.

Murji, Karim, and John Solomos. 2005. *Racialization: Studies in Theory and Practice*. New York: Oxford University Press.

Myler, Kathleen. 1983. "They Seek to Transform 'Jungle' into an Eden." *Chicago Tribune*, May 29, L1.

"Neighborhood Starting To Get Too Safe for Family To Afford." 2015. *Onion*, August 28. Accessed September 1, 2015 (http://www.theonion.com/article/neighborhood-starting-get-too-safe-family-afford-51197).

"Noise and Fury in Uptown." 2004. Editorial. *Chicago Tribune*, September 6, 22.

Nyden, Philip, Michael Maly, and John Lukehart. 1997. "The Emergence of Stable Racially and Ethnically Diverse Urban Communities: A Case Study of Nine U.S. Cities." *Housing Policy Debate* 8(2): 491–534.

Oliver, J. Eric. 2010. *The Paradoxes of Integration: Race, Neighborhood, and Civic Life in Multiethnic America*. Chicago: University of Chicago Press.

Olivo, Antonio. 2013. "African Immigrants Hope for a Chicago Community of Their Own." *Chicago Tribune*. Accessed February 14, 2019 (https://www.chicagotribune.com/news/ct-xpm-2013-01-14-ct-met-african-immigration-20130114-story.html).

Omi, Michael, and Howard Winant. 2014. *Racial Formation in the United States*. 3rd ed. New York: Routledge.

Oppenheim, Carol. 1974. "City's Newest Skid Row: Uptown." *Chicago Tribune*, September 29, 41.

Pacyga, Dominic A. 2009. *Chicago: A Biography*. Chicago: University of Chicago Press.

Pager, Devah. 2009. *Marked: Race, Crime, and Finding Work in an Era of Mass Incarceration*. Chicago: University of Chicago Press.

Palmer, A. T. 2001. "Restless in Rogers Park." *Chicago Tribune*, August 5, 16.

Papachristos, Andrew V. 2001. *A.D., After the Disciples: The Neighborhood Impact of Federal Gang Prosecution*. Peotone, IL: National Gang Crime Research Center.

Papachristos, Andrew V., David M. Hureau, and Anthony A. Braga. 2013. "The Corner and the Crew: The Influence of Geography and Social Networks on Gang Violence." *American Sociological Review* 78(3): 417–47.

Papachristos, Andrew V., Chris M. Smith, Mary L. Scherer, and Melissa A. Fugiero. 2011. "More Coffee, Less Crime? The Relationship between Gentrification and Neighborhood Crime Rates in Chicago, 1991 to 2005." *City and Community* 10(3): 215–40.

Park, Robert Ezra, and E. W. Burgess. 1925. *The City*. Chicago: University of Chicago Press.

Patterson, Orlando. 1997. *The Ordeal of Integration: Progress and Resentment in America's "Racial" Crisis*. Washington, DC: Civitas/Counterpoint.

Pattillo, Mary. 2007. *Black on the Block: The Politics of Race and Class in the City*. Chicago: University of Chicago Press.

Pattillo, Mary. 2013. *Black Picket Fences: Privilege and Peril among the Black Middle Class*. 2nd ed. Chicago: University of Chicago Press.

Paulsen, Krista E. 2004. "Making Character Concrete: Empirical Strategies for Studying Place Distinction." *City and Community* 3(3): 243–62.

Perry, Evelyn M. 2017. *Live and Let Live: Diversity, Conflict, and Community in an Integrated Neighborhood*. Chapel Hill: University of North Carolina Press.

Peterson, Paul E. 1981. *City Limits*. Chicago: University of Chicago Press.

Peterson, Ruth D., and Lauren J. Krivo. 2010. *Divergent Social Worlds: Neighborhood Crime and the Racial-Spatial Divide*. New York: Russell Sage Foundation.

Pettigrew, Thomas F. 1998. "Intergroup Contact Theory." *Annual Review of Psychology* 49(1): 65–85.

Phillips, Richard. 1976. "Chinatown North: Can It Revive Area?" *Chicago Tribune*, December 5, 40.

Picca, Leslie Houts, and Joe R. Feagin. 2007. *Two-Faced Racism: Whites in the Backstage and Frontstage*. New York: Routledge.

Pick, Grant. 1999. "The Streets Have Eyes." *Chicago Reader*. Accessed April 28, 2012 (http://www.chicagoreader.com/chicago/the-streets-have-eyes/Content?oid=900827).

Polsby, Nelson W. 1959. "The Sociology of Community Power: A Reassessment." *Social Forces* 37(3): 232–36.

Portes, Alejandro, and Min Zhou. 1993. "The New Second Generation: Segmented Assimilation and Its Variants." *Annals of the American Academy of Political and Social Science* 530: 74–96.

Pratt, Gregory. 2019. "Amid Departures and Upheaval, Progressive Candidates See Path to Chicago City Council." *Chicago Tribune*. Accessed April 17, 2019 (https://www.chicagotribune.com/news/local/politics/ct-met-chicago-city-council-progressive-tilt-20190117-story.html).

Putnam, Robert D. 2000. *Bowling Alone: The Collapse and Revival of American Community*. New York: Simon and Schuster.

Putnam, Robert D. 2007. "E Pluribus Unum: Diversity and Community in the Twenty-First Century." *Scandinavian Political Studies* 30(2): 137–74.

Quillian, Lincoln, and Devah Pager. 2001. "Black Neighbors, Higher Crime? The Role of Racial Stereotypes in Evaluations of Neighborhood Crime." *American Journal of Sociology* 107(3): 717–67.

Rahr, Sue, and Stephen K. Rice. 2015. "From Warriors to Guardians: Recommitting American Police Culture to Democratic Ideals." *New Perspectives in Policing, Harvard Executive Session on Policing and Public Safety, April 2015.* Accessed September 26, 2019 (https://www.ncjrs.gov/pdffiles1/nij/248654.pdf).

Rai, Candice. 2016. *Democracy's Lot: Rhetoric, Publics, and the Places of Invention.* Tuscaloosa: University of Alabama Press.

Rawls, Anne Warfield, and Gary David. 2005. "Accountably Other: Trust, Reciprocity and Exclusion in a Context of Situated Practice." *Human Studies* 28(4):469–97.

Recktenwald, William. 1991. "Groups Aim for Changes In Policing." *Chicago Tribune*, July 8, 1.

Reid, David. 2018. "Steve Bannon Tells France Right Wing to Embrace Racist Tag." *CNBC.* Accessed April 27, 2018 (https://www.cnbc.com/2018/03/12/steve-bannon-tells-france-right-wing-to-embrace-racist-tag.html).

Rhoden, William C. 2006. *$40 Million Slaves: The Rise, Fall, and Redemption of the Black Athlete.* New York: Crown.

Rich, Adrienne. 1979. "'Disloyal to Civilization': Feminism, Racism, and Gynephobia." *Chrysalis* 7: 9–27.

Riley, Chloe. 2015. "Crime and Affordable Housing—Issues That Just Won't Go Away in the 46th Ward." *Chicago Reader.* Accessed April 5, 2015 (http://www.chicagoreader.com/Bleader/archives/2015/04/03/crime-and-affordable-housingissues-that-just-wont-go-away-in-the-46th-ward).

Rios, Victor M. 2011. *Punished: Policing the Lives of Black and Latino Boys.* New York: New York University Press.

Roeder, David. 2006a. "Shiller on Tightrope over Development Plan in Uptown." *Chicago Sun-Times*, April 12, 65.

Roeder, David. 2006b. "Wilson Yard: 'Wonderful' or 'Debacle?'" *Chicago Sun-Times*, April 19, 63.

Roediger, David R. 1999. *The Wages of Whiteness: Race and the Making of the American Working Class.* Rev. ed. New York: Verso.

Rothschild, Joseph. 1981. *Ethnopolitics: A Conceptual Framework.* New York: Columbia University Press.

Ruklick, Joe. 2003. "Rogers Park Housing Advocates Charge TIF Task Force with Racism." *Chicago Defender*, August 21, 2.

Sampson, Robert J. 1999. "What 'Community' Supplies." Pp. 241–92 in *Urban Problems and Community Development*, edited by R. F. Ferguson and W. F. Dickens. Washington, DC: Brookings.

Sampson, Robert J. 2011. *Great American City: Chicago and the Enduring Neighborhood Effect.* Chicago: University of Chicago Press.

Sampson, Robert J., and Dawn J. Bartusch. 1998. "Legal Cynicism and (Subcultural?) Tolerance of Deviance: The Neighborhood Context of Racial Differences." *Law & Society Review* 32(4): 777–804.

Sampson, Robert J., Heather MacIndoe, Doug McAdam, and Simón Weffer-Elizondo. 2005. "Civil Society Reconsidered: The Durable Nature and Community Structure of Collective Civic Action." *American Journal of Sociology* 111(3): 673–714.

Sampson, Robert J., and Stephen W. Raudenbush. 1999. "Systematic Social Observation of Public Spaces: A New Look at Disorder in Urban Neighborhoods." *American Journal of Sociology* 105(3): 603–51.

Sampson, Robert J., Stephen W. Raudenbush, and Felton Earls. 1997. "Neighborhoods and Violent Crime: A Multilevel Study of Collective Efficacy." *Science* 277(5328): 918–24.

Sánchez-Jankowski, Martín. 1991. *Islands in the Street: Gangs and American Urban Society*. Berkeley: University of California Press.

Savage, Bill. 2009. "Borders and Boundaries." *Chicago Reader*. Accessed November 4, 2013 (http://www.chicagoreader.com/chicago/borders-and-boundaries/Content?oid=1103196).

Schilt, Kristen. 2010. *Just One of the Guys? Transgender Men and the Persistence of Gender Inequality*. Chicago: University of Chicago Press.

Schloss, Bert P. 1957. *The Uptown Community Area and the Southern White In-migrant*. Chicago: Chicago Commission on Human Relations.

Schütz, Alfred. 1967. *The Phenomenology of the Social World*. Evanston, IL: Northwestern University Press.

Scott, Marvin B., and Stanford M. Lyman. 1968. "Accounts." *American Sociological Review* 33(1): 46–62.

Sharkey, Patrick. 2013. *Stuck in Place: Urban Neighborhoods and the End of Progress toward Racial Equality*. Chicago: University of Chicago Press.

Sharkey, Patrick. 2018. *Uneasy Peace: The Great Crime Decline, the Renewal of City Life, and the Next War on Violence*. New York: Norton.

Shaw, Clifford R., and Henry Donald McKay. 1942. *Juvenile Delinquency and Urban Areas*. Chicago: University of Chicago Press.

Silverstein, Jason. 2016. "Pennsylvania Mayor to Step Down after Racist Facebook Posts." *NY Daily News*. Accessed April 27, 2018 (http://www.nydailynews.com/news/national/pennsylvania-mayor-step-racist-facebook-posts-article-1.2834949).

Simpson, Dick W. 2001. *Rogues, Rebels, and Rubber Stamps: The Politics of the Chicago City Council from 1863 to the Present*. Boulder, CO: Westview Press.

Sinclair, Upton. 1906. *The Jungle*. New York: Doubleday.

Skogan, Wesley. 2015. "Disorder and Decline: The State of Research." *Journal of Research in Crime and Delinquency* 52(4): 464–85.

Skogan, Wesley G. 1988. "Community Organizations and Crime." *Crime and Justice* 10: 39–78.

Skogan, Wesley G. 2006. *Police and Community in Chicago: A Tale of Three Cities*. New York: Oxford University Press.

Skogan, Wesley G., and Susan M. Hartnett. 1997. *Community Policing, Chicago Style*. New York: Oxford University Press.

Skogan, Wesley G., and Michael G. Maxfield. 1981. *Coping with Crime: Individual and Neighborhood Reactions*. Beverly Hills, CA: Sage.

Small, Mario L. 2004. *Villa Victoria: The Transformation of Social Capital in a Boston Barrio*. Chicago: University of Chicago Press.

Small, Mario L. 2009. *Unanticipated Gains: Origins of Network Inequality in Everyday Life*. New York: Oxford University Press.

Smith, Neil. 1996. *The New Urban Frontier: Gentrification and the Revanchist City*. London: Routledge.

Smock, Kristina. 2004. *Democracy in Action: Community Organizing and Urban Change*. New York: Columbia University Press.

Sobol, Rosemary Regina. 2014. "Charges Filed in Death of Photographer in Rogers Park." *Chicago Tribune*. Accessed May 30, 2018 (http://www.chicagotribune.com/news/local/breaking/chi-chicago-shooting-death-wil-lewis-20140713-story.html).

Sonnie, Amy, and James Tracy. 2011. *Hillbilly Nationalists, Urban Race Rebels, and Black Power: Community Organizing in Radical Times*. Brooklyn: Melville House.

de Souza Briggs, Xavier. 1998. "Brown Kids in White Suburbs: Housing Mobility and the Many Faces of Social Capital." *Housing Policy Debate* 9(1): 177–221.

de Souza Briggs, Xavier, Susan J. Popkin, and John M. Goering. 2010. *Moving to Opportunity: The Story of an American Experiment to Fight Ghetto Poverty*. New York: Oxford University Press.

Soyer, Michaela. 2016. *A Dream Denied: Incarceration, Recidivism, and Young Minority Men in America*. Berkeley: University of California Press.

Stafford, Zach. 2016. "Why Does Donald Trump Keep Talking about Chicago?" *Guardian*. Accessed January 17, 2017 (https://www.theguardian.com/commentisfree/2016/sep/30/donald-trump-chicago-violent-crime-statistics-race).

Stevens, Matt. 2018. "Starbucks C.E.O. Apologizes after Arrests of 2 Black Men." *New York Times*, April 15.

Stokes, Randall, and John P. Hewitt. 1976. "Aligning Actions." *American Sociological Review* 41(5): 838–49.

Stolle, Dietlind, Stuart Soroka, and Richard Johnston. 2008. "When Does Diversity Erode Trust? Neighborhood Diversity, Interpersonal Trust and the Mediating Effect of Social Interactions." *Political Studies* 56(1): 57–75.

Stone, Clarence N. 1989. *Regime Politics: Governing Atlanta, 1946–1988*. Lawrence: University Press of Kansas.

Struzzi, Diane. 1999. "Residents Blame Shiller for 46th Ward Shelters." *Chicago Tribune*, February 10, 4.

Stuart, Forrest. 2016. *Down, Out, and Under Arrest: Policing and Everyday Life in Skid Row*. Chicago: University of Chicago Press.

Sugrue, Thomas J. 2005. *The Origins of the Urban Crisis: Race and Inequality in Postwar Detroit*. Princeton, NJ: Princeton University Press.

Suttles, Gerald D. 1968. *The Social Order of the Slum: Ethnicity and Territory in the Inner City*. Chicago: University of Chicago Press.

Suttles, Gerald D. 1984. "The Cumulative Texture of Local Urban Culture." *American Journal of Sociology* 90(2): 283–304.

Sykes, Gresham M., and David Matza. 1957. "Techniques of Neutralization: A Theory of Delinquency." *American Sociological Review* 22(6): 664–70.

Taub, Richard P., D. Garth Taylor, and Jan D. Dunham. 1984. *Paths of Neighborhood Change: Race and Crime in Urban America*. Chicago: University of Chicago Press.

Tavory, Iddo, and Stefan Timmermans. 2014. *Abductive Analysis: Theorizing Qualitative Research*. Chicago: University of Chicago Press.

Tekippe, Abraham. 2013. "Notorious Uptown Apartment Building to Get $14 Million Rehab." *Crain's Chicago Business*. Accessed August 6, 2013 (http://www.chicagorealestatedaily.com/article/20130806/CRED03/130809879/notorious-uptown-apartment-building-to-get-14-million-rehab).

Tocqueville, Alexis de. 2000 [1835]. *Democracy in America*. New York: Harper Collins.

Trounstine, Jessica. 2013. "Turnout and Incumbency in Local Elections." *Urban Affairs Review* 49(2): 167–89.

"The Uptown Gamble." 1988. *Chicago Reporter* 17(11): 1.

US Department of Justice. 2017. *Investigation of the Chicago Police Department*. Washington, DC: US Department of Justice.

Valentino, Nicholas A., Fabian G. Neuner, and L. Matthew Vandenbroek. 2018. "The Changing Norms of Racial Political Rhetoric and the End of Racial Priming." *Journal of Politics* 80(3):757–71.

Van den Berghe, Pierre L. 1967. *Race and Racism: A Comparative Perspective*. New York: Wiley.

Vargas, Robert. 2016. *Wounded City: Violent Turf Wars in a Chicago Barrio*. New York: Oxford University Press.

Venkatesh, Sudhir A. 2000. *American Project: The Rise and Fall of a Modern Ghetto*. Cambridge, MA: Harvard University Press.

Venkatesh, Sudhir A. 2006. *Off the Books: The Underground Economy of the Urban Poor*. Cambridge, MA: Harvard University Press.

Venkatesh, Sudhir A. 2008. *Gang Leader for a Day: A Rogue Sociologist Takes to the Streets*. New York: Penguin Press.

Victor, Daniel. 2018. "When White People Call the Police on Black People." *New York Times*. Accessed May 29, 2018 (https://www.nytimes.com/2018/05/11/us/black-white-police.html).

Wacquant, Loïc. 2002a. "From Slavery to Mass Incarceration." *New Left Review* (13): 41–60.

Wacquant, Loïc. 2002b. "Scrutinizing the Street: Poverty, Morality, and the Pitfalls of Urban Ethnography." *American Journal of Sociology* 107(6): 1468–532.

Walton, John. 1993. "Urban Sociology: The Contribution and Limits of Political Economy." *Annual Review of Sociology* 19: 301–20.

Warr, Mark. 2000. "Fear of Crime in the United States: Avenues for Research and Policy." Pp. 451–89 in *Criminal Justice 2000: Measurement and Analysis of Crime and Justice*. Vol. 4, edited by D. Duffee. Washington, DC: U.S Department of Justice.

Warren, Mark R. 2001. *Dry Bones Rattling: Community Building to Revitalize American Democracy*. Princeton, NJ: Princeton University Press.

Washington, Laura. 2015. "Looking for Compassion in the 46th Ward." *Chicago Sun-Times*. Accessed April 5, 2015 (http://chicago.suntimes.com/politics/7/71/476274/looking-compassion-46th-ward).

Waters, Mary C. 1999. *Black Identities: West Indian Immigrant Dreams and American Realities*. New York: Russell Sage Foundation.

Weber, Max. 1978. *Economy and Society: An Outline of Interpretive Sociology*. Berkeley: University of California Press.

Wellman, Barry, and Barry Leighton. 1979. "Networks, Neighborhoods, and Communities." *Urban Affairs Review* 14(3): 363–90.

Welter, Gail D. 1982. *The Rogers Park Community: A Study of Social Change, Community Groups, and Neighborhood Reputation*. Chicago: Center for Urban Policy, Loyola University of Chicago.

Wenzel, Joseph, IV, and Courtney Zieller. 2018. "PD: Hartford Police Detective Terminated after Using Racial Slurs during DUI Arrest." *WFSB*. Accessed April 27, 2018 (http://www.wfsb.com/story/37217256/pd-hartford-police-detective-terminated-after-using-racial-slurs-during-dui-arrest).

West, Candace, and Sarah Fenstermaker. 1995. "Doing Difference." *Gender and Society* 9(1): 8–37.

West, Candace, and Don H. Zimmerman. 1987. "Doing Gender." *Gender and Society* 1(2): 125–51.

West, Candace, and Don H. Zimmerman. 2009. "Accounting for Doing Gender." *Gender and Society* 23(1): 112–22.

Western, Bruce. 2006. *Punishment and Inequality in America*. New York: Russell Sage.

Whyte, William F. 1993. *Street Corner Society: The Social Structure of an Italian Slum*. 4th ed. Chicago: University of Chicago Press.

Wilson, William J. 1978. *The Declining Significance of Race: Blacks and Changing American Institutions*. Chicago: University of Chicago Press.

Wilson, William J. 1987. *The Truly Disadvantaged: The Inner City, the Underclass, and Public Policy*. Chicago: University of Chicago Press.

Wimmer, Andreas. 2015. "Race-Centrism: A Critique and a Research Agenda." *Ethnic and Racial Studies* 38(13): 2186–205.

Winant, Howard. 2015. "Race, Ethnicity and Social Science." *Ethnic and Racial Studies* 38(13): 2176–85.

Wirth, Louis. 1938. "Urbanism as a Way of Life." *American Journal of Sociology* 44(1): 1–24.

Woodard, Benjamin. 2013a. "Astor House Residents, Fighting Eviction and Bed Bugs, Confront Ald. Moore." *DNAinfo*. Accessed July 2, 2013 (http://www.dnainfo.com/chicago/20130702/rogers-park/astor-house-residents-fighting-eviction-bed-bugs-confront-ald-moore).

Woodard, Benjamin. 2013b. "Astor House Residents Say New Building Owner Wants Them Out." *DNAinfo*. Accessed March 28, 2013 (http://www.dnainfo.com/chicago/20130328/rogers-park/astor-house-residents-say-new-building-owner-wants-them-out).

Woodard, Benjamin. 2013c. "Peterson Garden Project a 'Gentrification Bullet' for Howard St.: Critics." *DNAinfo*, October 23.

Woodard, Benjamin. 2014. "Developer Spends Nearly $1 Million in Upgrades at Astor House, Records Show." *DNAinfo Chicago*. Accessed September 14, 2018 (https://www.dnainfo.com/chicago/20140924/rogers-park/developer-spends-nearly-1-million-upgrades-at-astor-house-records-show).

Woodard, Benjamin. 2015. "Ald. Joe Moore Nearly Doubles Campaign Fund to $114,333 at End of Year." *DNAinfo*. Accessed January 22, 2015 (http://www.dnainfo.com/chicago/20150122/rogers-park/ald-joe-moore-nearly-doubles-campaign-fund-114333-at-end-of-year).

Zimring, Franklin E. 2007. *The Great American Crime Decline*. New York: Oxford University Press.

Zraick, Karen. 2018. "Man Labeled 'ID Adam' Is Fired after Calling the Police on a Black Woman at Pool." *New York Times*. Accessed July 11, 2018 (https://www.nytimes.com/2018/07/06/us/pool-racial-profiling-white-man.html).

Zukin, Sharon. 1980. "A Decade of the New Urban Sociology." *Theory and Society* 9(4): 575–601.

Index

Tables and figures are indicated by *t* and *f* following the page number

For the benefit of digital users, indexed terms that span two pages (e.g., 52–53) may, on occasion, appear on only one of those pages.